The
Jakarta
Method

The Jakarta Method

Washington's Anticommunist Crusade & The
Mass Murder Program That Shaped Our World

Vincent Bevins

PUBLICAFFAIRS

New York

PublicAffairs
Hachette Book Group
1290 Avenue of the Americas, New York, NY 10104
www.publicaffairsbooks.com
@Public_Affairs

Printed in the United States of America

Published by PublicAffairs, an imprint of Perseus Books, LLC, a subsidiary of Hachette Book Group, Inc. The PublicAffairs name and logo is a trademark of the Hachette Book Group.

The Hachette Speakers Bureau provides a wide range of authors for speaking events. To find out more, go to www.hachettespeakersbureau.com or call (866) 376-6591.

The publisher is not responsible for websites (or their content) that are not owned by the publisher.

Print book interior design by Amy Quinn

Library of Congress Cataloging-in-Publication Data
Names: Bevins, Vincent, author.
Title: The Jakarta method: Washington's anticommunist crusade and the mass murder program that shaped our world / Vincent Bevins.
Other titles: Washington's anticommunist crusade and the mass murder program that shaped our world
Description: New York: PublicAffairs, [2020] | Includes bibliographical references.
Identifiers: LCCN 2019046069 | ISBN 9781541742406 (hardcover) | ISBN 9781541724013 (ebook)
Subjects: LCSH: United States—Foreign relations—1945–1989. | Developing countries—Foreign relations—United States. | United States—Foreign relations—Developing countries. | Anti-communist movements—Developing countries—History—20th century. | Autonomy and independence movements—History—20th century. | Political violence—Developing countries—History—20th century. | Indonesia—History—Coup d'état, 1965. | Cold War. | United States. Central Intelligence Agency—History—20th century.
Classification: LCC E744 .B476 2020 | DDC 327.73009/04—dc23
LC record available at https://lccn.loc.gov/2019046069

ISBNs: 978-1-5417-4240-6 (hardcover), 978-1-5417-2401-3 (ebook)

LSC-C

10 9 8 7 6

For Bu Cisca and Pak Hong Lan Oei

Contents

Introduction

IN MAY 1962, A YOUNG girl named Ing Giok Tan got on a rusty old boat in Jakarta, Indonesia. Her country, one of the largest in the world, had been pulled into the global battle between capitalism and communism, and her parents decided to flee the terrible consequences that conflict had wrought for families like hers. They set sail for Brazil, having heard from other Indonesians who had already made the journey that this place offered freedom, opportunity, and respite from conflict. But they knew almost nothing about it. Brazil was just an idea for them, and it was very far away. Suffering through anxiety and seasickness for forty-five days, they made their way past Singapore, across the Indian Ocean to Mauritius, down past Mozambique, around South Africa, and then all the way across the Atlantic to São Paulo, the largest city in South America.

If they thought they could escape the violence of the Cold War, they were tragically mistaken. Two years after they arrived, the military overthrew Brazil's young democracy and established a violent dictatorship. After that, the new Indonesian immigrants in Brazil received messages from home describing the most shocking scenes imaginable, an explosion of violence so terrifying that even discussing what happened would make people break down, questioning their own sanity. But the reports were all true. In the wake of that apocalyptic slaughter in Indonesia, a young nation littered with mutilated bodies emerged as one of Washington's most reliable allies, and then largely disappeared from history.

What happened in Brazil in 1964 and Indonesia in 1965 may have been the most important victories of the Cold War for the side that ultimately won—that is, the United States and the global economic system now in operation. As such, they are among the most important events in a process that has fundamentally shaped life for almost everyone. Both countries had been independent, standing somewhere in between the world's capitalist and communist superpowers, but fell decisively into the US camp in the middle of the 1960s.

Officials in Washington and journalists in New York certainly understood how significant these events were at the time. They knew that Indonesia, now the world's fourth most-populous country, was a far more important prize than Vietnam ever could have been.[1] In just a few months, the US foreign policy establishment achieved there what it failed to get done in ten bloody years of war in Indochina.

And the dictatorship in Brazil, currently the world's fifth most-populous country, played a crucial role in pushing the rest of South America into the pro-Washington, anticommunist group of nations. In both countries, the Soviet Union was barely involved.

Most shockingly, and most importantly for this book, the two events led to the creation of a monstrous international network of extermination—that is, the systematic mass murder of civilians—across many more countries, which played a fundamental role in building the world we all live in today.

Unless you are Indonesian, or a specialist on the topic, most people know very little about Indonesia, and almost nothing about what happened in 1965–66 in that archipelago nation. Indonesia remains a huge gap in our collective general knowledge, even among people who do know a little about the Cuban Missile Crisis, or the Korean War, or Pol Pot, or can easily rattle off some basic facts about the world's most-populous country (China), the second most-populous (India), or even numbers six and seven (Pakistan and Nigeria). Even among international journalists, few people know that Indonesia is the world's largest Muslim-majority country, let alone that in 1965, it was home to the world's largest Communist Party outside the Soviet Union and China.

The truth of the violence of 1965–66 remained hidden for decades. The dictatorship established in its wake told the world a lie, and survivors were imprisoned or too terrified to speak out. It is only as a result of the efforts of heroic Indonesian activists and dedicated scholars around the world that we can now tell the story. Documents recently declassified in Washington have been a huge help, though some of what happened still remains shrouded in mystery.

Indonesia likely fell off the proverbial map because the events of 1965–1966 were such a complete success for Washington. No US soldiers died, and no one at home was ever in danger. Although Indonesian leaders in the 1950s and 1960s had played a huge international role, after 1966 the country stopped rocking the boat entirely. I know from thirteen years of working as a foreign correspondent and journalist that faraway countries that are stable and reliably pro-American do not make headlines. And personally, after going through the documentation and spending a lot of time with the people who lived through these events, I came to form another, deeply unsettling theory as to why these episodes have been forgotten. I fear that the truth of what happened contradicts so forcefully our idea of what the Cold War was, of what it means to be an American, or how globalization has taken place, that it has simply been easier to ignore it.

This book is for those who have no special knowledge of Indonesia, or Brazil, or Chile or Guatemala or the Cold War, though I hope that my interviews, archival research, and global approach may have delivered some discoveries that may be interesting for the experts too. Most of all I hope this story can get to people who want to know how violence and the war against communism intimately shaped our lives today—whether you are sitting in Rio de Janeiro, Bali, New York, or Lagos.

Two events in my own life convinced me that the events of the mid-1960s are very much still with us. That their ghosts still haunt the world, so to speak.

In 2016, I was working my sixth and final year as Brazil correspondent for the *Los Angeles Times*, and I was walking the halls of Congress in Brasília. Lawmakers in the world's fourth-largest democracy were preparing to vote on whether they would impeach President Dilma Rousseff, a former left-wing guerrilla and the country's first female president. Down the corridor, I recognized an unimportant but reliably outspoken far-right congressman by the name of Jair Bolsonaro, so I approached him for a quick interview. It was widely known by that point that political rivals were trying to bring President Rousseff down on a technicality, and that those organizing her ouster were guilty of far more corruption than she was.[2] Because I was a foreign journalist, I asked Bolsonaro if he worried the international community might doubt the legitimacy of the more conservative government that was set to replace her, given the questionable proceedings that day. The answers he gave me seemed so far outside the mainstream, such a complete resurrection of Cold War phantoms, that I didn't even use the interview. He said, "The world will celebrate what we do today, because we are stopping Brazil from turning into another North Korea."

This was absurd. Rousseff was a center-left leader whose government had been, if anything, too friendly with huge corporations.

A few moments later, Bolsonaro walked up to the microphone in the congressional chambers and made a declaration that shook the country. He dedicated his impeachment vote to Carlos Alberto Brilhante Ustra, the man who oversaw Rousseff's own torture as a colonel during Brazil's dictatorship. It was an outrageous provocation, an attempt to rehabilitate the country's anticommunist military regime and to become the national symbol of far-right opposition to everything.[3]

When I interviewed Rousseff a few weeks later, as she waited for the final vote that would remove her from office, our conversation invariably turned to the role of the United States in Brazil's affairs. Considering the many times and ways Washington had intervened to overthrow governments in South America, many of her supporters wondered if the CIA was behind this one, too. She denied it: it was the result of Brazil's internal dynamics.[4] But that is, in its own way, even worse: Brazil's dictatorship had transitioned to the type of democracy that could safely remove anyone—like Rousseff or Lula—whom the economic or political elites deemed a threat to their interests, and they could summon Cold War demons to go to battle for them when they pleased.

We now know the extent to which Bolsonaro's gambit succeeded. When he was elected president two years later, I was in Rio. Fights immediately erupted in the streets. Big burly men started yelling at tattooed women who wore stickers supporting the rival candidate, screaming, "Communists! Get out! Communists! Get out!"

In 2017 I moved in the exact opposite direction that Ing Giok Tan and her family had so many years before. I relocated from São Paulo to Jakarta to cover Southeast Asia for the *Washington Post*. Just months after I arrived, a group of academics and activists planned to put on a low-key conference to discuss the events of 1965. But some people were spreading the accusation on social media that this was actually a meeting to resurrect communism—still illegal in the country, over fifty years later—and a mob made their way toward the event that night, not long after I had left. Groups composed largely of Islamist men, now common participants in aggressive Jakarta street demonstrations, surrounded the building and trapped everyone inside. My roommate, Niken, a young labor organizer from Central Java, was held captive there all night, as the mob pounded on the walls, chanting, "Crush the communists!" and "Burn them alive!" She sent me texts, terrified, asking for me to publicize what was happening, so I did so on Twitter. It didn't take long for that to generate threats and accusations that I was a communist, or even a member of Indonesia's nonexistent Communist Party. I had become used to receiving exactly these kinds of messages in South America. The similarities were no coincidence. The paranoia in both places can be traced back to a traumatic rupture in the middle of the 1960s.

But it was only after I began work on this book, speaking with experts and witnesses and survivors, that I realized the significance of the two historical events was much greater than the fact that violent anticommunism still exists in Brazil, Indonesia, and many other countries, and that the Cold War created a world of regimes that see any social reform as a threat. I came to the conclusion that the entire world, and especially the countries of Asia, Africa, and Latin America that Ing Giok sailed past with her family, has been reshaped by the waves emanating from Brazil and Indonesia in 1964 and 1965.

I felt a heavy moral responsibility to research that story, and tell it right. In one sense, doing so is the culmination of over a decade of work. But specifically for this book, I visited twelve countries and interviewed over one hundred people, in Spanish, Portuguese, English, and Indonesian. I pored through the archives in the same number of languages, spoke to historians around the world, and did work with research assistants in five countries. I didn't have a lot of resources to write this book, but I gave it everything I had.

The violence that took place in Brazil, and Indonesia, and twenty other countries around the world, was not accidental, or incidental to the main events of world history. The deaths were not "cold-blooded and meaningless," just tragic errors that didn't change anything.[5] Precisely the opposite. The violence was effective, a fundamental part of a larger process. Without a full view of the Cold War and US goals worldwide, the events are unbelievable, unintelligible, or very difficult to process.

The remarkable film *The Act of Killing*, by Joshua Oppenheimer, and its sequel, *The Look of Silence*, smashed open the black box surrounding 1965 in Indonesia, and forced people in the country and around the world to look inside. Oppenheimer's masterful work employs an extreme close-up approach. I purposefully took the opposite approach, zooming out to the global stage, in the attempt to be complementary. I hope viewers of those films pick up this book to put them in context, and I hope readers will watch those films after they finish. I also owe Joshua a small personal debt for guiding my early research, but I owe much more to Indonesians and other historians, most of all Baskara Wardaya, Febriana Firdaus, and Bradley Simpson.

I decided that to really tell the story of these events and their repercussions—that is, the global extermination network they engendered— I had to try to somehow tell the wider story of the Cold War. It's very often forgotten that violent anticommunism was a global force, and that its protagonists worked across borders, learning from successes and failures elsewhere as their movement picked up steam and racked up victories. To understand what happened, we have to understand these international collaborations.

This is also the story of a few individuals, some from the US, some from Indonesia, and some from Latin America, who lived through these events, and whose lives were changed profoundly by them. My choice of focus, and the connections that I saw, were probably dictated to some extent by the people I was lucky enough to meet, and by my own background and language skills, but as far as I'm concerned, their story is just as much the story of the Cold War as any other is, certainly more so than any story of the Cold War that is focused primarily on white people in the United States and Europe.[6]

The story I tell here is based on declassified information, the consensus formed by the most knowledgeable historians, and overwhelming first-person testimony. I rely extensively on my own interviews with survivors, and of course I was not able to check every single one of the claims regarding their own lives, such as what things felt like, what they were wearing, or what date they were arrested. But none of the details I include contradict the established facts or the larger story that historians have already uncovered. To tell it as accurately as possible, to be faithful to the evidence and respectful to those who lived through it, I found it had to be done a certain way. First, the story is truly global; every life on Earth is treated as equally important, and no nations or actors are viewed, *a priori*, as the good or bad guys. Secondly, we've all heard the maxim that "history is written by the victors." This is usually, unfortunately, true. But this story by necessity pushes back against that tendency—many of the people at its center were some of the biggest losers of the twentieth century—and we cannot be afraid to let the facts of their lives contradict accepted popular understandings of the Cold War in the English-speaking world, even if those contradictions may be very uncomfortable for the winners. And finally, I avoid speculation entirely, resisting any urge to try to tackle the many unsolved mysteries by myself. We have to accept there's a lot we still don't know.

So this book does not rely on guessing. In the moments when my colleagues and I stumbled onto what seemed like big coincidences—seemingly too big, perhaps—or connections we couldn't explain, we stopped there and discussed them; we didn't just pick our own theory as to what caused them.

And we certainly did stumble onto some connections.

1

A New American Age

THE UNITED STATES, A WESTERN European settler colony in North America, emerged from World War II as by far the most powerful state on Earth. This was a surprise to most Americans, and to most of the world.

It was a young country. It was only about a hundred years previously that the government set up in former British colonies finished incorporating former French and Spanish territories into the new country, giving its leaders dominion over the middle strip of the continent. In comparison, their cousins back in Europe had been conquering the globe for almost five centuries. They had sailed around the planet, carving it up for themselves.

To say that the United States is a settler colony means that the land was overtaken by white Europeans over the course of several centuries in a way that differed from the way that most countries in Africa and Asia were conquered. The white settlers came to stay, and the native population was excluded, by definition, from the nation they built. In order for the new white and Christian country to take form, the indigenous population had to get out of the way.

As every American boy and girl learns, there was a strong element of religious fanaticism involved in the founding of the United States. The Puritans, a group of committed English Christians, did not travel across the Atlantic to make money for England. They sought a place for a purer, more disciplined version of the Calvinist society they wanted to build. One way to put this is that they wanted religious freedom. Another is that they wanted a society that was even more homogeneous, fundamentalist, and theocratic than the one that existed in seventeenth-century Europe.[1]

In the late 1700s, the leaders of the British colonies expelled the monarchy in a revolutionary war and created a remarkably effective system of self-governance that exists in slightly modified form today. Internationally, the country came to represent and champion revolutionary, democratic ideals. But internally, things were much more complicated. The United States remained a brutally white supremacist society. The consequence of the *a priori* dismissal of the native population was genocide.

Throughout the Americas, from Canada down to Argentina, European colonization killed between fifty million and seventy million indigenous people, around 90 percent of the native American population. Scientists recently concluded that the annihilation of these peoples was so large that it changed the temperature of the planet.[2] In the new United States of America, the destruction of the local peoples continued long after the declaration of independence from British rule. US citizens continued to buy, sell, whip, torture, and own persons of African descent until the middle of the nineteenth century. Women were only given the right to vote nationwide in 1920. They could actually do so, however, while the theoretical voting rights granted to black Americans were beaten back by racist terror campaigns and laws that were meant to exclude them from real citizenship. When the United States entered World War II, it was what we would now consider an apartheid society.[3]

In that war, however, the better angels of American nature came to the fore. It wasn't always clear that would be the case. In the 1930s, some Americans even sympathized with the Nazis, a hyper-militaristic, genocidal, and proudly racist authoritarian party governing Germany. In 1941, a senator from Missouri named Harry S. Truman said, "If we see that Germany is winning the war, we ought to help Russia; and if that Russia is winning, we ought to help Germany, and in that way let them kill as many as possible."[4] But when the US did join World War II, in an alliance with the British, French, and Russians against the Germans and Japanese, its troops fought to liberate prisoners from death camps and save Western Europe's limited democracies from tyranny. Apart from five hundred thousand who tragically lost their lives, a generation of American boys came back from that war rightfully proud of what they had done—they had looked an entirely evil system in the face, stood up for the values their country was built on, and they had won.

The end of World War II was the beginning of a new global order. Europe was weakened, and the planet was broken into pieces.

Three Worlds

The second most-powerful country in the world in 1945, the Soviet Union, also emerged as a victor in that war. The Soviets were intensely proud too, but their population had been devastated. Adolf Hitler, the leader of the Nazi party, despised their left-wing ideology and led a brutal invasion into their territory. Before the Soviets finally pushed them back—at Stalingrad in 1943, probably the turning point in the war, a year before the Americans landed in Europe—they had already suffered catastrophic losses. By the time the Red Army reached Berlin in 1945, occupying much of Central and Eastern Europe in the process, at least twenty-seven million Soviet citizens had died.[5]

The Soviet Union was an even younger country than the United States. It was founded in 1917 by a small group of radical intellectuals inspired by German philosopher Karl Marx, after a revolution overthrew a decrepit Russian monarchy ruling over an empire that largely consisted of impoverished peasants, and that was considered backward compared to the advanced capitalist countries of Western Europe, where Marx—and Vladimir Lenin, the first Soviet leader—actually thought the world socialist revolution was supposed to start.

These revolutionaries faced a civil war from 1918 to 1920, and employed what the Bolsheviks themselves called "terror" to defeat the White forces, a loose coalition of conservatives, Russian nationalists, and anticommunists, who were also engaging in mass murder. After Lenin died in 1924, his ruthless successor, Joseph Stalin, forcefully collectivized agricultural production, built a centrally planned economy, and used mass imprisonment and execution to deal with his real and perceived enemies. Millions died as a result in the 1930s, including some of the original architects of the revolution, and Stalin shifted the official ideology of the international Communist movement back and forth to suit his own political needs. But much of the worst of this remained secret. Instead, the Soviet Union's rapid industrialization and subsequent defeat of the Nazis—as well as the fact that it was communists who often resisted both fascism and colonialism earliest and most forcefully around the world—gave it significant global prestige in 1945.[6]

The Soviets became the world's second "superpower," but they were far weaker than the United States in every way that counts. By the late 1940s, the US produced a full half of the world's manufactured goods. By 1950, the US economy was probably as big as all of Europe and the Soviet Union combined.[7] As for military strength, the Soviet population had been decimated, and this was especially true for those who could be called on to fight in any war. Even though hundreds of thousands of Soviet women bravely fought the Nazis, the gender imbalance in 1945 drives home the devastation. By 1945, there were only seven men for every ten women between the ages of twenty and twenty-nine.[8] The US had superior military power, and demonstrated the apocalyptic damage it could unfurl from the air when it dropped atomic bombs on Hiroshima and Nagasaki.

That is what we are talking about when we discuss the "First World" and the "Second World" in the years after 1945. The First World consisted of the rich countries in North America, Western Europe, Australia, and Japan, all of which had gotten wealthy while engaging in colonialism. Their leading power, the United States, was late to that game, at least outside North America, but it certainly played. The young United States took control of the Louisiana territories, Florida, Texas, and the Southwest by waging war or threatening to attack.[9] Then, Washington took over Hawaii after a group of businessmen overthrew Queen Liliuokalani in 1893, and gained control of Cuba, Puerto Rico, and the Philippines in the Spanish-American War of 1898. The Philippines, the second-largest country in Southeast Asia, remained a formal colony until 1945, while Cuba moved into the informal US sphere of influence in Central America and the Caribbean—where US Marines intervened a dizzying twenty times, at least, by 1920—and Puerto Rico remains in imperial limbo to this day.[10]

The "Second World" was the Soviet Union and the European territories where the Red Army had set up camp. Since its founding, the USSR had publicly aligned itself with the global anticolonial struggle and had not engaged in overseas imperialism, but the world was watching how Moscow would exert influence over the occupied nations of Central and Eastern Europe.

And then there was the "Third World"—everyone else, the vast majority of the world's population. That term was coined in the early 1950s, and originally, all of its connotations were positive. When the leaders of these new nation-states took up the term, they spoke it with pride; it contained a dream of a better future in which the world's downtrodden and enslaved masses would take control of their own destiny. The term was used in the sense of the "Third Estate" during the French Revolution, the revolutionary common people who would overthrow the First and Second Estates of the monarchy and the clergy. "Third" did not mean third-rate, but something more like the third and final act: the first group of rich white countries had their crack at creating the world, as did the second, and this was the new movement, full of energy and potential, just waiting to be unleashed. For much of the planet, the Third World was not just a category; it was a movement.[11]

In 1950, more than two-thirds of the world's population lived in the Third World, and with few exceptions, these peoples had lived under the control of European colonialism.[12] Some of these countries had managed to break free of imperial rule in the nineteenth century; some earned their independence when fascist forces retreated at the end of World War II; some attempted to do so in 1945, only to be re-invaded by First World armies; and for many others, the war had changed little, and they were still unfree. All of them inherited economies that were far, far poorer than those in the First World. Centuries of slavery and brutal exploitation had left them to fend for themselves, and decide how they would try to forge a path to independence and prosperity.

The simple version of the next part of this story is that newly independent countries in the Third World had to fight off imperial counterattacks, and then choose if they would follow the capitalist model favored by the United States and Western Europe or attempt to build socialism and follow in the footsteps of the Soviet Union, hopefully moving from poverty to a position of global importance just as quickly as the Russians had. But it was more complicated than that. In 1945, it was still possible to believe they could be friendly with both Washington and Moscow.

A Vietnamese man named Ho Chi Minh, who had previously worked as a photo retoucher in Paris and as a baker in the United States, embraced revolutionary Marxism after he blamed the Western capitalist powers for refusing to acknowledge Vietnamese sovereignty at the Versailles Peace Conference following World War I.[13] He became an agent for the Communist International before he led the Viet Minh resistance movement against the

Japanese occupation in the 1940s. But when he arrived at the Ba Đình flower garden in downtown Hanoi after the two nuclear strikes on Japan by the US to declare independence on September 2, 1945, he opened with the following words: "'All men are created equal. They are endowed by their Creator with certain inalienable rights; among these are Life, Liberty and the Pursuit of Happiness.' This immortal statement was made in the Declaration of Independence of the United States of America in 1776. In a broader sense, this means: All the peoples on the earth are equal from birth, all the peoples have a right to live, to be happy and free."[14]

He was celebrating the revolutionary ideals that America's Founding Fathers had bequeathed to the USA, and that its leaders still deeply believed in. He was trying to tell the world that the Vietnamese only wanted what any other people wanted, that is, the right to govern themselves. He was also trying to survive in a very desperate situation. The French colonial army was on its way back to assert white rule over Indochina, and he knew that the last thing he needed was the most powerful country in human history also committed to crushing his independence movement. He was appealing directly to the stated values of the American people, just like many other leftists around the Third World did at the time.

After all, the United States had allied with the Soviet Union against Hitler. For the powerful men in that nation's capital, however, things were changing very quickly.

Washington's anticommunist crusade had actually started well before World War II. Just after the Russian Revolution, President Woodrow Wilson chose to join the other imperial powers in helping the White forces attempt to retake control from the Bolshevik revolutionaries. For two reasons. First, the core, foundational American ideology is something like the exact opposite of communism.[15] Strong emphasis is placed on the individual, not the collective, and an idea of freedom that is strongly linked to the right to own things. This had been, after all, the basis for full citizenship in the early American republic: only white men with property could vote. And secondly, Moscow presented itself as a geopolitical and ideological rival, an alternative way that poor peoples could rise into modernity without replicating the American experience.[16]

But in the years just after World War II, a series of events brought anticommunism to the very center of American politics, in an intensely fanatical new form.

Actually Existing Anticommunism

It started in Europe, in areas ravaged by World War II. It did not please leaders in Washington that Communist parties won the first postwar elections in both France and Italy.[17] In Greece, communist-led guerrillas who had fought the Nazis refused to disarm or recognize the government set up under British supervision, and civil war broke out. Then there was West Asia. In Turkey, the victorious Soviets demanded access to key waterways, sparking a small political crisis. In Iran, the northern half of which had been under Soviet control since 1941 (per agreement with the Western Allies), the Communist-led Tudeh Party had become the largest and best-organized political group in the country, and ethnic minorities were demanding independence from the Shah, or king, installed by the British.

President Truman had much less patience for the Soviet Union than his predecessor, and he was looking for a way to confront Stalin. Greece and Turkey gave it to him. In March 1947, he asked Congress for civilian and military support to those countries in a special address that outlined what would be known as the Truman Doctrine.

"The very existence of the Greek state is today threatened by the terrorist activities of several thousand armed men, led by Communists," he said. "I believe that it must be the policy of the United States to support free peoples who are resisting attempted subjugation by armed minorities or by outside pressures."[18]

Arthur Vandenberg, chairman of the Senate Foreign Relations Committee, had given some advice to Truman—in order to get what they wanted, the White House had to "scare the hell out of the American people" about communism. Truman took that advice, and it worked wonders. The anticommunist rhetoric only intensified, as the nature of the US political system provided clear incentives for its escalation. After Truman was re-elected in 1948, it just made political sense for the defeated Republican Party to accuse him of being "soft on communism," even though he was nothing of the sort.[19]

The specific kind of anticommunism that took shape in these years was partly based on value judgments: the widespread belief in the United States that communism was simply a bad system, or morally repugnant even when effective. But it was also based on a number of assertions about the nature of Soviet-led international communism. There was widespread belief that

Stalin wanted to invade Western Europe. It became accepted as fact that the Soviets were pushing for revolution worldwide, and that whenever communists were present, even in small numbers, they probably had secret plans to overthrow the government. And it was considered gospel that anywhere communists were acting, they were doing so on the orders of the Soviet Union, part of a monolithic global conspiracy to destroy the West. Most of this was simply untrue. Much of the rest was greatly exaggerated.

The case of Greece, the conflict Truman used essentially to launch the Cold War, is an important example. Stalin actually instructed the Greek communists to stand down and let the British-backed government take control after the Nazis left.[20] The Greek communists refused to heed his instructions. Fighting a right-wing government that wanted to annihilate them was more important to them than any loyalty to the Soviet Union. Similarly, the Soviet leader told the Italian and French Communists to lay down their arms (they did), and asked Yugoslavia's communist forces to stop supporting their Greek comrades, cede control of their country, and merge with Bulgaria (Yugoslavia's leader, Josip Tito, did not, causing such a huge rift that Stalin tried to kill him).[21] The leaders of Iran's Tudeh Party thought their country was ripe for revolution after World War II, but the Soviets told them to try no such thing, and the USSR had already decided by 1946 that Turkey was not worth the trouble. The Soviet leader had no plans to invade Western Europe. Stalin of course did not back off in those parts of the world out of some generosity of spirit or his deep respect for the right of national self-determination. He did so because he had made a deal with the Western powers at Yalta, and he was too afraid of antagonizing the United States to violate it. He was surprised to see that Washington acted as if he had antagonized them anyway.[22]

The right-wing Greek government got the backing of the United States, which far preferred a British ally over leftist guerrillas, and employed a chemical called napalm for the first time in history to crush rebels who had fought against Hitler's forces. The Royal Hellenic Air Force dropped the chemical poison over the verdant mountains of the Vitsi region, near the Albanian border. In Western Europe, the ancestral home of every US leader to date, Washington introduced the Marshall Plan, a brilliantly designed and magnificently effective economic aid package that put these rich countries on the path to American-style capitalist redevelopment.[23]

There existed many currents of socialism, Marxism, and communism in the world, and even parties that were theoretically loyal to the Soviet

Union acted independently when they saw fit. And Marxism as a guiding ideology, including in the Marxist-Leninist formulation cemented by Stalin, certainly did not prescribe that everyone everywhere make revolution at all times. In their worldview, you certainly didn't get socialism just because you wanted it.

Before Marx himself started writing, there was already a tradition of "utopian socialists." One of the main points of Marxism was to reject the idea that you could simply will the world you want into existence, and Marx laid out a theory in which societies moved forward through conflict between economic classes. In *The Communist Manifesto*, Marx and Friedrich Engels praised capitalism as a revolutionary force, saying that the emergence of the bourgeoisie had liberated humanity from the bonds of feudalism and unleashed powers hitherto unseen. He predicted that the capitalist mode of production would lead to the growth of a working class, which would then overthrow these bourgeois masters in the advanced capitalist countries. This is not how it actually worked out in Europe, but the Soviets still believed in the theory, and in the primacy of class development and economic relations. You had to get through capitalism to get to socialism, their theory went.

Well before the Russian Revolution, some Marxist parties in Europe, such as the Social Democrats in Germany, rejected the revolutionary path and committed themselves to forwarding the interests of the working class within parliamentary electoral systems. Even among the explicitly pro-Soviet parties in the new Communist International, or "Comintern," active from 1919 to 1943, applications of the official ideology varied, and the way that they actually acted was usually based on some combination of the possibilities offered by their local conditions, an interpretation of Marxist orthodoxy, and geopolitical concerns.[24]

The case of Mao Zedong in China is an important example. The Comintern provided training to both his Communist Party and the Nationalists, led by Chiang Kai-shek, directing them to organize along Leninist lines, meaning that they would be strictly disciplined and governed by the principle of "democratic centralism." The Chinese Communists were ordered by Moscow to work directly with the Nationalists in a broad "United Front," a concept that the Comintern itself had developed.[25] It was believed that because China was such an impoverished peasant society, the country was nowhere near the state of capitalist development that would make revolution possible.

The experiences of an older Communist Party inspired this approach. A Dutchman named Henk Sneevliet, the local Comintern boss, had helped found Asia's first Communist Party outside the former Russian Empire— the Indonesian Communist Party—and thought the Chinese party could learn from the success that Indonesian Communists had working with the Islamic Union mass movement.[26] Mao's job was to support the "bourgeois" Nationalists, and play a secondary role in the construction of a capitalist nation. A loyal Communist, Mao obeyed. This did not work out so well for the Chinese Communists. In 1927, Chiang turned on them. Starting with a massacre in Shanghai, Nationalist troops killed more than one million people, taking aim at Communists, peasant leaders, and organizers, across the country in a wave of "White Terror" over the next few years.[27] The Chinese Communists and the Nationalists teamed up again to fight off the occupying Japanese until the end of World War II, and afterward, Stalin ordered the Communists to stand down again.[28]

In Eastern Europe, Stalin took a very different approach, as he considered this area his rightful sphere of influence, because his troops had taken it from Hitler, and an important buffer against possible invasion from the West. After the announcement of the Truman Doctrine and the beginning of the Marshall Plan, Moscow engineered a communist coup in Czechoslovakia. The Western powers did not play fair in the territory their armies had occupied, either. After it became clear that so many Italians and French wanted to vote freely for Communist parties, the US intervened heavily in Western Europe to make sure that the leftists didn't take over. In Paris, the government, which was heavily dependent on US financial aid, ousted all its Communist ministers in 1947.[29] In Italy the US funneled millions of dollars to the Christian Democratic Party and spent millions more on anticommunist propaganda. Big stars like Frank Sinatra and Gary Cooper recorded spots for the US government's Voice of America radio station. Washington organized a huge writing campaign from Italian Americans to friends and relatives back in the home country, with form letters including messages such as "A communist victory would ruin Italy. The United States would withdraw aid and a world war would probably result" and "If the forces of true democracy should lose in the Italian election, the American Government will not send any more money to Italy."[30] The Communists lost.

By the end of the 1940s all of the area that had been liberated by the Red Army consisted of one-party Communist states, and all of the area controlled by Western powers was capitalist with a pro-American orientation, regardless of what the people may have wanted in 1945.

After a famous Winston Churchill speech, many in the West began to say that Eastern European socialist states were behind an "Iron Curtain." Italian Communist leader Palmiro Togliatti, whose party remained popular for decades, said that the United States was a nation led by ignorant "slaveholders" who now wanted to buy entire nations just as they had bought human beings.[31] Stalin, as a Marxist-Leninist, certainly thought that communism would eventually win. The laws of history made that inevitable. But for that very reason—and because the Soviets had been so weakened by the war—he had no intention of invading Western Europe. He thought that the next world war would break out between the imperialist Western powers, as his own theories seemed to indicate.[32]

But in China, Mao decided to ignore Stalin's directives this time, continuing to wage a civil war after the end of World War II. In 1949, he finally defeated the Nationalists, whose venality, brutality, and incompetence had long troubled their backers in Washington. Like Ho Chi Minh in August 1945, Mao had also been under the illusion that he could have good relations with the United States. He was wrong, of course.[33] After his victory, the emergency of "Red China" led to violent recriminations back in the United States.

Global McCarthyism

McCarthyism is named after Senator Joseph McCarthy, who led a wild search for communists in the US government in the early 1950s, but it's best understood as a process that started before that man famously began drunkenly berating people in front of the entire nation, and its consequences extended long after he was exposed as a liar.[34] The House Un-American Activities Committee (HUAC) began its activities in 1938, and only finished in 1975. The famous public trials weren't simply "witch hunts," in which mobs went after entities that don't exist; there really were communists in the United States. They were active in labor unions, Hollywood, and some parts of the government, and the Communist Party USA had attracted many black and Jewish members. They were never hugely popular in the 1930s, but what changed after World War II was that communists were no longer welcome at all.

McCarthyism was a top-down process, driven especially by the presidency and the FBI. In 1947, FBI Director J. Edgar Hoover, who had been hugely influential in creating and disseminating the anticommunist consensus, addressed HUAC and gave voice to some of the fundamental assumptions of that ethos.[35] He said that communists planned to organize a military revolt in the country, which would culminate in the extermination of the police forces and the seizure of all communications. He said:

> One thing is certain. The American progress which all good citizens seek, such as old-age security, houses for veterans, child assistance, and a host of others, is being deployed as window dressing by the Communists to conceal their true aims and entrap gullible followers. . . . The numerical strength of the party's enrolled membership is insignificant . . . for every party member there are ten others ready, willing, and able to do the party's work. . . . There is no doubt as to where a real Communist's loyalty rests. Their allegiance is to Russia.[36]

Hoover had presented a logical death trap. If anyone accuses you of being communist, or communist-adjacent, no defense is possible. If you are simply promoting mild social reform, well, that is exactly what a communist would do, in order to conceal their true motives. If your numbers are insignificant, that is only further proof of your deviousness, as your comrades are all lurking in the shadows. And if there are a lot of you, or you're openly, proudly communist, that's just as bad.

As McCarthyism took off, anything smelling even remotely like communism was expelled from polite American society. A young actor named Ronald Reagan imposed a loyalty oath on all the members of the Screen Actors Guild, the powerful union he led at the time. At the levels of government that mattered, everyone who remained was a fanatical anticommunist—which meant that some of the smartest experts in the State Department, the US diplomatic service, were purged. Because of the "loss" of China to communism, longtime Asia specialists in particular were accused of harboring left-wing sympathies.[37]

As one Brazilian historian puts it, the USA had not invented the ideology, but in the years after World War II, the country was transformed into the global "fortress of anticommunism," expending considerable resources on promoting the cause, and serving as a reference and source of legitimacy for like-minded movements around the world.[38]

By the end of the 1940s, the lines defining the First and Second World had become relatively stable. What was still in flux, however, was the future of the Third World.

The Jakarta Axiom

After the Truman Doctrine and the beginning of McCarthyism, there was no question that communists, and communist governments, were the enemy of Washington. No matter what they hoped for in 1945, Ho Chi Minh and Mao were not going to be welcomed onto the world stage. It was not so clear, on the other hand, what the men running the US government would do with the growing wave of radical Third World movements that were opposed to European imperialism, were not communist, but resisted forming an explicit alliance with Washington against Moscow. This was a very common phenomenon. Many leaders of Third World independence movements associated the United States with its Western European imperialist allies; others believed the Soviet Union was an important friend in the struggle against colonialism. Even if they did not want to be ruled by the Soviets, they wanted as many allies as they could get.

In 1948, the outcome of a small power struggle in the former Dutch East Indies seemed to offer a solution. On the island of Java, independence forces were battling an army that had arrived from the Netherlands in the attempt to reconquer its colonies in Southeast Asia. They had lost this vast archipelago to the Japanese during World War II, and refused to recognize the government set up by locals in 1945. During the war of independence, right-leaning republican forces clashed with communists within the revolutionary movement around the city of Madiun, East Java. The communists were defeated, with the support of independence leader Sukarno, and the head of the Indonesian Communist Party was killed in what became known as the Madiun Affair.[39] The huge nation that Sukarno would go on to lead after the Dutch were finally expelled in 1949, now called Indonesia, was seen as willing enough to put down communist uprisings to be of long-term advantage of the United States.

Under Truman, the US foreign policy establishment saw Sukarno's nascent Indonesia as the axiomatic case of a sufficiently anticommunist anticolonial movement, and so the name of its capital, Jakarta, came to signify this principle of tolerance for neutral Third World nations. As Cold War historian Odd Arne Westad put it, Washington adopted the "Jakarta Axiom."[40]

This position was not very stable, nor were the real-world actions of the United States satisfactory to the leaders of the new Third World. A young congressman from Massachusetts named John F. Kennedy had the curiosity, ambition, and money to travel the world trying to get an idea of their attitudes, and what he got was an earful.

Jack Kennedy, or JFK, was a rare bird among the US elite. He was a Catholic, and he was much more than the "First Irish Brahmin"—he was the first member of American royalty to descend from the masses of people who had come to the country as impoverished immigrants rather than as colonizers.[41] His father, Joseph Kennedy, had fought prejudice and probability to build a huge fortune in finance and real estate, and by the time young Jack went off to fight in World War II, he had been on a grand tour of Europe, swung through most of South America, and graduated from Harvard.

Joe Kennedy understood one fundamental truth about political power in the United States. You can buy it. He spent a "staggering sum" on Jack's 1946 congressional race, according to one of his cousins. He told two reporters: "Politics is like war. It takes three things to win. The first is money and the second is money and the third is money." Joe's assistant liked to hand out cash in public toilets, just to be on the safe side.[42] Jack, who like his father was considered a playboy by those who knew him, won easily. But US politics can't run on money alone—he did also need to maintain public support. The nature of his working-class Catholic constituency pushed him a bit to the "liberal" side of the aisle, however, into an alliance with those who had supported Franklin Delano Roosevelt's New Deal.

But Jack certainly had no time for the reds. During his first campaign, he said, "The time has come when we must speak plainly on the great issue facing the world today. The issue is Soviet Russia."[43] He saw labor unions as self-serving and infiltrated by communists, and let their members know it in congressional hearings. And in 1954, when a special Senate committee recommended that Joseph McCarthy be condemned for breaking Senate rules, John F. Kennedy was the only Democrat not to vote against him.[44] However, perhaps because he was so well traveled, or perhaps because he was Irish, and knew in some very small way what it felt like to come from a people who had been oppressed somewhere, JFK viewed the Third World differently from most of the Washington elites. While so many others saw any deviation from an explicit alliance with the US as communist subversion of the global order, JFK believed that emerging nations were insisting on their right to forge their own path, and that this was entirely understandable.

In 1951, he went on a trip to Morocco, Iran, Egypt, Indochina, Malaya, Burma, India, and Pakistan, and came to the conclusion that the United States had failed to understand the importance of "nationalistic passions . . . directed primarily against the Colonial policies of the West."[45]

Later that year, he went on another one of his long jaunts, this time to Israel, Iran, Pakistan, Singapore, French Indochina, Korea, Japan, and Indonesia. He observed that the US "was definitely classed with the imperialist powers of Europe." Washington desperately needed to align with the emerging nations, but that was difficult because Americans were "more and more becoming colonialists in the minds of the people."[46]

Reflecting on the situation in Vietnam, he reported that the United States had "allied ourselves to the desperate effort of a French regime to hang on to the remnants of Empire." He said, "If one thing was borne into me as a result of my experience in the Middle as well as the Far East, it is that Communism cannot be met effectively by merely the force of arms."[47]

But it was in India that Jack and his brother Bobby really got a lecture from one of the world's new class of leaders. Jawaharlal Nehru, India's first prime minister, like Gamal Abdel Nasser, who came to power in Egypt in 1952, favored the construction of a socialist society. Both these leaders rejected the Leninist model and wanted to forge their own path, but when push came to shove, they often preferred to align with the Soviets rather than with the Americans and their European allies. Even if he had known about the worst tragedies of the 1930s in the Soviet Union, it would be hard to blame Nehru for distrusting the Western powers. During World War II, British policies created a famine that took the lives of four million people.

British Prime Minister Winston Churchill blamed the Indians for the famine his own government caused, saying it was their fault for "breeding like rabbits," and asked why Gandhi—whom Churchill loathed—hadn't died yet.[48]

When Jack and two younger siblings dined with Nehru in 1951, the Indian leader was imperious, acting bored and unimpressed, and only showed interest in their sister Pat, Bobby Kennedy reported. When JFK asked Nehru about Vietnam, the Indian leader dismissed the French war as an example of doomed colonialism, and said the US was pouring its aid money down a "bottomless hole." He gently lectured the Kennedys, as if he were speaking to children, and Bobby wrote down in his notes, in an exasperated tone, that Nehru told them communism offered the people of the Third World "something to die for." Bobby continued jotting down Nehru's comments in his journal: "We [Americans] have only status quo to offer these people."[49]

Smiling Jones and Wisner's Weirdos

As the United States woke up to its position of unprecedented global power, there were a few ways its government could interact with the rest of the world. The president was in charge of the Department of War, or the Pentagon, which soon became the Department of Defense. There was the State Department, the US foreign ministry and diplomatic service, which had been in operation since 1789. But there was no dedicated spy service—there was no permanent institution engaged in gathering information abroad and licensed to carry out secret operations, covert action seeking to change the course of events around the world. The Americans did not have the centuries of experience running a global empire the British did, or even the experience of ongoing, self-defensive spycraft the Soviets inherited from the Russian Empire. But Washington created a new intelligence agency very quickly, using the country's vast wealth to fund it generously and young men who cut their teeth abroad during World War II to staff it.

One of the most important new hires was Frank Wisner, who had a story he would tell every time he was trying to explain why he did what he did for the United States government. Wisner had flown into Romania in September 1944 to work as station chief for the Office of Strategic Services (OSS), the temporary spy agency that Washington set up during the war. Once there, he heard, and believed, that the Soviets were scheming to take control of the country, but his bosses back home were in no mood to hear that their allies were up to no good. In January 1945, Stalin ordered that thousands of men and women of German descent be taken back to the Soviet Union to be "mobilized for work." Wisner knew some of them personally. As the forced evacuation began, he rode frantically around the city, as he told it, trying to save them. But he failed. Thousands of people were herded onto boxcars and sent to labor camps. According to his family, those scenes would haunt him for the rest of his troubled life.[50]

Wisner, sometimes just called "Wiz," was born in 1909 to a wealthy family with a lot of land in Missouri, one of the states in the US South governed by Jim Crow laws, which discriminated against African Americans. He grew up in an insular, privileged household. As a child, he didn't even put on his own clothes—he would lie down, raise his arms and legs, and his black maid would put his shirt and trousers on for him.[51] Frank's favorite book was *Kim*, by Rudyard Kipling, which told its story against the backdrop of the "Great Game" between the British and Russian Empires.[52] Wiz was sent off to the aristocratic Woodberry Forest School in Virginia. He desperately lifted weights to add bulk to his wiry frame and was intensely competitive. At the University of Virginia, he was tapped to the join the Sevens, a secret society so baroque that it only revealed the names of its members at their death. He was intense, but could come alive, especially at parties liberally lubricated with alcohol. Wiz became a lawyer at a white shoe firm on Wall Street. Restless, and driven by an intense sense of moral purpose, he enlisted in the Navy a year before the Japanese attacked the United States at Pearl Harbor.[53]

The OSS liked to hire elite corporate lawyers from the best schools, and Wisner fit the bill. He got into the intelligence service with the help of an old professor, and took to the life like a fish to water. In Romania, he wasn't only gathering information and attempting to save Germans. He was hobnobbing with royalty, drinking and dancing, living in a mansion, and doing magic tricks.[54] He was also socializing alongside the more experienced Soviet agents. After he left Romania, it became clear that Russian spies had infiltrated his entire operation.[55]

Back on Wall Street after the war, Wisner was once more bored and listless. So he jumped at the opportunity to serve his country again, and to fight the communists.[56] He took over a new covert operations organization innocuously named the Office of Policy Coordination (OPC) and began activities in Berlin.

At the same time, a very different man named Howard Palfrey Jones, working in the opposite arm of the US foreign policy apparatus, arrived in Berlin along with Allen Dulles, Wisner's old OSS boss. Jones was a diplomat and a veteran who had witnessed the brutality of German National Socialism early. On a trip to Germany in 1934, he was beaten by Nazi soldiers because he failed to salute the Nazi flag properly.[57] He was already a grown man when World War II started, and served in Germany. Immediately after the war, he entered the State Department. Unlike Wisner, who was a die-hard crusader, Jones had an entirely different approach to the rest of the world. Rather than viewing every situation in terms of a black-and-white global struggle, he sought to engage deeply with the complexities of each situation. And he was having a great time.

In almost every picture taken of him, Howard Palfrey Jones looks like a big, good-natured goofball. He has a wide grin on his face, looking just very pleased to be there, whether among Javanese dancers or rubbing elbows with fellow diplomats. His contemporaries described him in similar terms. He would strut around the world in white sharkskin suits, doing his best to use the local language and make friends with everyone. Even those who considered him an enemy—that is, the communists—called him Smiling Jones, and warned comrades not to be taken in by his wholesome demeanor.[58]

Jones was born into a middle-class family in Chicago in 1899. The city was bustling and chaotic, and he grew up causing all kinds of trouble with a mix of kids—sons of immigrants from Poland, Italy, Bohemia, and Norway—in the neighborhood.[59]

By global standards, his childhood was an absolute dream. But compared to the likes of Wisner and Kennedy, he was just a regular guy. And when asked later in life to describe the experience he was most proud of, he went straight to the time he tried to take on racism in the US. After college at the University of Wisconsin, he became a newspaper editor in Evansville, Indiana. The paper found that the Ku Klux Klan, a brutal white supremacist organization, was running a web of criminal activities and controlled the police. The editors prepared an exposé, and the KKK grand eagle called to threaten Jones directly. He ran the story anyway, and the Klan burned crosses throughout the town. Half the paper's advertisers pulled out of the paper.[60]

The State Department was different from the hard-charging outfits Wisner worked for. But even compared to most diplomats at State, Jones was especially engaged and empathetic. He was called, perhaps a bit dismissively, the master of the "soft sell," which meant that he presented the official position of the US government as gently as possible. For him, foreign policy had to be based on deep knowledge of what the local people wanted, and this meant that no one-size-fits-all approach could work. He certainly believed it was acceptable for Washington to try to change the world and pursue its own interests. But how could you do so without understanding each culture on its own terms?

In Berlin in 1948, Jones and Wisner were both working on the big issue of the day in Germany—financial affairs in the divided country. Wisner pressed hard for an adversarial stance toward Moscow. He supported the creation of a new currency in the Western-occupied areas. In June 1948, the Allied governments decided to unilaterally issue a currency for West Germany, the deutsche mark, catching the Soviets off guard and likely forcing the long-term split of the country into two.[61]

Afterward, Jones was sent to work in Taiwan, where Chiang Kai-shek's Nationalists had set up a government. Because they refused to recognize Mao's communist government on the mainland, the US government recognized this as the "real" China, even though Taiwan had its own population and identity before they arrived. This was no democracy. In February 1947, the new government massacred thousands of people opposed to Nationalist rule, beginning another period of White Terror and intermittent repression of dissidents, often justified on anticommunist grounds, that continued for years.[62]

By 1951, Wisner's OPC had been absorbed into a newly formed, permanent organ called the Central Intelligence Agency, and his title had become deputy director of plans. Wiz was the man in charge of clandestine operations. His team—often called his "gang of weirdos" elsewhere in Washington—started looking for ways to fight the Cold War, in secret around the world, however they could.

Wisner was a real blue blood. But most of the ranks of the early CIA were from an even higher strata of American society. Many were Yale men, of the type who would look down on other Yale men if they didn't come from the right boarding school or enter the right secret society. But when it came to anticommunism, Wiz had most of them beat. Arthur Schlesinger Jr., who was an OSS sergeant in Germany, said, "I myself was no great admirer of the Soviet Union, and I certainly had no expectations of harmonious relations after the war. But Frank was a little excessive, even for me."[63]

The CIA boys and their wives built a lively social life around Washington, DC. More urbane and liberal than most people in that city at the time, they would organize spirited dinner parties at their houses in Georgetown. They'd invite over CIA agents, defense officials, and influential journalists. After the meal, the women would retire to one room, while the men talked politics in another, which was the style at the time.[64] They also liked to get very drunk, just like James Bond. As a matter of fact, they looked up to the Secret Intelligence Service, or MI6, the British agency that had accumulated so much expertise in spycraft while maintaining the British empire for centuries. And some of them loved James Bond himself. Tracy Barnes, one of the Agency's founding figures, loved the character created by Ian Fleming in 1953, and would pass out copies of the novels to his family at Thanksgiving.[65]

Paul Nitze, the man who wrote the so-called blueprint of the Cold War, described the upper-class imperial values that children soaked up at the Groton School, a private institution which was modeled on elite English schools and gave the CIA many of its key early members.

"In history, every religion has greatly honored those members who destroyed the enemy. The Koran, Greek mythology, the Old Testament. Groton boys were taught that," said Nitze. "Doing in the enemy is the right thing to do. Of course, there are some restraints on ends and means. If you go back to Greek culture and read Thucydides, there are limits to what you can do to other Greeks, who are a part of your culture. But there are no limits to what you can do to a Persian. He's a Barbarian." The communists, he concluded, "were barbarians."[66]

From the beginning the CIA had two basic divisions. On one side was the gathering of intelligence through espionage. Their job was something akin to providing a private news service for the president. On the other side was covert action—the rough stuff, the active attempts to change the world. That was Frank Wisner's territory.

Wiz started out by building a network of spies and "stay-behind" agents in Western Europe, whose job was to rise to action if the Soviets ever did invade.[67] In Germany, the CIA had no problem recruiting former Nazis, including those who had run death squads, as long as they were anticommunist. Then Wisner looked for a way to penetrate Soviet territory. He recruited desperate, homeless Ukrainian refugees, many of whom had fought with the Nazis, to parachute into communist territory and revolt against the Russians. None of them survived.[68] But that didn't stop Wisner. The Agency sent hundreds of Albanian agents back to their homeland. Almost all were captured or killed. It almost seemed as if the Soviet-aligned government was waiting for them. They were. Kim Philby, a British agent who worked closely alongside Wisner and the rest of the CIA, had been a Soviet mole the whole time. Almost every single one of Wisner's early operations had been compromised somehow. Wisner sent more men into Albania even after he found this out. They were caught and put on trial.

Slowly but surely, Wiz and the CIA boys realized that actual Soviet territory was mostly rock solid. They were certainly failing to penetrate it. If they wanted to fight communism—and they did, very badly—they had to look elsewhere. The Third World offered that opportunity. The problem these men overlooked, according to a mostly sympathetic history written by journalist Evan Thomas, was "the fact that they knew almost nothing about the so-called developing world."[69]

2

Independent Indonesia

A New Life for Francisca

In 1951, Francisca came back to her home country. At twenty-four years old, she and her new husband moved into what was basically a garage at the Air Force airport, ten miles outside the center of town. This was much rougher than what she was used to, but they had a cousin who hooked them up with the space, and they took it. Every day, she woke up at six in the morning, rode her bicycle to the nearest station, caught a bus, then jumped on the back of a little six-seater car with a motorcycle engine, and rode in to work. There was only a little bit of traffic in those days, and almost no Muslim women covered up in *hijab*, but with heavy humidity and temperatures around ninety degrees almost every day of the year, commuting in Jakarta has always been a sweaty, difficult affair.

She didn't mind any of this one bit. Francisca, like so many other Indonesians, was overcome with excitement. After hundreds of years of exploitation and slavery, she had her own country, and it was just one year old.

As she made her way across town every day, she didn't think about the comfortable life she had given up. The only thing she cared about was that she was building up Indonesia from nothing. "We have to live life to the utmost, to do everything we can," she thought. "When you're working toward a cause like this, one that's so much bigger than you, it hardly feels like work at all."[1]

Francisca Pattipilohy was born in 1926, and she was technically royalty. Indonesia has often been governed by numerous small kingdoms (and some large kingdoms), and her family were members of the upper class on Ambon, a quiet and comfortable little island surrounded by white sand and bright blue ocean, 1,500 miles northeast of Jakarta. Those aristocracies were often granted special privileges within the Dutch colonial structure, but her father chose to forgo them and make his life as an architect in the capital, which was then called Batavia. The larger island of Java is one of the world's most densely populated pieces of land, with a dazzling constellation of cities, many of which are thousands of years old, but Batavia was never an important city for any of its local kingdoms. It was an outpost of the major pepper port of Banten when the Dutch East India Company, one of the most important organizations in the development of both global capitalism and colonialism, took over in 1619.[2] The mega-city that exists now was largely a Dutch construction, and it still feels different from the rest of Java.

Francisca's father thrived as an architect, and was able to afford a nice home in the city. He did so well, in fact, that Francisca was able to attend colonial school with Dutch children. At home, she loved to spend time in her father's library, reading the children's books he had bought for her. She was the only little girl in the family, so she was alone in the house a lot. Almost all the children's stories then were in Dutch, telling tales of white children back in Holland or Germany. She dove so deeply into *Grimm's Fairy Tales*, books about cowboys and Indians, and Hans Christian Andersen that she truly believed they referred to her own country. She thought that the Rhine flowed through some part of Indonesia until she was a teenager. But she read nothing about other Indonesians. At home, she would speak both the colonial language, Dutch, and some of the tongue her family had brought from Ambon. Her family was Protestant, as plenty of Indonesians in the "outer islands" are, and she studied at a private Christian school nearby. She was intensely smart and fiercely curious. When she spoke about the fun of learning something new, the pitch of her voice would always rise with excitement.

She also learned very quickly what it meant to be a brown girl in a colony run by white people. There were only five "native" students in her class, and the hierarchy of status was obvious. But it was outside school one Sunday that the brutal reality of her condition was driven home. It was especially hot. She went along with a friend from school and her Dutch family to the local pool, to spend the day swimming. As they handed their tickets to the man at the gate, he stopped her. Indonesians were not allowed. Her relative wealth didn't matter, nor did the fact that the other girls protested. She was a native.

In 1942, when she was just sixteen, the Japanese arrived. Under Emperor Hirohito, the Japanese had become an aggressive imperialist power allied with the Nazis, and were sweeping through much of Southeast Asia, setting up occupation governments. At first, some Indonesians welcomed them, including the leaders of the country's small independence movement, which had been bubbling up for decades. At least the Japanese were Asians, the thinking went. Their victory had proved whites were not invincible, and they might treat locals better than the Dutch had. The day after their invasion, Francisca's father came home and announced to the family, "They are our liberators."[3]

But young Francisca saw, before most of the country, that this was an illusion. Just days later, the family was going for a walk in their quiet leafy neighborhood, called Menteng, when a Japanese guard nearby started screaming at her father. He, of course, didn't understand Japanese, and he didn't know he was supposed to bow. So he didn't. The guard came up to him and struck him hard, on the face, in front of his whole family. "After that, we hated the Japanese," Francisca would say later. "We knew their true purpose."

Others got it much worse. By the thousands, Indonesian women were forced into sexual slavery, made to work as "comfort women" for the occupying Japanese troops. The Dutch were put into concentration camps. Francisca was put into a different school.

The new school was a bit of a shock, for two reasons. First, she was considered equal to the other students. Second, she learned to speak Bahasa Indonesia, which means "the Indonesian language," a version of Malay that is now Indonesia's official tongue.[4] Francisca had always excelled at language, but here she was starting from zero. She wasn't alone, though. Only a small minority of Indonesians spoke it as their first language. It had been used as a lingua franca at ports and in trade for a while, but most people spread across the country's thirteen thousand wildly diverse islands didn't know it.[5]

Soon after the Japanese left in 1945, a man named Sukarno declared independence very close to Francisca's house.[6] He had been hesitant to do it. So three youth leaders in the independence movement, impatient with his decision, kidnapped him and fellow independence leader Hatta—this was considered a brusque but broadly acceptable way of forcing someone's hand at the time—until Sukarno committed to proclaiming the creation of independent Indonesia.

Maybe he was right to be a bit worried. Not long after the speech, Sukarno's independence movement was in trouble. Just as the French did in Indochina, the Dutch came back, attempting to reassert colonial rule. The Netherlands called the attempts at reconquest "police actions," in terminology that managed to be both condescending and euphemistic, and they were brutal. As the Japanese had, the Dutch employed mass violence to suppress support for the new republic. The independence leaders, a mix of nationalists, leftists, and Islamic groups, hopped around the archipelago, making alliances with local kingdoms and mounting resistance.[7]

In the middle of all this, in 1947, Francisca went to Holland to study in the small university town of Leiden. She attended the Royal Institute of Eastern Countries, set up to study European colonial possessions. Right away, she got involved in the Indonesian student organization, as almost everyone did. And right away, she met a man named Zain, five years her senior.

She didn't like him at first. She had considered herself "some kind of a feminist" from an early age, and had no intention of marrying, ever. She had seen that even the smartest, best-educated women in the Dutch East Indies never got to put to use all the wonderful things that they learned once they got married. She wanted to work. Zain was handsome, sure, even gallant, but he was a little too self-assured, maybe, a little too bossy when he asked her to take the role of treasurer within the student organization. She wasn't going to let anyone think she was impressed with him, like so many other girls were. So at first, a bit coyly, she rejected his advances.

But then she got to know him. They'd spend hours and hours talking, about history, and the anticolonial struggle, and the ways her childhood had been unjust, twisted by European domination. How they could fight to make things right. This was exciting. He was exciting, she was willing to admit that. They began working together tirelessly, united by a common cause. That cause, of course, was independence.

Somewhat ironically, direct contact with Europe had always been important for fomenting revolutionary movements in the Third World. The Indonesian independence movement had early roots in Holland, and it was in Paris that Ho Chi Minh got his political education. When studying or working back in the imperial capitals, colonial subjects often came into contact with ideas that were never allowed to reach their territories. Much of colonialism had relied on the logic of "Do as I say, not as I do." Or in practice, "Do as white say, not as white do." So while Europeans themselves were extending education to their entire populations, and their intellectuals were debating the merits of socialism and Marxism, much of this was banned in the colonies. The natives might get ideas. For example, in the Congo, brutally controlled by the Belgians since King Leopold II established the Free Congo State in 1885 (and the United States rushed to be the first country in the world to recognize the colony), authorities banned left-leaning publications and liberal lifestyle magazines that circulated freely back in Europe, and were scared even by the fact that working-class blacks lived together in urban areas. Wouldn't this lead to subversion, or worse, Bolshevism? Congolese pupils learned about the Belgian royal family, but not the American civil rights movement, and the French Revolution was explained very carefully, so as not to make that whole affair seem too attractive in African editions of textbooks.

The justification given by European authorities in the Congo went like this: "All those in our colony are unanimous in stating that the blacks are still children, both intellectually and morally."[8]

For Francisca and Zain, who began dating in earnest in the late 1940s, the colonial independence struggle was intimately tied to left-wing politics. So she, a wholehearted supporter of Indonesian freedom, fell naturally into socialist circles, as the two struggles had long been married together. In the 1930s and 1940s, practically no Europeans supported colonial independence except the leftists. The Indonesian Communist Party, the *Partai Komunis Indonesia* (PKI), was founded in 1914 as the Indies Social Democratic Association with the help of Dutch leftists, worked alongside Sukarno and pro-independence Muslim groups in the 1920s, and then engaged in active antifascist work during the Japanese occupation.[9]

Francisca heard a little bit about socialism at the student meetings, and she liked what she heard, but she didn't get too involved in any of the more intricate ideological battles. She didn't take part in debates over the so-called "Madiun Affair" and the clashes between communists and Sukarno's republican forces within the revolutionary movement. It was much easier to take sides when the Netherlands launched a second attempt to reconquer Indonesia. In protest, all the students with Dutch scholarships returned them, and Francisca joined them in walking out of their classes. Then, that same year, she jumped at the opportunity to attend the second World Festival of Youth and Students in Budapest. It was organized by the World Federation of

Democratic Youth. She knew, of course, that "Democratic" in this usage basically meant "socialist," and that Hungary was allied with the Soviet Union, but none of that made the prospect of the journey any less exciting.

Not all of the Indonesian students could afford to attend, but she had the money for a ticket, so she jumped on the train and crossed what the Americans were now calling "the iron curtain." She didn't see one. For her, the trip was a wonder, and she stared out the windows as postwar Germany, then Austria and Hungary, flew by. Europe was in tatters; but still, Budapest was enchanting. And there, no one treated her like a second-class citizen, like they did in her home country. But nothing prepared her for the youth festival itself. She met left-wing students from all over the world, from nations across Asia, from Africa, and even from the United States! This was a real shock to her, as she'd really only seen Americans in the movies.

She began talking to the students from the US, and was even more shocked to see a black man and a white woman together. She didn't know much about international politics, but she knew all about the racism back in the United States. So she asked them, "How did you come here together? Isn't it difficult for you? Don't they keep you apart?"

They chuckled, and nodded. "Well, yes, but we manage," the American woman said.

Next, she met students from Korea and the Congo. Among the Congolese delegation, she swears she met a charming young man by the name of Lumumba, but she didn't know much else about him at the time.[10] The students put on dances and cultural performances from all over the world. They were a display of international unity, as well as the pride that each nation felt. When she described this show afterward, her voice got so high it practically became a whistle.

In 1950, she and Zain eloped. They had to sneak off to Prague to get married, because Dutch authorities would have required her to get her father's permission, and he was still withholding it for some reason or another—they didn't care much why. The trip was another little adventure, and they got to put their language skills to use, because their humble ceremony had to be in German. No problem. By that time, Zain knew English, Indonesian, Dutch, and Batak (the language native to his family on the island of Sumatra), and Francisca was now fluent in German, French, Indonesian, Dutch, and English on top of a bit of *Bahasa Ambon*.

Francisca's father came around to her new husband soon enough, and gave them his blessing. More importantly for them, they both established themselves quickly as productive members of a brand-new society. Upon returning to a new, independent Indonesia, Francisca started working as a librarian—a dream job, because she could be surrounded once more by books. It wasn't hard for her to land a position. The new republic was starving for qualified workers, and was still relying on Dutch librarians to work alongside her. As a result of intentional Dutch neglect, the Indonesian people were badly deprived of education. By the time the Dutch withdrew, only around 5 percent of the Indonesian population of sixty-five million could read and write.[11]

Francisca said, "I think this was one of the worst crimes of colonialism. After three and a half centuries of Dutch occupation we were left with almost no knowledge of our own people, and our own culture."

Meanwhile, Zain started working in journalism, and got a job at a paper called *Harian Rakyat*, or *The People's Daily*. This was the newspaper run by the Indonesian Communist Party, the PKI. It was a great job for Zain to land, and Francisca was very happy for him. There was nothing strange about working for a communist paper at that time, as far as she was concerned. She knew he was close to the Communist Party, and probably a member, but none of it was a big deal. After the 1948 clash, the Communist Party had reorganized and integrated into the new nation. The PKI was one branch of a multiparty patriotic revolution. The PKI was part of Sukarno's new Indonesia.

Because of his language skills, Zain was assigned an extremely interesting beat at the paper. He began writing about international affairs, translating stories from abroad for a local audience. And for someone concerned with Third World liberation and the fight against "imperialism"—to use the language his paper used—the early 1950s were an incredibly interesting time.[12]

US troops were in Korea, in a war few people had expected to break out. After the Japanese left the Korean Peninsula, which they had dominated even more brutally than they did Indonesia, the country was divided in two. During Japanese rule, what was left of the Korean Communist Party (Stalin had much of its leadership executed in the late 1930s) waged fierce guerrilla warfare against the occupiers across Korea and Manchuria until they were forced into exile in Siberia. One of these Communists, Kim Il-sung, took over in the North in 1945.[13] In the South, the occupying US forces plucked up Syngman Rhee, a Christian and anticommunist who had lived in the US for decades, and installed him as leader. His authoritarian government targeted leftists and massacred tens of thousands of people on Jeju, an island that had been controlled since the war by independent "people's commit-tees," using the threat of communism as justification.[14] In 1950, war erupted at the dividing line. Northern communist troops rapidly pushed into Seoul, leading the United States to take to the UN to gather forces for a counter-attack. For reasons that are unclear, Stalin instructed his ambassador to sit out the vote at the UN rather than protest, and the US easily won the vote. The US-UN troops pushed North Korea back to the original borders, but then proceeded north in an attempt to take the whole country. The Soviets offered little help, but to Washington's surprise, Mao's tired and ragged Red Army mobilized to help the Korean communists, largely because they felt they owed the Koreans a debt for the assistance Kim's insurgents had offered them against the Japanese in Manchuria. During the resulting three-year stalemate, the US dropped more than six hundred thousand tons of bombs on Korea, more than was used in the entire Pacific theater in World War II, and poured thirty thousand tons of napalm over the landscape. More than 80 percent of North Korea's buildings were destroyed, and the bombing cam-paign killed an estimated one million civilians.[15]

In Korea, the CIA boys also tried out some of the same tools they had unleashed in Eastern Europe. Thousands of recruited Korean and Chinese agents were dropped into the North during the war. Once again, the infiltra-tion was a total failure. Later, classified CIA documents concluded that the operations "were not only ineffective but probably morally reprehensible in the number of lives lost."[16] The CIA only found out later that all the secret information the Agency gathered during the war had been manufactured by North Korean and Chinese security services.

Once again, the CIA's well-funded covert operations came up short against actual, battle-hardened communist soldiers dedicated to achieving victory. In Iran, however, where there was no such contingent, the young CIA found its first big win.

Operation Ajax

At the end of 1952, Frank Wisner met with Monty Woodhouse, an English spy working in Tehran. The Brits had a problem and needed help. Since the end of World War II, they had been overseeing the formal deconstruction of much of their empire, but they certainly didn't expect that to mean they would lose control over the natural resources, too. In Iran, new Prime Minister Mohammad Mossadegh was overseeing the nationalization of oil production. And he had already caught MI6 trying to overthrow him for it.

Mossadegh and the Iranians had a lot of reasons to resent the British. During their period of imperial glory, Iran suffered a famine that took the lives of two million people. And after World War II, the British set up an arrangement in which they took twice as much income from petroleum as Iran, while local oil workers lived in shanties without running water. When Mossadegh and Iran's elected parliament maneuvered around the Shah the British had put in place, London began looking for a way to claw back what it considered its own. The Americans, Wisner included, were wary of getting tied up in British imperial affairs. But their allies from across the pond appealed to their anticommunism. Mossadegh had legalized the well-organized, Communist-led Tudeh Party (along with all other political parties), and the Brits suggested to the Americans that, perhaps, the Tudeh could take over if they weren't careful, or even that the Soviets might invade.

Changes at the White House at the beginning of 1953 were a very big help to the supporters of regime change. Newly elected Republican President Dwight Eisenhower appointed John Foster Dulles to serve as secretary of state and tapped his younger brother, Allen Dulles, to lead the CIA. John Foster had two lifelong obsessions, according to historian James A. Bill: fighting communism and protecting the rights of multinational corporations. These came together in Iran. "Concerns about communism and the availability of petroleum were interlocked. Together, they drove America to a policy of direct intervention," Bill wrote.[17]

The Dulles brothers and the CIA got the green light. Kermit Roosevelt, the grandson of President Theodore Roosevelt, whom Wisner had hired in 1950, took charge of the mission, which they decided to call Operation Ajax. He had a million dollars to spend in Iran as he pleased, a huge sum for the kind of help he wanted to buy. The CIA bribed every politician it could, and looked for a general willing to take over and install the Shah as dictator. Agents paid street thugs, strongmen, and circus performers to riot in the streets. When CIA station chief Roger Goiran argued the US was making a historic mistake by aligning itself with British colonialism, Allen Dulles recalled him to Washington.

The CIA created pamphlets and posters proclaiming that Mossadegh was a communist, an enemy of Islam. They paid off journalists to write that he was a Jew. The CIA hired gangsters to pretend to be Tudeh Party members and attack a mosque. Two of Roosevelt's Iranian agents, who were handling some of the hired muscle, tried to turn down further work at one point, saying the risk was becoming too great. But Roosevelt convinced them by saying that if they refused, he'd kill them.

For his part, the Shah was not convinced any of this was a good idea. He took off to Rome at one point, infuriating the Americans who wanted to make him king. But he returned to the palace in August 1953, rigged parliamentary elections, and served both the CIA and international oil companies well as ruler of the country. The Soviets did not rush to intervene in the country in which they were supposedly so powerful. In Washington, there were celebrations all around, and Kermit Roosevelt was declared a hero. Wisner had finally proved to the men upstairs that there was a real use for his gang of weirdos.[18]

In 1954, the CIA wrapped up another successful operation, nearby in the Philippines. The left-wing "Huk Rebellion" that began under Japanese occupation continued after both the Japanese left and the US (officially) handed over power to Filipinos. Anti-occupation "Huk" guerrillas were opposed to the new president, who had been an active collaborator with the Axis powers, and the ongoing oligarchical control of the economy by hugely powerful feudal landowners. US military adviser Edward Lansdale, who would later inspire the character of Colonel Edwin Barnum Hillendale in Burdick and Lederer's Ugly American, wrote in his diary that the Huks "believe in the rightness of what they're doing, even though some of the leaders are on the communist side . . . there is a bad situation, needing reform. . . . I suppose armed complaint is a natural enough thing."[19] The US helped the Philippines devise and implement a counterinsurgency operation, and made considerable progress, including the use of more napalm.[20] In a bit of bizarre psychological warfare, Lansdale also collaborated closely with Desmond FitzGerald—a Wisner recruit at the CIA—to create a vampire.

As part of a range of psychological operations alongside the war on the guerrillas, CIA agents spread the rumor that an aswang, a bloodsucking ghoul of Filipino legend, was on the loose and destroying men with evil in their hearts. They then took a Huk rebel they had killed, poked two holes in his neck, drained him of his blood, and left him lying in the road.[21]

After years of conflict, the Huks gave up, and the Philippines settled into right-leaning pro-American stability that would last decades. With special privileges granted to US corporations, the woeful condition of the Filipino people described by Lansdale remained entirely unchanged.

The People's Daily reported on the events in Iran and the Philippines, of course.[22] Even though Washington's real activities were secret at the time, Zain's newspaper and the global left-wing press were often closer to getting the story of Washington's interventions right than US newspapers, which largely saw it as their duty to peddle the official line that Wisner and his team passed on to them.[23]

Zain, working late nights back in Jakarta every day, exhausted himself in this period, being one of a few people who could read and translate all the reports coming in. He was rarely at home with Francisca, as he was always rushing back to the newsroom, working night shifts. *Harian Rakyat*, or *The People's Daily*, was always a lean operation, twenty to thirty people working in downtown Jakarta at all hours.[24]

For a communist newspaper in a heady postrevolutionary environment, *The People's Daily* was a remarkably lighthearted read. There were cartoons poking fun at the bumbling Western imperialists, original works of fiction published every day, a children's section, and educational inserts with explanatory essays on global left-leaning figures like Albert Einstein and Charlie Chaplin. International news, the area that Zain oversaw, was a huge part of the coverage, and the paper paid special attention to events in the rest of the Third World.

News from Amerika

1953 was the end of the Jakarta Axiom; independent countries were no longer tolerated just because they had left-wing forces in check. With the overthrow of Mossadegh in Iran, the new rule under Eisenhower was that neutral governments were potential enemies, and Washington could decide if and when an independent Third World nation was insufficiently anticommunist. Wiz and his boys, emboldened by the success in Tehran, turned their attention to Central America, where they would score the victory that would serve as a template for future covert interventions into the next decade.

A decade before, the Guatemalans had a small revolution. A series of strikes led to the overthrow of Jorge Ubico, a pro-Nazi dictator who had worked hand in hand with the landed aristocracy and foreign corporations for two decades to keep peasants in a system of forced labor—in other words, slavery. The left, including the Guatemalan communist party, called the *Partido Guatemalteco del Trabajo*, or PGT, had long been involved organizing workers in opposition to him. The revolution arrived in 1944, when the United States under FDR was in an alliance with the Soviet Union, and very busy fighting World War II. Perhaps for that reason, the new government didn't ring many alarm bells for US politicians.[25]

From 1944 to 1951, popular schoolteacher Juan José Arévalo took control of the very young democracy in Central America's largest country. But it was the election of Jacobo Árbenz, who took power in 1951, that really turned heads up North.

Árbenz was a middle-class soldier who became a large landowner himself, and to the extent that he ever held any radical ideas, they were probably due to the influence of his California-educated Salvadoran wife, María Vilanova, a more complex and fascinating figure than he. A polyglot social campaigner shocked by inequality, she rejected Central American high society, read intensely and widely, and formed links with leftist figures from around Latin America. Árbenz accepted the small but well-organized PGT as a part of his ruling coalition. But Guatemala voted against the Soviet Union's actions at the UN, and the new president made it clear in his inaugural speech that his goal was to "convert Guatemala with a predominantly feudal economy into a modern capitalist state."[26]

This was no small task. When his government passed a 1952 land reform, this effort ran up against very powerful interests. The government began to buy back large, unused land holdings and distribute them to indigenous people and peasants. Processes of these kind were seen by economists around the world as not only a way of benefiting regular people, but of putting the whole country to productive use and unleashing the forces of market enterprise. But the law stipulated that Guatemala would make payments based on the land's official value, and the United Fruit Company—a US firm that basically controlled the country's economy for decades—had been criminally undervaluing its holdings to avoid paying taxes.

The powerful company howled in protest. United Fruit was extremely well connected in the Eisenhower administration, and started a public relations campaign denouncing Árbenz as a communist in the US, and brought US journalists on press junkets, which were successful in getting deeply critical stories published in outlets like *Time, U.S. News & World Report,* and

Newsweek.[27] The CIA again asked Kermit Roosevelt to oversee operations. He refused this time, telling his superiors that future coups wouldn't work unless the people and the army in the country "want what we want."[28] Frank Wisner chose Tracy Barnes instead.

Washington made three coup attempts, and it was the third one that worked.[29] In November 1953, Eisenhower removed the ambassador in Guatemala City and sent in John Peurifoy, who had been in Athens since 1950 and had thrown together a right-wing government favorable to both Washington and the Greek monarchy. Leftists there called him the "Butcher of Greece."[30]

In Guatemala, the North Americans did their best to create a pretext for intervention. The CIA planted boxes of rifles marked with communist hammers and sickles so they could be "discovered" as proof of Soviet infiltration. When the Guatemalan military, unable to find any other suppliers, did actually buy some weapons (that turned out to be worthless) from Czechoslovakia, Wisner's boys were relieved. Now they had their excuse. Árbenz uncovered plans for the third coup attempt in January 1954, and had them published in the Guatemalan press. The CIA men were so confident that they kept going anyway, issuing denials to the US press. They organized a tiny rebel force around General Carlos Castillo Armas, an unimpressive man despised even by the conservative officers in the Guatemalan military. They began broadcasting false reports, on US-controlled radio stations, of a military rebellion marching toward victory, and dropped bombs on Guatemala City. This was psychological warfare, not a real invasion—the ragtag group over the border in Honduras and El Salvador had no chance of actually entering and defeating the real military, and the bombs that US pilots dropped on the capital became nicknamed *sulfatos*, or sulfate laxatives, because their job was not to do damage, but to make Árbenz and everyone around him so afraid they would fill their pants.[31]

Miguel Ángel Albizures, nine years old, heard the bombs explode near him, and the shock seared a feeling of fear deep into his brain. He was having breakfast before school in the capital, at one of the public eateries set up by Árbenz, when it started. He was terrified—yes, so shocked, so afraid he felt like he could shit himself, exactly as intended—and ran to take cover under the pews in the closest Catholic church.[32]

Árbenz, realizing that the US was determined to oust him, began to contemplate giving in. His government frantically offered to give United Fruit what it wanted. But it was too late for concessions. The communists and a few others urged Árbenz not to hand over power. In vain, a twenty-five-year-old Argentine doctor living in Guatemala City at the time, named Ernesto "Che" Guevara, volunteered to go to the front, then tried to organize civilian militias to defend the capital.

Instead, the president resigned on June 27, 1954, and handed over power to Colonel Díaz, head of the Armed Forces. Díaz had met with Ambassador Peurifoy, and believed he would be an acceptable replacement to the United States. He told Árbenz he had an understanding with the North Americans, and that if he took power, at least they could avoid losing the country to the hated Castillo Armas, which helped persuade the president to step down.[33]

That deal didn't last long. Just a few days after Díaz took power, CIA station chief John Doherty and his deputy, Enno Hobbing—former *Time* bureau chief in Paris—sat him down. "Let me explain something to you," said Hobbing. "You made a big mistake when you took over the government." Hobbing paused, then made himself very clear. "Colonel, you're just not convenient for the requirements of American foreign policy."

Díaz was shocked. He asked to hear it from Peurifoy himself. According to Díaz, when Peurifoy came over, at four in the morning, he backed up Doherty and Hobbing. He also showed Díaz a long list of Guatemalans who would need to be shot immediately.

"But why?" Díaz asked. "Because they're communists," Peurifoy responded.[34]

Castillo Armas, the US favorite, took over. Slavery returned to Guatemala. In the first few months of his government, Castillo Armas established Anticommunism Day, and rounded up and executed between three thousand and five thousand supporters of Árbenz.[35]

Eisenhower was elated. Even though Wisner had been anxious throughout the operation, this was another triumph for his approach. After he and Barnes met with the president, they burst back into Barnes's living room in Georgetown and "did a little scuffling dance."[36]

The People's Daily paid very close attention to the events in the small country, half a world away. Day after day, the situation in Guatemala was at the top of the front page, and the headlines were clear and precise: "*Amerika Menjerang Guatemala*" (America threatens Guatemala), and then a long explanatory article, "This Is Guatemala," featuring a map of the faraway region, and then referring to "American aggression."[37]

The US press covered it differently. The *New York Times* referred to the coup plotters as "rebels," while calling the Árbenz government "reds" or a "Communist threat," and saying that the US government was "helping" mediate peace talks, rather than organizing the whole thing. Most historians today would quickly recognize that this small Indonesian communist newspaper reported the events more accurately than the *New York Times*.[38]

There is a reason for that. Sydney Gruson, an enterprising *Times* correspondent, was planning to launch an investigation of the "rebel" forces. Frank Wisner wanted him stopped. He asked his boss, Allen Dulles, to speak with the *New York Times* higher-ups, which he did. Believing he was performing a patriotic act, *Times* publisher Arthur Sulzberger ordered Gruson to stay away.[39]

There's also a reason that Zain and his colleagues paid so much attention to Guatemala. A front-page story in *The People's Daily* on June 26 said that what was happening in Guatemala "threatens world peace, and could threaten Indonesia as well."[40]

An internal State Department document, now publicly available, should dispel the notion that Washington thought Guatemala was an immediate "communist threat." According to Louis J. Halle in a note to the director of the policy planning staff, the risk was not that Guatemala would act aggressively. The risk was that Árbenz would provide an example that inspired his neighbors to copy him. The note reads, "The evidence indicates no present military danger to us at all. Although we read public references to the facts that Guatemala is three hours' flying time from the oil-fields of Texas and two hours' flying time from the Panama Canal, we may console ourselves that Guatemala's capability for bombing either is nil. The recent shipment of arms makes no difference to this conclusion, nor would repeated shipments . . ."

The real risk, Halle said quite clearly, was that communist "infection" could

> spread through the example of independence of the U.S. that Guatemala might offer to nationalists throughout Latin America. It might spread through the example of nationalism and social reform. Finally and above all, it might spread through the disposition the Latin Americans would have to identify themselves with little Guatemala if the issue should be drawn for them (as it is being drawn for them), not as

that of their own security but as a contest between David Guatemala and Uncle Sam Goliath. This latter, I think, is the danger we have most to fear and to guard against.[41]

The question of land reform was an exemplary and recurring case of "Do as I say, not as I do." When General MacArthur was running Japan immediately after World War II, he pushed through an ambitious land reform program, and US authorities oversaw redistribution in South Korea in these years as well. In strategic, US-controlled nations, they saw the necessity of breaking up feudal land control in order to build dynamic capitalist economies. But when carried out by leftists or perceived geopolitical rivals—or when threatening US economic interests—land reform was more often than not treated as communist infiltration or dangerous radicalism.

The Dulles brothers had worked on Wall Street, and both had actually done work for the United Fruit Company. To this day, there is a debate as to whether or not the CIA engineered the coups in Iran and Guatemala for cynical economic reasons—to help business buddies and American capitalism more generally—or if the Agency really felt threatened by "communism." There can be more than one explanation. The leader of the PGT, Guatemala's communist party, said that "they would have overthrown us even if we had grown no bananas."[42] Wisner's discussions at home, with his family, indicated he really felt that the Iranian Tudeh and Guatemalan PGT were somehow a danger to his country.[43]

But the motivation didn't matter much to the millions of people reading about the events back in Asia, nor to the Latin Americans watching up close. Whatever their reasons, the United States established a reputation as a frequent and violent intruder into the affairs of independent nations.

That young doctor, Che Guevara, believed he learned an important lesson in 1954. He came to the conclusion that Washington would never allow mild social reform, let alone democratic socialism, to flower in its backyard, and that any movement for change would have to be armed, disciplined, and prepared for imperialist aggression. Then twenty-six years old, he wrote to his mother that Árbenz "did not know how to rise to the occasion." The Guatemalan president, Che said, "did not think to himself that a people in arms is an invincible power. He could have given arms to the people, but he did not want to—and now we see the result." Che took off to Mexico City, and began to formulate a more radical revolutionary strategy based on what he had seen in Guatemala.[44]

Back in Indonesia Francisca, though not following the news as closely as Zain, felt that the Indonesian revolution was far from complete. They had only been free from white colonialism for five years, she thought, and there was no guarantee the freedom would last. But she was usually busy working at the library and caring for their first daughter. Zain would come home late, and they would mostly sit around and talk about the books they were reading, mostly European literature, rather than discuss international news. Zain had enough of that at work. But she knew that their situation was fragile, and that the Western powers were not inclined to simply cede freedom to the peoples of the Third World. The brutal French invasion in Vietnam was more proof of that. President Sukarno was always on the radio, putting his considerable rhetorical skills to use to drive home the point that Indonesians still had to fight. The way it looked from Indonesia was that in both Iran and Guatemala, nascent democratic movements had tried to assert new independence in the global economy, and the new Western power had reacted violently, and crushed them back into the subservient role they had always played. Sukarno liked to call this "neocolonialism," or the enforced conditions of imperial control without formal rule. Thoroughly modern, he loved neologisms and acronyms, and later coined NEKOLIM—that is, neocolonialism, colonialism, and imperialism—to name the enemy he believed they all faced.

In 1954, after Ho Chi Minh's surprisingly well-organized forces emerged victorious at the battle of Dien Bien Phu, the French finally gave up in Vietnam. In Geneva, the US was helping to hammer out the division of that country, under the stipulation that a national referendum would take place to reunite its two halves by 1956. In Jakarta, Sukarno was about to meet one of the West's new representatives. Always sunny-faced and eager, Howard Palfrey Jones landed in July.

Presiden Sukarno

When Smiling Jones arrived in Jakarta for the first time, he was enchanted. A "teeming, steaming metropolis," he called it. He also recognized, very quickly, that America's supposed enemies operated here. He was sent to be chief of the Economic Aid Mission, and saw that in Independence Square, where Sukarno had made his famous 1945 proclamation, now across from the US Chancery, every tree was plastered with a poster bearing the hammer and sickle. The same was true in front of his house, and when he got a chance to drive around the island of Java, he often found his car passing under arches of hammer-and-sickle streamers.

Even though Sukarno, Indonesia's charismatic first president, was friendly with Washington and had always operated in varying degrees of opposition to the PKI, a minority party among many, the apparent boldness of the Communist Party—just advertising openly like that, rather than hiding in the shadows—was worrying to the US.

A few days after he got there, Pepper Martin, a senior foreign correspondent at *U.S. News & World Report* gestured toward the communist symbols, turned to Jones, and said, "It looks as if it's all over but the shouting, doesn't it?"[45] Jones would learn soon that it was far from over. And when he met Sukarno for the first time, he was blown away by just how complicated things were. Jones himself, like everyone else in the US government, was an anticommunist, and thought it was his job to fight that system. But he thought the major failure of US diplomacy at the time was a persistent inability to understand the differences between Third World nations, and the nature of Asian nationalism. He believed that after World War II, the US was "too involved in the complexities of intimate relations with our allies of that war, to hear the cry of peoples halfway around the word." He wrote, "We didn't understand and made little attempt to comprehend the political, economic and social revolution that was sweeping Asia."[46]

Unlike many other Americans, Jones refused to dismiss the beliefs and practices of the locals, *a priori*, as backward. He paid close attention. Of course, he lived a very different life from the Indonesians. State Department officials lived in colonial mansions, and had maids and cooks and drivers. Almost any US citizen in the Third World would have been considered incredibly rich, even if they were not working for Uncle Sam.

Once, one of the pools began to leak constantly. The local embassy staff knew what to do. They called a *hadji*, a Muslim who had made the pilgrimage to Mecca, who came and meditated. He told the Americans the premises had not been ritually consecrated. Jones recounted, without hesitation or skepticism, that they held a *slametan* ceremony, appeasing the surrounding spirits by planting a rooster head on each corner of the pool. It never leaked again. Jones, a Christian Scientist who himself had watched his mother recover miraculously after bouts of prayer, never questioned there may be forces at work in Indonesia most Americans didn't fully comprehend.[47]

When interacting with other US government officials, Jones would proudly correct them when they would mislabel Asians or their political affiliations. Most crucially, he thought Americans failed to understand what nationalism was in the context of emerging countries, and its difference from communism. Nationalism in the Third World meant something very different from what it had meant in Germany a decade prior. It was not about race, or religion, or even borders. It was built in opposition to centuries of colonialism. Exasperated, Jones often stressed that to Americans, this might look like an instinctive anti-Western disposition, and that young nations might make early mistakes when forming a government. But wouldn't Americans feel the same way, and demand the right to make their own mistakes?

When Jones finally met *Presiden Sukarno*—as he is called in Indonesian—he was deeply impressed. He wrote: "To meet him was like suddenly coming under a sunlamp, such was the quality of his magnetism." He quickly noticed, he said, Sukarno's "enormous brilliant brown eyes, and a flashing smile that conveyed an all-embracing warmth." He would watch, amazed, as Sukarno spoke eloquently on "the world, the flesh, and the devil: about movie stars and Malthus, Jean Jaures and Jefferson, folklore, and philosophy," then wolf down a huge meal, and dance for hours. Even more impressive to Jones, who had lived a relatively comfortable life, was that this remarkable man—about the same age as Jones—learned to eat this way, and became so steeped in knowledge, while spending years behind bars for opposing Dutch colonial rule.[48] Along the way, he had learned to speak in German, English, French, Arabic, and Japanese, in addition to Bahasa Indonesia, Javanese, Sundanese, Balinese, and Dutch.[49]

When Sukarno opened his mouth in any of these languages, the whole country stopped to listen, and Jones noticed that this had gone to his head. Sukarno told him once, after surviving yet another assassination attempt, "There is only one thing I can think of after yesterday. . . . Allah must approve of what I am doing, otherwise I would long ago have been killed."[50]

Sukarno was born in 1901 in East Java. His mother was from Bali, and therefore Hindu; and his father, from an upper-middle class of Javanese civil servants, was Muslim, like the vast majority of the island. On Java at the time, Muslims could be roughly divided into two categories. There were

the *santri*, the stricter, orthodox Muslims, more influenced by Arab religious culture. Then there were the *abangan*, whose Islam existed on top of a
deep well of mystical and animistic Javanese traditions. Sukarno grew up in
the latter tradition.[51] From an early age, he was well steeped in the wisdom
of the *wayang*, the all-night shadow puppet shows that function here in the
same kind of way that epic poetry functioned in classical Greece.

Though not from the elite, Sukarno was able to study in good colonial
schools. Officially, he studied architecture, but on his own, he studied political philosophy. He began to move in Indonesian nationalist circles, which
welcomed a broad range of anticolonial schools of thought. *Sarekat Islam*,
the Islamic Union, was the central nationalist organization at the time; it had
conservative Islamic thinkers, as well as many who were loyal to the Communist Party. Then called the Indies Communist Party, the party had often
disobeyed directions from Moscow when its leaders saw fit, and saw Muslim
unity as a revolutionary, anticolonial force. There were committed Muslim
Communists who wanted to create an egalitarian community—inspired to
varying degrees both by Marx and the Koran—but felt that foreign infidels
were holding them back. And for almost everyone in the country, "socialism" by definition implied opposition to foreign domination and support for
an independent Indonesia.[52]

This brought Indonesians together. At one December 24 PKI convention
at *Sarekat Islam* headquarters, they decorated the walls with red and green
(for Christmas Eve), and dyed a hammer-and-sickle design in traditional
Javanese *batik* style.[53]

Sukarno by nature was a syncretist, always more interested in mixing
and matching and inclusion than shrill ideological disputes. In 1926, he
penned an article titled "Nationalism, Islam, and Marxism," in which he
asked: "Can these three spirits work together in the colonial situation to become one great spirit, the spirit of unity?" The natural answer for him was
yes. Capitalism, he argued, was the enemy of both Islam and Marxism, and
he called upon adherents of Marxism—which he said was no unchanging
dogma, but rather a dynamic force that adapted to different needs and different situations—to struggle alongside Muslims and nationalists.[54]

The next year, he founded the Indonesian Nationalist Party (PNI),
which sat in the middle of the currents struggling against Dutch imperial
rule—with the Communists to his left, and the Muslim groups to his right.
Sukarno's natural predilection toward inclusion was extremely well suited

to the historical moment. Indonesia is an archipelago whose islands sprawl across two million square miles of sea and are home to hundreds of distinct nationalities speaking more than seven hundred languages. Nothing brought them together other than the artificial boundaries imposed by a racist foreign power. The young nation needed a shared sense of identity more than anything else.

Sukarno was the prophet of that identity. In 1945, he provided an ingenious, impassioned basis for what it meant to be Indonesian when he put forward the Pancasila, or five principles. They were, and remain: belief in God, justice and civilization, Indonesian unity, democracy, and social justice. In practice, they combine the broad affirmation of religion (that would likely mean Islam, Hinduism, Christianity, or Buddhism), revolutionary independence, and social democracy. They certainly didn't exclude the communists, either, since the vast majority of them were *abangan* Muslims like Sukarno, or Balinese Hindus like his mother. Even if a tiny minority of high-level communists might have been without religion, they were happy enough to sign off on Pancasila within a few years. Later the chairman of the PKI would justify this by offering a very novel spin on Marxism, saying that within Indonesia, widespread belief in one God was an "objective fact" and that "communists, as materialists, must accept this objective fact."[55]

The Republic of Indonesia adopted a national slogan—*Bhinneka Tunngal Ika*, meaning "unity in diversity" in Old Javanese, the language spoken by the largest number of people, most of whom live in the middle of that central island. Pancasila, or *Pantja Sila*, is itself derived from Sanskrit, which was used in the pre-Islam days across the Nusantara archipelago, when much of the islands were strongly influenced by cultural and religious elements originating on the Indian subcontinent. ("Indonesia" itself simply means "Indies islands," and is derived, like the name "India," from the Indus River).

It was under Sukarno's watch that the young country chose to make Bahasa Indonesia the official Indonesian language. A leader of less wisdom might have been inclined to make his native Javanese into the official tongue, but this is a hard language to learn and easily could have been seen as a kind of chauvinistic or even colonial imposition from the strongest island. Instead, Indonesia picked an easy, seemingly neutral language, and most of the country learned it within a generation or two. This was a significant achievement; nearby countries in Southeast Asia still have not established truly national languages.[56]

Sukarno was a left-leaning Third World nationalist, and he was more of a visionary than a nuts-and-bolts administrator, as Howard Jones and the rest of the Americans would learn soon enough. True to his conciliatory nature, he was committed to maintaining a friendship with both the United States and Moscow, and he certainly was not trying to aggravate the leadership in Washington.

Jones struck up a kind of friendship with Sukarno, despite the fact that many of his American colleagues thought they were "losing" Indonesia to communism. Indeed, he surprised many of the locals, including those on the more radical left, by simply calling them up for a chat. By now, the left automatically viewed the US with suspicion—the days of Ho Chi Minh's overtures to Washington were over. Jones quickly came to the conclusion that in order to be effective, the aid programs he was managing could not in any way appear to be paternalistic or offend Indonesians' fierce pride in their independence. As for the point of that aid in the first place, he was quite open with the Indonesians—Washington didn't want Indonesia to enter the "Communist bloc."[57]

Sukarno was unquestionably president, but ruling required constant maneuvering within an unwieldy parliamentary system. He led a coalition government, and though the PKI supported the arrangement, there were several other parties that were much more influential, and the PKI had no representatives in his cabinet.[58] As was his wont, Jones continued to correct other American officials who didn't comprehend Asia on its own terms. He understood when the Indonesian president told him, "I am a nationalist, but no Communist." Smiling Jones was proud—and dismayed—that he was "the one American who was convinced Sukarno was not a Communist."[59]

As leader of such a large Third World country, Sukarno was relatively well known back in Washington. But a year after Jones landed, Sukarno would put on an event that would launch him onto the global stage, and change the meaning of the Indonesian revolution forever.

Bandung

That term, "Third World," was born in 1951 in France, but it really only came into its own in 1955, in Indonesia.

As historian Christopher J. Lee has written, it was the *Konferensi Asia-Afrika*, held in Bandung in April, that really solidified the idea of the Third

World.[60] This remarkable gathering brought the peoples of the colonized world into a movement, one that was opposed to European imperialism and independent from the power of the US and the Soviet Union.

It didn't happen automatically; it was the result of concerted efforts by a few of the world's new leaders. In 1954, Indonesia got together with Burma (Myanmar), Ceylon (Sri Lanka), Pakistan, and India, led by Jawaharlal Nehru, the same leader who gave the Kennedy brothers a lecture over dinner. They formed the Colombo Group, named after the Sri Lankan capital, where they met, and began planning a bigger meeting. Indonesia's prime minister initially proposed a 1955 conference as a response to the founding of SEATO, the US-sponsored copy of NATO in Southeast Asia. But the invitation list soon expanded rapidly, as Nehru invited China (this necessarily excluded Taiwan), while apartheid South Africa and both Koreas (technically still at war) as well as Israel (whose presence might have upset Arab nations) weren't invited.

The people who came together at the Bandung Afro-Asian Conference represented about half the United Nations, and 1.5 billion of the world's 2.8 billion people. As Sukarno declared in his opening speech, delivered in bursts of accented but perfect English, it was the "first intercontinental conference of colored peoples in the history of mankind!"[61] Some of the countries there had recently achieved independence while others were still fighting for it. Brazil, the largest country in Latin America, attended as a friendly "observer" from outside Asia and Africa.

The very existence of the conference elevated Sukarno and Nehru to the status of global leaders. It was also a catapult to worldwide relevance for Gamal Abdel Nasser, who had taken over in Egypt, the world's largest Arab country, just three years earlier. Like Nehru, Nasser was secular and left-leaning, and insisted on his right to make alliances with every country, including the Soviet Union. By attending, Mao's foreign minister, Zhou Enlai, sought to legitimate the communist People's Republic of China among its neighbors and take the side of the Third World.[62]

The content of the meeting led to a flowering of global organizations, some of which are active to this day. They were inspired by the "Spirit of Bandung," which Sukarno put forward very clearly in the rest of that powerful opening speech:

We are gathered here today as a result of sacrifices. Sacrifices made by our forefathers and by the people of our own and younger generations.

For me, this hall is filled not only by the leaders of the nations of Asia and Africa; it also contains within its walls the undying, the indomitable, the invincible spirit of those who went before us. Their struggle and sacrifice paved the way for this meeting of the highest representatives of independent and sovereign nations from two of the biggest continents of the globe. . . .

All of us, I am certain, are united by more important things than those which superficially divide us. We are united, for instance, by a common detestation of colonialism in whatever form it appears. We are united by a common detestation of racialism. And we are united by a common determination to preserve and stabilize peace in the world. . . .

Sukarno wore a tailored white suit, glasses, and small *peci* hat, and as he spoke, world leaders sitting around the small chambers clapped, and leaned in to take in more. He had their attention as he turned his legendary rhetorical skills against Western imperialism:

How is it possible to be disinterested about colonialism? For us, colonialism is not something far and distant. We have known it in all its ruthlessness. We have seen the immense human wastage it causes, the poverty it causes, and the heritage it leaves behind when, eventually and reluctantly, it is driven out by the inevitable march of history. My people, and the peoples of many nations of Asia and Africa, know these things, for we have experienced them. . . .

Yes, some parts of our nations are not yet free. That is why all of us cannot yet feel that journey's end has been reached. No people can feel themselves free, so long as part of their motherland is unfree. Like peace, freedom is indivisible. There is no such thing as being half free, as there is no such thing as being half alive. . . .

Almost everyone in the room knew exactly what he meant. The people in the room that day would spend the rest of their lives describing the energy he had summoned in the crowd. He went on:

And, I beg of you, do not think of colonialism only in the classic form which we of Indonesia, and our brothers in different parts of Asia and Africa, knew. Colonialism has also its modern dress, in the form of economic control, intellectual control, actual physical control by a small but alien community within a nation. It is a skillful and determined enemy, and it appears in many guises. It does not give up its loot easily. Wherever, whenever, and however it appears, colonialism is an evil thing, and one which must be eradicated from the earth.

Sukarno and the organizers had gone to great trouble to avoid antagonizing or frightening the most powerful country on earth with their openly anti-imperialist rhetoric. So they scoured their American history books, and asked the Americans they knew, looking for a way to connect the date of the conference to the United States.[63] They found one. The president continued:

The battle against colonialism has been a long one, and do you know that today is a famous anniversary in that battle? On the eighteenth day of April, one thousand seven hundred and seventy-five, just one hundred and eighty years ago, Paul Revere rode at midnight through the New England countryside, warning of the approach of British troops and of the opening of the American War of Independence, the first successful anticolonial war in history. About this midnight ride the poet Longfellow wrote: "A cry of defiance and not of fear, A voice in the darkness, a knock at the door, and a word that shall echo for evermore. Yes, it shall echo for evermore."

As Howard Jones understood, the Bandung Conference put forward an entirely different type of nationalism from the type that existed in Europe. For leaders like Sukarno and Nehru, the idea of the "nation" was not based on race or language—it indeed could not be in territories as diverse as theirs—but is constructed by the anticolonial struggle and the drive for social justice. With Bandung, the Third World could be united by its own common purposes, such as antiracism and economic sovereignty, Sukarno believed. They could also come together and organize collectively for better terms within the global economic system, forcing rich countries to lower their tariffs on Third World goods, while the newly independent countries could use tariffs to foster their own development.[64] After centuries of exploitation, these nations were far, far behind the rich world, and were going to force that to change.

There were twenty-nine countries officially participating, plus states attending as observers. Both Vietnamese states took part, because at this point they were still officially in peaceful coexistence until the 1956 referendum to reunite them. Cambodia's Norodom Sihanouk, like Sukarno a strong supporter of independence from both Washington and Moscow, was there. The Syrian Republic, Libya, Iran (now under the Shah), and Iraq (still a kingdom) sent representatives, and Pakistani Prime Minister Mohammed Ali came along. Momolu Dukuly took a seat for Liberia, the country founded by former American slaves in the nineteenth century.

Sukarno himself often linked the anticolonial struggle to the fight against global capitalism. But the Bandung Conference was also a small blow to his supporters in the PKI, since Indonesia's Communist Party favored a direct alliance with the Soviet Union. Because of his language skills, Francisca's husband, Zain, was one of the Indonesian journalists lucky enough to cover the conference. He wrote it up for *The People's Daily*, which showered praise on the event, despite this small slight.

"Long live the friendship and cooperation between the peoples of Africa and Asia!" the paper exclaimed on opening day, featuring a cover illustration of a man, his muscular frame held together by the flags of the Third World, turning the wheel of history. The next day, after Sukarno's opening speech, *The People's Daily* printed caricatures of figures representing Britain, the USA, the Netherlands, and France in a daze, suffering from a bad headache, with a slightly forced little pun underneath. The "Afro-Asian" (AA) conference, Zain's paper joked, made the imperialist powers desperate for Aspirin-Aspro (AA), because watching the unity of the independent young nations made their heads pound.[65]

From the United States, the keenest observer of the conference was Richard Wright, the black novelist and journalist. The former communist and author of *Native Son* wrote an entire book on his experience there, which went on to influence much anticolonial and antiracist thought. Once he found out about "a meeting of almost all of the human race living in the main geopolitical center of gravity of the Earth," a conference of "the despised, the insulted, the hurt, the dispossessed—in short, the underdogs of the human race," he wrote, he had to go and document it.[66]

Before leaving for Bandung, Wright spoke to North Americans and Europeans aghast at the idea of the conference, certain that a meeting of those nations could only amount to "racism in reverse," hatred of whites inspired by the Communists, or a global antiwhite alliance.[67] Even Wright himself was skeptical of the Bandung mission until he saw the legacy of colonialism and heard the speeches. He realized quickly that locals would speak to him entirely differently when there were no white people in the room. Wright met an Indonesian who had worked as an engineer for three months in New York, but barely left his apartment—he was too afraid of racist confrontations on the street.[68] Then Wright came across a 1949 book designed to teach Indonesian to colonial officials and tourists—except it didn't contain any words allowing conversation. It was mostly a list of orders, all punctuated with exclamation marks.

> Gardener, sweep the garden!
> That broom is broken! Make a new broom!
> Here are the dirty clothes!

And then, in a section called "Hold the Thief":

> All the silver is gone
> The drawers of the sideboard are empty[69]

Wright also realized just how little anticommunism there was in Asia, compared to his native United States. Even the head of *Masjumi*, the Muslim party receiving CIA funding, told him the West's predominant "fear of communism" made trusting First World leaders difficult.

"We shall always have our misgivings about the real aims of the West, of which we have had good reasons to be suspicious in our past history," the *Masjumi* leader said. "No real success can be expected from a cooperation based on such weak grounds," meaning a partnership based purely on Washington's desire to find anybody to oppose the communists.

Not everything went smoothly at Bandung. The Cold War hung over the conference, and not everyone could agree on how to mark themselves out from the major powers. Nehru, for example, resisted attempts by Western-oriented Third World states, such as Iraq, Iran, and Turkey, to condemn Soviet movements in Asia as colonialism. The delegates failed to come to an agreement as to how they could practically support territories still under colonial domination. In the end, they came up with ten basic principles that would come to govern relations between Third World states:

1. Respect for human rights and the United Nations Charter.
2. Respect for sovereignty and territorial integrity of all nations.
3. Recognition of the equality of all races and the equality of all nations large and small.
4. Non-intervention: abstention from interference in the internal affairs of another country.
5. Respect for the right of each nation to defend itself.
6. Abstention from the use of collective defense to serve the particular interests of any of the big powers, and abstention from exerting pressure on other countries.
7. Refraining from acts or threats of aggression against any country.
8. Settlement of all international disputes by peaceful means.
9. Promotion of mutual interests and cooperation.
10. Respect for justice and international obligations.

Most famously, the Bandung Conference provided the structure that would grow into the global Non-Aligned Movement, which was founded in 1961 in Belgrade. But in Asia and Africa, Bandung led to changes that were felt immediately. Collectives, communications networks, and international organizations sprung into existence. Leaders began to broadcast radio messages throughout the two continents, carrying the message of the "Spirit of Bandung" to peoples still struggling against colonialism. Most notably, Nasser pointed his *Radio Cairo* broadcasts south toward sub-Saharan and East Africa with this message.[70] In the Congo, people began listening to *La Voix de l'Afrique* from Egypt and All India Radio, which featured broadcasts in Swahili, as a man named Patrice Lumumba was beginning to form the *Mouvement National Congolais*, a very "Spirit of Bandung" independence movement that rejected ethnic divisions and sought to build the Congolese nation out of anticolonial struggle.[71]

In 1958, the first Asian-African Conference on Women was held in Colombo, and launched a transnational Third World feminist movement. For the 1961 Cairo Women's Conference, Egyptian organizer Bahia Karam wrote in her introduction to the proceedings: "For the first time in modern history, feminine history that is, that such a gathering of Afro-Asian woman has taken place . . . it was indeed a great pleasure, an encouragement to meet delegates from countries in Africa which the imperialists had never before allowed to leave the boundaries of their land."[72] The press in Egypt, for example, began to focus on the lives of women from around the Third World, including Indonesia, discussing the "ties of sisterhood and solidarity between the women of Africa and Asia."[73]

And the Bandung Conference countries would go on to found the Afro-Asian Journalist Association, an attempt by people from the Third World to cover the Third World without relying on the white men, usually sent from rich countries to work as foreign correspondents, who had been telling their stories for decades, if not centuries.

Within Indonesia, Sukarno had cemented himself in the minds of the people as the leader of a new kind of revolution. Francisca, absolutely inspired, would be able to recite parts of Sukarno's opening speech at Bandung by heart long afterward.

In Washington, the attitude was very different. The response was racist condescension. State Department officials called the meeting the "Darktown Strutters Ball."[74]

But to Eisenhower, Wisner, and the Dulles brothers, Sukarno's behavior was no joke. For them, by now, neutralism itself was an offense. Anyone who wasn't actively against the Soviet Union must be against the United States, no matter how loudly he praised Paul Revere.

Now a senator, John F. Kennedy made his opposition to this approach very public in a set of speeches given in the years after Bandung. In a speech harshly criticizing the French for attempting to hold on to Algeria by force, he said that "the single most important test of American foreign policy today is how we meet the challenge of imperialism, what we do to further man's desire to be free. On this test more than any other, this nation shall be critically judged by the uncommitted millions in Asia and Africa, and anxiously watched by the still hopeful lovers of freedom behind the Iron Curtain."[75]

JFK's star was rising, and this kind of position was rare among US politicians. President Sukarno noticed what he said. But Kennedy was in the opposition. And one more event in 1955, in Indonesia, alarmed the anticommunists in power in Washington even more.

The CIA spent a million dollars trying to influence the parliamentary elections in September of that year. The Agency's chosen partners, the *Masjumi*, were solidly to the right of Sukarno. Nevertheless, Sukarno and his supporters did well.[76] Even worse for the Americans, the PKI came in fourth place, with 17 percent of the votes cast. It was the best performance in the history of the Indonesian Communist Party.

3

Feet to the Fire, Pope in the Sky

Soccer with Sakono

In March 1956, the new leader of the Soviet Union, Nikita Khrushchev, shocked the communist world. In an initially "secret speech" to the Communist Party, he issued a lengthy, unflinching denunciation of crimes committed by Stalin.[1] Stalin had been unprepared for World War II, he claimed. He tortured his own comrades and forced them into confessing to crimes they had never committed, as an excuse to have them shot and secure his grip on power.

Stalin had died just three years earlier. When he did, so many people rushed toward his funeral procession that some were crushed—at the time, many citizens of the Soviet Union and other communist countries felt real affection for the man, and a deep identification with the collectivist, socialist project overall.[2] To hear him attacked, by the leader of the world's foremost Marxist-Leninist party no less, was an unexpected blow to communists around the world.

Some leftists, especially in Western Europe, reacted by distancing themselves from the Soviet project altogether. Others, most notably Mao, accused Khrushchev of distorting or exaggerating Stalin's misdeeds for his own benefit. He began to claim Khrushchev was guilty of the crime of "revisionism" of Marxist-Leninist doctrine, the first crack in a growing split between the two countries.[3] Under its new leader, the Soviet Union pursued peaceful co-existence with the West, warmed to nonaligned countries, and expanded its aid to Third World countries like Indonesia, Egypt, India, and Afghanistan.

Officially, the PKI went along with Khrushchev into a post-Stalinist, more moderate future. But in practice, the communist world was even more divided than it had been at the beginning of the Cold War. The Indonesian communists, confident in the importance of their country and growing in size and strength, were even more certain than before that they didn't need to take orders from abroad.

After the failed Madiun uprising in 1948, the PKI had reorganized under the leadership of D. N. Aidit. Self-confident and gregarious, Aidit was born off the coast of Sumatra into a devout Muslim family and became a Marxist during Japan's occupation. With Aidit as its leader, the PKI transformed into a mass-based, legal, ideologically flexible movement that rejected the armed struggle, frequently ignored Moscow's directions, stuck close to Sukarno, and embraced electoral politics. The party was doing things very differently from the Russian or the Chinese communist parties. The PKI's goal, both publicly and privately, was to form an antifeudal "united national front" with the local bourgeoisie, and not to worry about implementing socialism "until the end of the century."[4]

Internationally, the PKI was committed to anti-imperialism; and locally, party members were growing their movement by winning democratic elections.

As 1956 progressed, the communist world was divided further, when Khrushchev sent tanks into Hungary to crush an uprising and reassert Soviet control. The violence of October and November 1956 was a public relations debacle for Moscow. It was also a deep personal failure for Frank Wisner. Though the US denied this publicly, the CIA had been encouraging the Hungarians to revolt, and many did so thinking they would receive support from Washington. When the Dulles brothers decided against this course of action, seemingly hanging the protesters out to dry, Wisner felt personally betrayed.

His behavior became increasingly erratic. William Colby, a senior CIA officer in Rome, said in 1956 that "Wisner was rambling and raving, totally out of control. He kept saying, all these people are getting killed." His son noticed that he appeared overworked and was deeply emotionally involved in the events in Europe. Wiz began acting in ways the people working with him had a hard time understanding. They thought it might have been be-cause of an illness caused by a bad plate of clams he had in Greece.[5]

While Second World communism was suffering from fissures, the Third World was further united by a bit of First World bumbling. After Nasser nationalized the Suez Canal, France and Britain invaded—against Wash-ington's wishes—to reassert control of the waterway and oust the Egyptian leader. They were joined by the young state of Israel, whose creation had been supported by both Washington and Moscow, but eventually had to back down because of US pressure. Despite Eisenhower's anger with the new Jewish state, Washington steadily increased support for Israel from the mid-dle of the 1950s for Cold War reasons. It was the nascent alliances between the USSR and radical Arab nationalist regimes, we know now, that formed the basis for a growing US-Israel alliance.[6]

Something else happened in 1956. Or rather, it didn't happen. The divi-sion between North and South Vietnam was supposed to be resolved by an election that would unite the country under a single government. But Ngo Dinh Diem, the Catholic leader of majority-Buddhist South Vietnam whom the United States had handpicked before he turned out to be hopelessly cor-rupt and dictatorial, knew that he would lose badly to Ho Chi Minh. So Diem decided to cancel the vote. Washington went along with this, just as it did when Diem fraudulently declared he had won an election in 1955 with 98.2 percent of the vote.[7] From that moment on, the government in North Vietnam, and many communists in the South, believed they had the right to directly oppose Diem's US-backed regime.

In the same turbulent year, Sukarno went to Washington. It's not clear whether or not the Indonesian leader himself knew this, but the visit did not go well. The impression he made with the most powerful people on the planet was not a good one. Back home in Indonesia, Sukarno's sexual ap-petites were famous, but they shocked the Americans. John Foster Dulles, a deeply prudish Presbyterian, found him "disgusting." Frank Wisner, who usually didn't take his work home with him, confided to his son that "Su-karno wanted to make sure his bed was properly filled, and the Agency was not without the ability to satisfy the Indonesian ruler's lust."[8]

To make things worse, he went from Washington straight to Moscow and Beijing. He believed this his right as an independent world leader, of course, but this was not the kind of thing the Eisenhower administration tolerated.

In the fall of 1956, Wisner told Al Ulmer, head of the CIA's Far East Division, "I think it's time we held Sukarno's feet to the fire."[9]

In elections the following year, the Indonesian Communist Party did even better than it had in 1955. The PKI was the most efficient, professional organization in the country. Crucially, in a country plagued with corruption and patronage, it had a reputation for being the cleanest of all the major parties.[10] Its leaders were disciplined and dedicated, and Howard Jones saw quickly that they actually delivered on what they promised, especially to peasants and the poor. Jones was not the only one in the US government who understood why the Communists kept winning. The vice president at the time, Richard Nixon, gave voice to the general feeling in Washington when he said that "a democratic government was [probably] not the best kind for Indonesia" because "the Communists could probably not be beaten in election campaigns because they were so well organized."[11] And most importantly, Jones recognized that the PKI was going into the countryside, delivering the kind of programs that spoke directly to the people's needs. The party was "working hard and skillfully to win over the underprivileged," he worried.[12]

Sakono Praptoyugono, the son of farmers in a village in Central Java, remembers the impact of these programs very well. Sakono—not to be confused with Sukarno, the president—was born in 1946 in the Purbalingga Regency, the sixth of seven children, while the Dutch were still trying to crush Indonesia's independence movement. After Indonesia was established, his father got a bit of rice from the revolutionary government, and their family worked a small plot of land. While his parents were peasants who spoke only Javanese, the young republic gave Sakono a chance to study, and he took to it like a fish to water.[13]

You might call Sakono something of a teacher's pet. He was the kind of kid who read the whole newspaper every day, and organized extra classes for him and his friends after school. He absolutely loved studying history, and politics, and by the age of nine, he was already following Sukarno's near-constant radio speeches—he was a huge fan—and the results of national elections.

Short and solidly built with twinkling eyes, Sakono was the kind of guy who rattles off facts and quotes and phrases from foreign languages, smiling the whole time, so excited he may not notice when others may want to talk about something else. He read *The People's Daily*, or *Harian Rakyat* to him, and he started an extracurricular study group under a young member of the PKI, which was engaged in constant outreach in his town.

The most important of the PKI programs in his region was carried out by the Indonesian Farmers Alliance (BTI), which sought to enforce peasants' rights within the existing legal framework and push for land reform. BTI members told Sakono and his family that "the land belongs to those who work it, and it can't be taken away," and even more importantly, they surveyed and recorded holdings, made sure laws were enforced, and helped improve agricultural efficiency.

Twice a week, Sakono and two of his friends got together for three hours with a man named Sutrisno, a tall, happy-go-lucky party member with brown curly hair, to study basic politics in the Marxist tradition. Sakono learned about feudalism, and that the inefficient distribution of land his family lived under would be replaced if Indonesia ever transitioned to socialism. They studied the concepts of neocolonialism and imperialism, and learned about the capitalist United States. Sutrisno told them about Khrushchev and Mao, and the "revisionist" debate, but said that the PKI had chosen the peaceful path to power in the context of President Sukarno's revolution. Sakono could not afford to buy issues of *Harian Rakyat*, the paper Zain wrote for, so he'd go read it at the newsagent's house for free.

As teenagers often do, Sakono got a bit obsessed. His love for left-wing theory suffused every part of his life. He and his friends would play soccer in the middle of town (there was no proper field in their small Javanese village, of course), and as they kicked the ball back and forth, he told himself he was learning important political lessons. "Soccer was the people's sport, because it was cheap," he would remember later. "And sport builds the collective spirit, it teaches you to work with others, that you can't accomplish anything alone. I realized soccer taught me that if you have something you want to accomplish, you have to cooperate."

The PKI claimed it was organized along Leninist lines, but it wasn't really. It was a "broad mass party," in its own terminology, growing far too quickly to maintain the strict hierarchical discipline Lenin himself argued for.[14] The party had active members, or cadres, like Sakono's teacher Sutrisno, who took a pledge to uphold party ethics, and it also ran a number of affiliated organizations, like the BTI, which were meant for mass civilian participation. The industrial counterpart to BTI was SOBSI, the affiliation of union members that included much of the country's working class, whether they cared about Marxism or not. Then there was LEKRA, the cultural organization, which provided an essential service in small towns where there was little to do—it put on concerts, and plays, and dances, and comedy shows, which would often go on all night and provide the best (and perhaps only) entertainment in town.[15] "Oh, everyone went," Sakono said. "It didn't matter what your politics were. If it was happening, you had to come and watch."

Broadly speaking, all these Communist-affiliated organizations supported President Sukarno, though not uncritically. The Indonesian Women's Movement, or *Gerwani*, opposed the traditional practice of polygamy, which Sukarno embraced very publicly while president. *Gerwani* became one of the largest women's organizations in the world. It was organized along feminist, socialist, and nationalist lines, and focused on opposing traditional constraints put on women, promoting the education of girls and demanding space for women in the public sphere.[16]

In Sakono's part of Central Java, the Women's Movement was focused on the most basic of issues. A young woman named Sumiyati, who joined the organization as a teen in her village in Jatinom, was taught how to sing, dance, play sports, and, most of all, defend "feminist ideals, and the rights of women to fight to destroy the shackles that bound them, and our rights to learn and to dream." On the question of polygamy in general, the movement was uncompromising in its opposition. On the question of Sukarno's specific polygamy, it made compromises.

"No man is perfect," Sumiyati learned. "This is a time of transition and we have to struggle for the changes we want to see. We move forward step by step, we can't expect the world to turn over as easily as we turn the palm of our hands."[17]

At absolutely no point did cheerful, studious Sakono think his leftism made him a subversive. If anything, he was almost a nerd, a kind of overenthusiastic young fan of the country's revolution. "The Communists are the good guys," he often thought. They were doing well in elections, and were friends with his hero, President Sukarno.

In his studies, Sakono also developed a sophisticated understanding of the relationship between economic conditions and ideology. "You see, the Communist Party in the United States never grew because it didn't have the right roots," he concluded. "But in Indonesia we have so much injustice and exploitation. There's a relation between the material conditions of our society and the ideology which flowers here. And injustice is very fertile soil for its roots to grow."

By 1957, Indonesia's left already considered Washington an obstacle to the nation's development, if not an all-out enemy. But soon, things got much worse. Rebellions against Sukarno's government broke out on the "outer islands" to the northeast of Java and Bali, as well as on the island of Sumatra. The rebellions were both economically and ideologically motivated, demanding more control over the income from their regions, as well as the prohibition of communism—which greatly pleased Washington.

Because the rebels had such good weaponry, people like Sakono and his teacher believed the USA was helping them. "It's the strategy of *divide et impera*," he said, using the Latin for "divide and conquer." "It is the Cold War," he said. "Let me explain—'Cold War' is the name they have given to the process by which America tries to dominate countries like Indonesia."

Bombs over Ambon

As the Indonesian left became more certain that Washington was somehow behind the growing civil war, Sakono's village received a copy of *Harian Rakyat* with a cartoon on the front page. The headline above the illustration read "Two systems—Two sets of morals." On the left, the Soviet Union was launching something upward: Sputnik, the first satellite ever sent into orbit by humankind, which had been a fabulous propaganda tool for global communism all year. On the right, the United States was dropping something from the sky: bombs, onto Indonesia.[18]

Howard Jones was working a stint in Washington as all this was going on, until he got a metaphorical tap on the shoulder. President Eisenhower asked him to return to Indonesia. This time, he would be United States ambassador. And as soon as he got there, he had to face a government that was increasingly suspicious of the United States.

Just days after Smiling Jones presented his credentials in March 1958, Sukarno's foreign minister asked to speak with him. Subandrio, a thin, bespectacled, and thoughtful diplomat who had tried to rally international support from London during Indonesia's independence struggle, asked the new US ambassador, as politely as possible, to explain a cache of weapons that had been air-dropped to the rebels. There were machine guns, STEN guns, and bazookas, and the weapons bore the mark of a manufacturer in Plymouth, Michigan.

Jones said he didn't know anything about them, and pointed out that US weapons were available for purchase on the open market all over the world.

Subandrio backed off, saying he did not want to imply that Washington was arming those who sought to break up Indonesia. Carefully and articulately, however, he would refer back to the issue several times, as delicately as possible. Subandrio was taking extreme care not to confront or offend the new ambassador. This is the stereotypically Javanese way of broaching sensitive topics; one dances around them suggestively, even with close friends, and this was a representative of the most powerful nation on earth. It slowly became clear to Jones that the foreign minister was convinced the rebels were receiving external support, but he wasn't saying it outright. Finally, he did. Subandrio submitted that the Indonesians believed someone was behind the rebellion, but took his accusation no further. Jones knew his bosses were sympathetic to the rebellion—everyone did—but he had nothing to admit, and the meeting ended.

Soon after, Jones met with Hatta, the second-most important Indonesian revolutionary behind Sukarno. Like Subandrio, Hatta wore glasses and the flat *peci* cap, the Indonesian version of the fez—a very popular look among Indonesia's early revolutionaries. The two men talked about the logistics of the rebellion, and Hatta made it clear he shared Washington's commitment to fight communism. But, he said, this rebellion was an entirely different matter, and they considered it a threat to Indonesia itself. They finished the meeting. But just as Jones was turning to leave, he slipped the new ambassador a piece of information that spoke directly to his concerns.

"From the standpoint of America, you could not have a better man as chief of staff of the Indonesian Army," Hatta said, referring to General Nasution. "From your standpoint, Nasution is fine."

"What do you mean by that, Dr. Hatta?" Jones replied.

"The communists call me their Enemy Number One," Hatta said. "They call Nasution Enemy Number Two."

Jones had a revelation. "Then what has happened in Indonesia is that . . . anticommunists are fighting anticommunists. Communism is not a major issue of this dispute." That was right. The Army was perhaps the most anticommunist force in the country, apart from the most radical Islamists. A few of its top generals had even studied in the United States.[19]

As the rebellion dragged on, protesters began to gather in front of Jones's ambassadorial mansion, convinced the US was behind the rebels.[20] The *New York Times* had Washington's back, lambasting Sukarno and his government in a May 9 editorial for doubting assurances the US would never intervene in the conflict.[21] Jones dealt with the protesters as well as he could. But the rebellion was not happening in the capital, where things were mostly comfortable. The fighting was raging to the west, on the large island of Sumatra, and on the smaller islands to the northeast.

Most crucially, planes were circling over Ambon, the home island of Francisca's family, and dropping fiery death onto its residents. Day after day, bombs fell onto Indonesian military and commercial shipping vessels. Then, on May 15, the explosions hit a market, killing both morning shoppers and Ambonese Christians attending church.[22]

On May 18, 1958, the Indonesians managed to shoot down one of the planes, and a single figure floated slowly toward a coconut grove. His white parachute got caught in the branches of a tall palm tree, where he was stuck for a moment—then he fell to the ground and broke his hip. He was quickly found and captured by Indonesian soldiers, who probably saved him from being killed on the spot by furious locals.

His name was Allen Lawrence Pope; he was from Miami, Florida; and he was a CIA agent.[23] Howard Jones didn't know it, but Frank Wisner's boys had been actively supporting the rebels since 1957.[24] The two men, and their differing approaches to fighting communism, had come into direct conflict.

After Wiz returned from sick leave in 1957, he had warned the Dulles brothers that the rebellion would be an unpredictable, potentially explosive affair. They ignored his concerns, and gave Wisner the authority to spend $10 million to back a revolution in Indonesia. CIA pilots took off from Singapore, an emerging Cold War ally, with the goal of destroying the government of Indonesia or breaking the country into little pieces. They chose not to tell Howard Jones's predecessor, John Moore Allison, about the covert action because, as Wisner put it, the plans "might elicit an adverse reaction from the Ambassador." Instead, they transferred him to Czechoslovakia, and brought in the oblivious Jones.[25]

Jones was brought back so that he could keep smiling to the Indonesians while another arm of his own government dropped tons of exploding metal onto small, tropical islands. Jones noticed that the Indonesian newspaper *Bintang Timur* (Eastern Star) came up with a nifty drawing to illustrate this posture. They drew John Foster Dulles in a boxing ring. On one of his gloves, they wrote, "Goodwill Jones," and on the other, they wrote, "Killer Pope."[26]

Throughout the course of the CIA's history, this dynamic would often be repeated. The Agency would act behind the back of the diplomats and experts at the State Department. If the CIA was successful, the State Department would be forced into backing the new state of affairs the Agency had created. If the secret agents failed, they would just move on, leaving the embarrassed diplomats to clean up the mess.

That's what happened with Jones. For reasons we still don't understand, Allen Pope was carrying identifying papers when he was captured. He was put on trial, and he became a very potent symbol of US involvement in the rebellions, and apparent proof that the Indonesians—especially the left—had been right all along. Even so, Ambassador Jones received orders to issue categorical denials that the US had controlled any missions that impinged on Indonesia's sovereignty, including Pope's.

Not long after, Jones was authorized to offer Indonesia's prime minister thirty-five thousand tons of rice if the government "took positive steps to curb Communist expansion within the country."[27] Taken together, it was a carrot-and-stick approach, but with the stick very poorly hidden.

The 1958 operation in Indonesia was one of the largest in the CIA's history, and it was patterned on the successful coup in Guatemala—in other words, it was exactly what the *People's Daily* writers such as Zain had been worried about four years earlier, as they carefully reported on the events in Central America.[28]

But this one failed. The Indonesian Army put down the rebellions, greatly increasing their power within the country as a result, and no more US military missions were uncovered.

Sukarno, of course, felt deeply betrayed. He put it in very personal terms. He said, "I love America, but I'm a disappointed lover."[29]

Jones did not enjoy the position that Wisner's CIA operations put him in one bit. Reflecting later on the tragic, absurd failure of the operation, Jones turned back to the nature of his country to find an explanation. "Washington policymakers had not been privy to all the facts nor really grasped the inwardness of the situation, but had proceeded on the assumption that Communism was the main issue," he wrote. "This was the all too common weakness of Americans—to view conflict in black and white terms, a heritage, no doubt, from our Puritan ancestors. There were no grays in the world landscape. There was either good or evil, right or wrong, hero or villain."[30]

Jones stressed that the Indonesians only turned to the Communist Bloc for economic and military aid after they had exhausted their attempts to get the same kind of help from America.[31] In 1955, the Soviet Union had offered substantial aid, but Indonesia, pursuing a strictly neutral position, said it wouldn't take any more than the Americans offered. Even then the government hesitated, unsure if it should take anything from the Soviet Union at all—until 1958, the year Allen Pope and other CIA operatives burned Indonesians alive, when they took it.

The playbook that Wisner's team had developed in Iran and Central America had failed badly in this much larger country, one that was playing a fundamental role in global affairs. In the most credible way possible, Washington had been exposed in Asia as an aggressor against one of the world's leading neutral powers. Very little of this made the news back home, but people in the Third World knew.

Frank Wisner began to act increasingly erratically toward the end of 1958. Sometimes he would appear too excited, talking too quickly. Sometimes his eyes would just glaze over. Back in Georgetown, he saw a psychiatrist. He was prescribed a generous dose of psychoanalysis, and underwent shock therapy.[32]

Jones, along with the US military attaché in Indonesia, took Subandrio's advice. He emphasized to Washington that the United States should support the Indonesian military as a more effective, long-term anticommunist strategy. The country of Indonesia couldn't be simply broken into pieces to slow down the advance of global socialism, so this was a way that the US could work within existing conditions. This strategic shift would begin soon, and would prove very fruitful.

But behind the scenes, the CIA boys dreamed up wild schemes. On the softer side, a CIA front called the Congress for Cultural Freedom, which funded literary magazines and fine arts around the world, published and distributed books in Indonesia, such as George Orwell's *Animal Farm* and the famous anticommunist collection *The God That Failed*.[33] And the CIA discussed simply murdering Sukarno. The Agency went so far as to identify the "asset" who would kill him, according to Richard M. Bissell, Wisner's successor as deputy director for plans.[34] Instead, the CIA hired pornographic actors, including a very rough Sukarno look-alike, and produced an adult film in a bizarre attempt to destroy his reputation.

The Agency boys knew that Sukarno routinely engaged in extramarital affairs. But everyone in Indonesia also knew it. Indonesian elites didn't shy away from Sukarno's activities the way the Washington press corps protected philanderers like JFK. Some of Sukarno's supporters viewed his promiscuity as a sign of his power and masculinity. Others, like Sumiyati and members of the *Gerwani* Women's Movement, viewed it as an embarrassing defect. But the CIA thought this was their big chance to expose him. So they got a Hollywood film crew together.[35]

They wanted to spread the rumor that Sukarno had slept with a beautiful blond flight attendant who worked for the KGB, and was therefore both immoral and compromised. To play the president, the filmmakers (that is, Bing Crosby and his brother Larry) hired a "Hispanic-looking" actor, and put him in heavy makeup to make him look a little more Indonesian. They also wanted him bald, since exposing Sukarno—who always wore a hat—as such might further embarrass him. The idea was to destroy the genuine affection that young Sakono, and Francisca, and millions of other Indonesians, felt for the Founding Father of their country.

The thing was never released—not because this was immoral or a bad idea, but because the team couldn't put together a convincing enough film.[36]

West New Guinea

After the Allen Pope fiasco, relations between Indonesia and the United States also took a nosedive, and it was Jones who was left to save them. With characteristic energy, Sukarno quickly set to work on befriending the cheerful new ambassador. After just a few months, in October 1958, Jones and his wife invited the president to their bungalow on the Puncak, in the mountains in West Java, for a small luncheon. To their surprise, Sukarno showed up with eighty security guards and twenty drivers, and promptly set about charming two American marines accompanying Jones.

They feasted on chicken and beef satay, vegetables and mangosteen, papayas, mangos, and rambutan, and the president asked for some music and dancing. Sukarno requested fast, Moluccan rhythms—that is, music from

Ambon and the surrounding islands, the ones the CIA had just bombed. Soon, the Americans and Indonesians were all whirling, and sweating, and moving to the sounds of kettles, which they all were banging with their spoons and bayonets.[37]

The budding friendship helped to put the attacks of 1958—which everyone knew were not Jones's fault—behind the two of them. But that wasn't the only issue threatening the US-Indonesia relationship.

Decolonization was far from finished in Southeast Asia. When the Dutch finally gave in to the revolutionaries in 1949, they ceded control of most of their territory to the young republic. But they did not give up their claim to a giant piece of land to the east of Java and north of Australia—that is, the western half of New Guinea, the second-largest island in the world. Indonesia as it stood was already an incredibly diverse country, but the people of Papua (or New Guinea) are visibly different both physically and culturally from people from the other islands. They are darker-skinned, with curly hair, and the Dutch colonial administration had barely penetrated into their territory (the Dutch never had the whole island—the eastern half, now Papua New Guinea, was controlled at the time by Australia).

To Sukarno, the issue was incredibly simple. The Dutch had absolutely no business being anywhere but back home in Holland. Indonesia was a democratic, multiethnic national republic. Race didn't matter, and neither did Papua's level of economic development. For years, his government in Jakarta tried to negotiate with the Dutch, to no avail. Then from 1954 to 1958, Sukarno argued the case at the United Nations. At home, this meant organizing protests and creating as much pressure on the Netherlands as possible. Washington, not wishing to alienate the Dutch, important Cold War allies in Western Europe, neglected to back Indonesia's claim.

For the Indonesians, this was an issue of national pride. It was so crucial that at the end of 1957, the Indonesian government—frustrated with seven years of being ignored—expelled all the remaining Dutch citizens from the country.[38] This was always going to be a blow to the economy. After only eight years of independence, and just the beginning of a public education system, Indonesia had not trained everyone needed to run the enterprises set up over centuries of colonialism.

Francisca remembers that by the time the Dutch left, her library, and her social life, became Indonesian-dominated for the first time. Her country had been transformed radically in less than two decades, from one where she was part of a minority of brown students sitting in a white classroom to one where she was running a library entirely with fellow Indonesians. This was the world where she would raise her young children—and she now had three.

In naming them, she and Zain mixed local traditions with their international ideals. The first, they named Damaiati Nanita—"*damai*" means "peace" in Bahasa Indonesia. The second, Francisca wanted to name Candide, after the famous work by Voltaire, which she had devoured in Europe. So they named the child Kandida Mirana. The second name, which Zain chose, included "*mir*," the Russian word for "peace" (peace was becoming a theme). The third child, their first son, took the Christian names Anthony and Paul from Francisca's family tradition on the Moluccan islands. Then they expanded them to Anthony Paulmiro, so that once more, their son would carry *mir*, or peace. They were among a new group of Indonesians, the first ever born in the country.

Around them in Jakarta, a whole generation that had been raised on the values forged in 1945 was coming up. Students, workers, and regular people of all stripes had been rallying against "imperialism," in all its forms. Jones was dealing with them right in front of his home.

Benny Widyono, a well-to-do economics student, found himself in one of these demonstrations while attending college in Jakarta. He joined a crowd, which carried him into Lapangan Banteng Square (a new name—it was previously Waterloo Square), and was electrified by the movement taking place all around him. The people were standing up for themselves, and *demanding* full independence. They weren't asking the Western powers. They were telling them. Benny's parents, who had quietly built a business under Dutch rule, and had suffered under Japanese occupation, never could have imagined that just over a decade later, Benny would be out in the streets, openly protesting imperialism in Jakarta.

Howard Jones traveled throughout the entire country, asking Indonesians if they really cared about the issue of Papuan independence from the Dutch. The answer was unequivocal. Yes, they really did. But that wasn't going to change Washington's position. He recounts that locals came to him, time and time again, and asked, with genuine mystification: "We just don't understand America. You were once a colony. You know what colonialism is.

You fought and bled and died for your freedom. How can you possibly support the status quo?"

After over a decade representing the United States in Asia, Jones had no answer. The behavior of the United States lent weight to the charge, he realized, "that we had become an imperial power ourselves."[39]

4

An Alliance for Progress

Benny

Benny Widyono was born in 1936 in Magelang, Central Java, into a family of Chinese descent. Immigrants from China, particularly the south, started moving to the islands of Southeast Asia centuries earlier. They often fled starvation or bandits, looking for work or at least refuge in a land where it was always warm and it seemed you could always just pick coconuts from the trees when you were hungry. Some Chinese came to Southeast Asia as early as the eleventh century, and immigration continued until much more recently.[1]

Across the region, some ethnic Chinese ended up as workers or shopkeepers or small business owners. Some became quite wealthy indeed, moving to the top of the emerging business class. Their position in modern Southeast Asian society has sometimes been compared, in the very broadest sense, to that of Jews in Europe. Since the ethnic Chinese were immigrants, and neither peasants nor royalty, without an official place in the old feudal system, they had to work a bit harder and were forced early into industries that would grow in exponential terms as capitalism developed later. They experienced periodic waves of racism—not only because it was perceived they had undue wealth—that would push them into ethnic enclaves, inspiring even more suspicion.

Benny's family members were not shopkeepers. They were rich. His father farmed tobacco, to this day one of the most important crops in

Indonesia. During the Japanese occupation, he was jailed and tortured for sending contributions to Chiang Kai-shek's Nationalist forces back in China, leaving him with a lifelong disability. But after the Dutch left, business began to boom for the family again, and they employed a lot of workers. Growing up, young Benny would watch the Javanese men hauling huge sacks, bigger than their own skinny bodies, back and forth from the fields all night long. They begged the boss for higher wages, but he had no incentive to offer a raise—he was the only employer in town, and there was no real way for them to work anywhere else.

Benny had a warm, inviting face, and he was always eager to laugh at the ridiculousness of life. But these scenes stuck with him. He went off to study economics in Jakarta, under some of the country's leading academics. He began to learn about exploitation and monopolies, accumulation and profit. Then on a visit home from university over the holidays, Benny had an interaction with his father that would probably be familiar to anyone who has sent kids off to college, or gone to college themselves.

Benny turned his radical new ideas on his dad. He called him an exploiter.

"He almost kicked me out of the house!" Benny would remember later, before bursting into laughter. The whole idea behind the economics degree was that he would take over the family business, and there he was, with his newfangled left-wing notions, saying he was too good for it. But eventually, he and his father got over this little fight, and another relative ended up taking over the family business, so no harm was done.

Benny was raised Catholic, even though his father was Confucian. But Benny took his mother's faith, and ended up in one of Jakarta's elite Catholic high schools. The students there were all wealthy, and mostly anticommunist. Some were solidly conservative. But whatever their political stripes, almost all of them supported Sukarno and his opposition to international imperialism. At school in Jakarta, even the right-leaning students felt real sympathy for the great leader of the revolution, and were intensely proud of their young democracy.

But in 1959, as Benny was finishing his undergraduate studies, the nature of Indonesian democracy changed: it took a big step backward.

A few months after the regional rebellions backed by the CIA were defeated, Sukarno declared that the country would be moving to a system he had been discussing for a few years called "Guided Democracy." As he put it, the system was a national response to the weakness of liberal democracy. Liberalism and party democracy, he complained, were a Western import that pitted everyone against each other, forcing each person to fight for their own selfish interests. That was not the Indonesian way, he claimed.[2] He wanted a decision-making process based on the traditional village assembly, in which everyone got together and chose a course of action after careful consideration. Every party would be represented in the cabinet—called a *gotong royong* cabinet, after the traditional village practice of doing collective work—and there would be a "National Council" representing civil groups like workers, peasants, intellectuals, religious groups, and entrepreneurs. The idea was that minority considerations could never be excluded.

However, when Sukarno declared the system would be put in place in July 1959, he was overstepping his constitutional powers. He cemented himself as the leader of the government, and major parties—such as the *Masjumi* (the Muslim party that received CIA funds in 1955, then supported the regional rebellions) and the Socialist Party—were effectively excluded from the new system. Western-style elections would not occur again under President Sukarno.

Some back in Washington used Indonesia's slide toward a kind of illiberal populism as retroactive justification for their opposition to Sukarno's government. But the move to Guided Democracy happened after the CIA bombed the country and discussed killing its leader. The Indonesian Communist Party (PKI), Washington's *bête noire* in Southeast Asia, was the political group that most wanted voting to continue.[3] The PKI had no interest in ending elections in Indonesia for one simple reason—it was doing better and better in them. In Singapore, British intelligence concluded in 1958 that if votes were held, the Communist Party would have come in first.[4]

It was the military, the most anticommunist force in the country, now building an increasingly intimate partnership with Washington after Ambassador Jones's recommendations, that forced the cancellation of the vote that was planned for 1959.[5] The regional conflicts had enormously increased the influence of the Army in Indonesian society over the past two years. The Armed Forces were granted emergency powers to fight the rebels, and the prestige of the forces under General Nasution got a big boost after they effectively put down attacks on the central government.[6] As Guided Democracy went into effect, the Army became one of a few key actors in Indonesian society. The military was to the right of the president, the Communists were on the left, and Sukarno provided a delicate balance by playing political forces against each other.

Washington took Howard Jones's advice, and moved closer to the Indonesian Armed Forces to construct an anticommunist front. In 1953 and 1954, there were about a dozen Indonesian officers training in the United States, and that number dropped to zero in 1958, the year Allen Pope bombed Ambon. In 1959, zero became forty-one, and by 1962, there were more than one thousand Indonesians studying operations, intelligence, and logistics, mostly at the Fort Leavenworth Army base.[7]

This new approach dovetailed with a growing consensus within the United States that the military should be given more power and influence in the Third World, even if it meant undermining democracy. In the 1950s, an academic field of study called Modernization Theory began to gain influence in Washington. In its basic approach, Modernization Theory replicated the Marxist formulation that societies progress through stages; but it did so in a way that was highly influenced by the anticommunist, liberal American milieu in which it emerged. The social scientists who pioneered the field put forward that "traditional," primitive societies would advance through a specific set of stages, ideally arriving at a version of "modern" society that looked a whole lot like the United States.[8]

Technocratic and resolutely antipopulist, Modernization Theory was prodemocracy when possible, but its proponents increasingly came to the conclusion that it might be better to just have some determined elite, say US-friendly generals, provide the crucial force for the difficult jump to "modernity."

In 1959, the State Department completed a major study informed by this logic. The recent history of Latin America, the study claims, "indicates that authoritarianism is required to lead backward societies through their socioeconomic revolutions. . . . The trend towards military authoritarianism will accelerate as developmental problems become more acute." The National Security Council met to discuss the report with the president, and to shower its conclusions with lavish praise. In Indonesia especially, they began to view the Army as they viewed themselves: as a bulwark against communism, and a modernizing political and economic force.[9]

At the same time, young Indonesians were brought to study in universities in the United States through various scholarship and funding programs. The idea, as with similar programs around the Third World, was to show the young intellectuals how things worked in the US, which would hopefully inspire them to take pro-American ideas back home. Since 1956, the Ford Foundation had been providing fellowships that brought young Indonesian economists to the US.[10]

In 1959, much to his surprise, Benny received a scholarship to study in the United States. This was a very welcome development, as he was unsure about his future at home and still in a bit of a fight with his family. But he wouldn't be going to California, as he would have liked. He was awarded a scholarship to attend the University of Kansas, in Lawrence. He had never set foot outside of Indonesia before.

The United States was a bit weird, he wrote in endless letters to his high school sweetheart. For some reason, he had to do a physical education class as part of his economics master's degree. On the one hand, Americans ate huge amounts of meat, which he didn't mind. But these people in Kansas would drink big glasses of cow's milk with their food, which he never understood. His life was that of a typical poor grad student—living in dingy dorms and trying to have as much fun as possible in between class and endless research. He and the other Indonesian students craved Indonesian food, but there was nothing like that in Kansas. There was just one "stupid, stupid Chinese restaurant" in the American style in the little university town, he told his friends.

But Lawrence was just forty minutes from the Fort Leavenworth Army base, where members of the Indonesian military were getting their training. And Washington was treating them very nicely. To Benny and his broke student friends, it seemed like the military men were being downright wined and dined by the US government. They had cars, and they had cash, so they would drive to meet the students in the college town, pool Uncle Sam's money to buy the best ingredients, and cook up a little Indonesian feast in the dorms. They were mostly Army generals—some of whom had even fought to crush the regional rebellions the CIA had backed. The young academics and the Army guys didn't talk too much politics, but it became clear to the grad students that the idea was to "groom them to be anti-Sukarno generals," in Benny's words. "They were all well-trained, and Americanized, and many of them became anticommunists there in Kansas."

The students and military brass spent most of their time bonding over the food, and their homesickness. And, getting drunk and heading into town for some fun. The Indonesian boys loved getting together and heading to Kansas City, where they could hit up the strip clubs. Indonesia is not a prudish country, but this type of show was something you couldn't catch back home.

Benny also witnessed another distinctly American spectacle: the US political process unfolding, viewed from the heartland. Not long after he arrived, John F. Kennedy took on Richard Nixon in a presidential contest. Benny and his buddies could watch the famous debate that aired on television on September 26, 1960, in which JFK, confident and attractive, proved perfectly suited to the medium, while Nixon, stuffy and sweaty, came across very poorly. But it was also the faltering economy, anxiety about the Soviet Union, the influence that vice presidential candidate Lyndon B. Johnson had in the South, and the support of minority voters that helped to win it for JFK. Just barely. He only got around 110,000 more votes than Nixon, out of sixty-nine million votes cast.[11]

Patrice, Jack, Fidel, Nelson, Nasution, and Saddam

After the prudish Eisenhower, the United States elected a president who was a womanizer, just like Sukarno. The two would meet soon, and get along well. But Kennedy's election seemed to herald serious changes for US foreign policy, especially toward the Third World. Sukarno, like many Indonesians, viewed young Jack as a rare American ally in the fight against colonialism because he had read JFK's denunciations of French colonial rule in Algeria.[12]

As a candidate, JFK had run on solidly anticommunist credentials, of course. It was the United States. But in his inauguration speech, he also made a pledge to the Third World. "To those people in the huts and villages of half the globe struggling to break the bonds of mass misery, we pledge our best efforts to help them help themselves, for whatever period is required—not because the communists may be doing it, not because we seek their votes, but because it is right," Kennedy said. "If a free society cannot help the many who are poor, it cannot save the few who are rich. To our sister republics south of our border, we offer a special pledge—to convert our good words into good deeds—in a new alliance for progress."[13]

However, JFK wasn't going to build a United States government from scratch. He would be inheriting the state as it existed—and the CIA operations already underway around the globe. On January 17, 1961, three days before he was sworn in, as he was still writing that lofty speech, the whole world got a stark reminder of that when Patrice Lumumba, the young, energetic, and popular leader of the Congo, was executed.

Lumumba had become prime minister in the wake of a decolonization process that was even more chaotic than Indonesia's had been a decade earlier. The end of Belgian control left the few independence leaders in the Congo scrambling to set up a government. Lumumba was dynamic and renowned for the fast-paced speeches that rolled over the radio waves across the territory. When the nation won independence, he was compared to the Sputnik satellite, and regular people looked forward to nothing less than a cosmic turnabout.[14]

The debonair Lumumba was more of a classical liberal than a leftist. Often wearing a bowtie, he was an *évolué*, a member of the class of Congolese who dressed to the nines, suiting up in European attire. He was an economic nationalist, not a committed internationalist revolutionary. Khrushchev observed that "Mr. Lumumba is as much a communist as I am a Catholic."[15]

But just months after his election, the young, inexperienced politician made a serious mistake, at least given the rules of the global Cold War. As Belgian forces (and mining interests) backed a white-supported secession movement in the Katanga Province, Lumumba turned to the United Nations for help. The UN offered nothing more than a strongly worded resolution— but Lumumba was desperate, and thought he deserved troops. So on July 14, 1960, he sent a cable to Moscow asking for further assistance. It was immediately leaked to the CIA.

As David Van Reybrouck notes in his astounding history of the Congo, "It would be hard to overstate the importance of this move. At a single swoop, this telegram opened up a new front in the Cold War: Africa." Did Lumumba and his team realize the impact the telegram would have? "Probably not. Inexperienced as they were, they were simply trying to obtain foreign assistance in solving a conflict concerning national decolonization."[16]

That wasn't Lumumba's only mistake, however. He made another big one in Washington, at least according to legend within the Agency. After a frenzied set of meetings in Washington, he made a personal request. Like Sukarno four years earlier, he wanted to have an exchange with a sex worker, the story goes. This inspired "revulsion," adding to the distaste US officials already felt for him. In the middle of the twentieth century, black men in the

US were brutally tortured and murdered for alleged sexual transgressions involving white women, including for simply whistling. Washington didn't like the way Lumumba talked politics, either. Under Secretary of State C. Douglas Dillon said "he was gripped by this fervor that I can only describe as messianic."[17] New CIA Deputy Director for Plans Richard M. Bissell called him a "mad dog." On July 21, Allen Dulles said it was safe to assume he had been "bought by the communists."[18]

On August 25, the White House gave the order, and the CIA drew up plans to have him killed.[19]

Bissell asked Dr. Sidney Gottlieb, the CIA's in-house scientist—the same man who had overseen MK-Ultra, a program that kidnapped poor black men in the United States and dosed them with LSD to see if the Agency could control their minds—to prepare a poison.[20] The CIA made plans to inject it into Lumumba's food or toothpaste.[21] That operation fizzled, so the Agency ran an operation to lure Lumumba out of United Nations protection, where he could be killed by local rivals.[22] Although ultimately without direct Agency participation, this is what happened. Lumumba lost UN recognition on November 22, and five days later fled house arrest in Leopoldville. Troops loyal to Joseph Mobutu, the CIA-backed Army chief of staff and former friend of Lumumba, caught up with Lumumba, kidnapping him and delivering him to the Belgian-backed rebels in Katanga. Working with four Belgians, Katangan rebel forces stuffed Lumumba into the back of a car, then unloaded him near a shallow well. They shot him three times, and shoved him into the hole.[23]

Lumumba's death made waves all around the world. People marched in the streets in Oslo, Tel Aviv, Vienna, and New Delhi. Belgian embassies were attacked in Cairo, Warsaw, and Belgrade. Moscow named a university after him. Mobutu took over the second-largest country in sub-Saharan Africa, staged public executions of his rivals, built a dictatorship, and became one of Washington's closest Cold War allies in Africa.[24]

But for Kennedy, it was tiny little Cuba, just ninety miles from Florida, that occupied his attention for the first months of his presidency.

When Fidel Castro's guerrilla forces overthrew the Batista dictatorship in January 1959, his movement was neither openly communist nor aligned with the Soviet Union. Indeed, he was accompanied by Che Guevara, the committed Marxist who had come to the conclusion, while watching the

Guatemalan coup in 1954, that the United States could not be trusted. Capitalist imperialism, Che believed, would wage war on any democratic socialist project, and therefore armed struggle and a tightly controlled state were the only options open to Third World revolutionaries. But at the very beginning, Castro hoped for decent relations with Uncle Sam, and some in Washington even welcomed his victory. This fell apart quickly. Washington responded to Castro's agrarian reforms and nationalizations by imposing severe trade restrictions, which led Cuba to turn to the Soviet Union for badly needed fuel imports.

During JFK's campaign, he attacked Eisenhower for being weak on Cuba.

The Bay of Pigs invasion, whose planning began before Kennedy took office, was a fiasco for the United States, and for JFK, for two reasons. The first reason was bureaucratic breakdown. The CIA failed to communicate the true chances of success to the president, and failed to come to a clear agreement as to the support its Cuban mercenaries would need after they landed on Cuba's shores and attempted to incite an anti-Castro uprising. The preparations alone created all kinds of problems, even before the invasion began. The CIA considered calling off the operation, but warned the president that the mercenaries they were training in Guatemala would speak out publicly against Kennedy if they were demobilized.[25] And in Guatemala, the presence of the Cubans led to a military revolt against the US-backed dictatorship, setting off a brutal war that had been slowly preparing to explode since the coup in 1954. The second reason was that the United States thought Cubans would genuinely rise up to support an anticommunist revolt.

In April 1961, three months after JFK took office, the opposite happened, and the soldiers of fortune were immediately arrested. Che Guevara might not have known how to build a socialist country quickly, famously struggling as finance minister; but he certainly wasn't naïve enough to leave the country vulnerable to the same kind of Yankee scheme he had witnessed firsthand in Guatemala.

It seems very possible the US officials could have toppled Castro, as they toppled so many other governments in the region over the years, if they had applied more pressure, or developed another strategy entirely. But the Bay of Pigs failure was so spectacular, and so obvious, that their hands were tied. The United States had shot its shot, and couldn't try anything so public again.

For days after the invasion, Kennedy's "anguish and dejection" were evident to everyone around him. Under Secretary of State Chester Bowles said that Kennedy was clearly "quite shattered." Kennedy himself related that it was the worst experience of his life.[26] He said he felt personally guilty for those who had died in the invasion. And it was a national humiliation. After the Bay of Pigs, two things changed for the JFK presidency, which had started with such idealism. From then on, he would have to deal with the CIA Wisner had created and with the problems it had bequeathed to him, and he would now govern while being accused of being soft on communism himself.

Even Khrushchev ridiculed Kennedy for the failure in Cuba. Although Castro is not a Communist, "You are well on the way to making him a good one," the Soviet leader told JFK. Privately, Khruschev told Communist allies he feared Kennedy was no match for the huge military-industrial complex in the US, and worried the young president couldn't keep the "dark forces" of his country at bay.[27]

It was just four days after the Bay of Pigs invasion, as JFK was still piecing his presidency together, that President Sukarno came to visit. For the Indonesian president, the parallels between the Bay of Pigs and what Indonesia had gone through in 1958 were obvious. But being the polite Javanese man that he was, he did not bring it up. The White House, in turn, took the advice from Jones's embassy to shower Sukarno with pomp and circumstance, while the Secret Service catered to Sukarno's "insatiable demand for call girls."[28] Sukarno could not get JFK to budge on West New Guinea, but reportedly was impressed with the man himself. Kennedy, reportedly, called Sukarno "an inscrutable Asian."[29]

Just after his meeting with Sukarno, the young president sent a letter to Jones in Jakarta laying out clearly that he was in charge of the US presence in Indonesia, including "all other United States Agencies."[30] It was clearly part of an attempt to wrest control over foreign relations away from the CIA after the Bay of Pigs failure.

Elsewhere in Southeast Asia, the Agency's actions had been felt viscerally. Secret American plotting was exposed in Cambodia, badly undermining US credibility in the region. For years, Norodom Sihanouk had railed against Eisenhower's anticommunism, believing the Americans were trying to get rid of him for maintaining a neutral stance. His claims were dismissed as far-fetched or absurd at the time. But he was right. In 1959, a CIA agent was instructed to liaise with Sihanouk's interior minister to organize a coup, which never succeeded.[31]

The South Vietnamese government of Ngo Dinh Diem also tried and failed to organize a coup in Cambodia, with US approval. After that failed, Sihanouk received a gift box. Maybe it was an attempt to patch things up. Instead, it exploded when his staff opened it, killing two men.[32] The parcel bomb, the third attempt to destroy Sihanouk, was traced to a US base in Saigon, but may have been sent without US knowledge. However—and this crucial dynamic repeats itself throughout the Cold War—the incident would not have happened if the South Vietnamese thought Washington would disapprove. Broad US plotting often led to events the Americans did not specifically predict. Either way, Sihanouk's relationship with the US was damaged beyond repair.[33]

Kennedy's White House, and especially his brother Bobby, became obsessed with destroying Castro, and put the CIA to the task. Robert McNamara, who served as secretary of defense from 1961 to 1968, later called the Kennedys' approach to Cuba "hysterical." At a party, Desmond Fitz-Gerald, who had helped to create the vampire terror campaign in the Philippines, told a friend about his new job on the Cuba task force, "All I know is I have to hate Castro."[34] The CIA had already sanctioned outlandish attempts on Castro's life. Under Eisenhower, they tried poisonous cigars, and attempted to make his beard fall out (they apparently thought that Cubans would respect him less clean-shaven). The Agency had contracted the mafia to murder Castro (Robert Maheu, the former FBI agent who set up that meeting with the mob, was the same CIA freelancer who had arranged for the fake Sukarno sex tape).[35] After the Bay of Pigs, the Agency built upon this tradition. They created a scuba diving suit contaminated with spores, but couldn't get it to the Cuban leader. One plan revolved around an exploding seashell.[36] The Miami CIA station became the largest in the world, and offered cash bounties for dead communists. Edward Lansdale, the same man who had created vampire victims in the Philippines, discussed spraying civilian sugar workers in Cuba with biological warfare agents, as well as faking the Second Coming of Christ.[37]

Bobby Kennedy, whom Bowles considered "aggressive, dogmatic, and vicious," was willing to employ even more drastic measures to shape Latin America as he thought fit. After the assassination of Dominican dictator Rafael Trujillo, the Kennedy brothers debated the merits of sending in the

Marines. Because this would not look good, Bobby suggested they simply blow up the US consulate themselves. That could provide the rationale for the invasion.[38]

Kennedy did launch his Alliance for Progress economic cooperation program in Latin America, as well as the Peace Corps and the Agency for International Development. But his administration's active engagement to fight communism ended up being primarily with local militaries. His administration wholeheartedly embraced Modernization Theory and hired economist W. W. Rostow, author of the suitably titled *The Stages of Economic Growth: A Non-Communist Manifesto*, as one of JFK's advisers. Under Kennedy, the most important alliance for progress was made with armed forces around the world, and their task was to lead their countries closer to a US-style economic system.

Bobby played a special role in adopting the State Department's recommendation that Third World militaries should focus on "counterinsurgency" in addition to nation-building—that is, fighting wars against internal enemies and playing a broader political role in society at large. From the start, US officials held up Indonesia as a crucial testing ground for this vision.[39] The Kennedy administration provided increasing levels of assistance to the Indonesian military, which was meant to serve as a counterweight to support that Sukarno was now receiving from the Soviets. Despite the Kennedy brothers' obsession with Cuba, in 1961, the National Security Council listed Indonesia and West New Guinea among its most "urgent planning priorities," because it was there that they believed Moscow and Washington were competing most directly for influence. Within a few years, Indochina would dominate international headlines, but until the middle of the 1960s most officials considered Indonesia far more important than Vietnam or Laos.[40]

After returning to Indonesia from Washington, Sukarno did not let the issue of West New Guinea go. At the end of 1961, he gave a speech titled "Triple Command of the People," or *Trikora*, demanding the dismantling of the Dutch "puppet state" and calling for the mobilization of the "entire Indonesian people" to regain the territory. General Nasution and other military leaders were wary of provoking war with the Dutch, but organized citizen militias and the Navy clashed with Dutch ships. As Jones had been telling Washington, this was not about a piece of land for Sukarno—it was about completing his revolution and the legitimacy of his state, and Indonesians would go to war over this if they had to. Exasperated that his allies in

Holland were proving so stubborn, and seeing this as a small price to pay to avoid losing Indonesia altogether to the Soviet orbit, Kennedy finally pushed the Dutch into a negotiation to hand over the territory.

For Indonesia, at least, this was a shift from the days of Eisenhower and the Wisner method. Rather than attempting to destroy him, Kennedy gave Sukarno what he knew he needed. At the same time, the power and influence of the anticommunist Indonesian military, in constant coordination with US officials with Washington, rose steadily in the background. Kennedy's positive engagement took the form of a "civic action program" (CAP) in Indonesia, which included the covert training of "selected personnel and civilians" and a range of anticommunist activities whose nature, more than fifty years later, is still a classified secret.[41] The CAP proved crucial in the creation of a *negara dalam negara*, a "state within a state," led by the generals. The process had begun when the military got emergency powers to fight the CIA in 1958. Now, the military received equipment and training from the US to engage in fishing, farming, and construction, which increased its economic interests and role around the country.[42]

In Africa, the US took a different direction. With CIA assistance, white South African authorities arrested Nelson Mandela in 1962. US officials also set the Middle East on a new path, in 1963. Outside Indonesia, the largest Communist Party in the Bandung countries was the Iraqi Communist Party (ICP), which had grown in opposition to dictator Abd al-Karim Qasim. The ICP thought of making a bid for revolution—and the Soviets advised against it. But Washington backed a successful coup by the anticommunist Baath Party, which immediately moved to crush the ICP. The CIA supplied lists of communists and alleged communists to the new regime, which slaughtered untold numbers of people. A Baath Party member named Saddam Hussein, only twenty-five years old, reportedly took part in this US-backed anticommunist extermination program.[43] Some communists were shot in their homes, while others were taken to prison; those who survived jail said Hussein had a reputation for being the worst of the torturers—they prayed to be taken in for interrogation on his nights off. The new Baath regime overturned the land reform that Qasim had passed.[44]

In Kansas, the Indonesian officers kept pouring into the country, and pouring into Benny's dining room. Presumably, they were now studying counterinsurgency strategies in addition to soaking up US anticommunist ideology more generally. But that's not what Benny remembers about those days. They all had one big last night before he went off to get a PhD, get married, and start a family. In between Missouri and Kansas, there's a street called State Line Road. Benny, his student friends, and the anticommunist generals-in-training walked across to Missouri for some cocktails. The Army guys wanted to find a specific club they liked, one with full nudity. They all got drunk, and the soldiers got their way.

5

To Brazil and Back

Squeezed Out

In the same years that Benny was in Kansas, life for Indonesians of Chinese descent like him got increasingly difficult back home. They had long suffered from intermittent explosions of racism, but as lines in the sand were drawn and redrawn under Sukarno's Guided Democracy, there seemed to be less and less space for them. The first major blow was a 1959 law, passed just as Benny was heading to Kansas, that took some economic rights away from foreign nationals. In practice, this included the country's large ethnic Chinese population. It was not Sukarno who pushed for this—it was the military—but he let the racist law, a deviation from Indonesia's foundational values, pass. The Army also organized violent anti-Chinese riots—for which it did not seek Sukarno's approval. The military used US funds to plot these pogroms.[1] The situation was terrifying.

Many Indonesians of Chinese descent began to look for a way out. This included the Tan family, whom we met briefly in the introduction. Tiong Bing and Twie Nio lived in Jakarta, not too far from Francisca's home. Tiong Bing, the father of the family, had come from a line of farmers but worked as an engineer in the largely Chinese section of North Jakarta, where life had become tense. Many in their community moved to China, but their family was looking for a different opportunity. Prospects for Canada or the US were grim. They had heard, however, that some Chinese Indonesians had gone to

Brazil, which offered good opportunities and relative freedom from discrimination.[2] The trickle of immigration started in the early 1960s, and as a result stories of Brazil made their way back to Jakarta, and to the Tans.

So the family decided to board the *Tjitjalengka*, a big old Dutch hospital ship that had been used to carry prisoners of war during World War II, with their three children. Tiong Bing never actually got permission to leave his engineering job, his daughter Ing Giok remembers. He just ran away. His exit papers might have even been faked. "We'll figure it all out after we get on the boat," he told the kids. It wasn't easy to keep three little girls healthy and happy as they inched their way around the globe. Ing Giok kept throwing up. But six weeks later, they pulled into the port of Santos, in the state of São Paulo.

The China of the 1960s

Ing Giok was only a little girl when she first saw Brazil, and it was a very different place from what she was used to. Perhaps for those reasons, the country's major characteristics jumped out at her more clearly than they would to North Americans, or even to Brazilians.[3] First, she realized very quickly that Brazil is a Western European settler colony, with extreme inequality and a very obvious racial hierarchy. This all became apparent as her family moved into an apartment in Brooklin, the São Paulo neighborhood named after the New York borough, and her parents got her into an upper-middle-class Catholic school.

There, most of the kids were white. And it was clear that these white people ran the country. In the streets around her were people with dark or black skin, mostly descended from slaves, and still obviously treated like second-class citizens. She was part of a third group, a community of more recent immigrants that was classed somewhere between the white and black people—allowed to ascend to the middle class, but always treated with a healthy dose of ridicule. The kids called her "Japa": São Paulo has a large Japanese community, and she was often confused with Brazilians of Japanese descent, who were higher on the racial ladder than the blacks. And she knew there was a fourth race somewhere far away, although she had little contact with them: Brazil's indigenous people, who were discussed as though they were barely human.

Other things were new to her. Brazil had only one language—Portuguese—and it came from Europe, not from Brazil. White colonizers had brought it with them, and it had functionally annihilated all the local languages. This was very different from Indonesia, of course, which spoke to itself in a hurricane of intermixed indigenous languages that had essentially blown Dutch away before she was born. And there was just one religion—Christianity. The colonizers had brought it, and Brazil's local traditions were practiced only in the jungle far away, somewhere she knew she wasn't expected to go. It was all very different from Indonesia, which had five or six religions, depending on how you counted.

It was pretty obvious what Ing Giok was supposed to do: study hard, move up toward the part of society occupied by the white people, and adopt their manner of doing things. She was a smart girl, and so she did well.

The Tan family did not realize until they arrived in 1962 that Brazil was in political crisis. At least, it surely looked that way to the United States. By far the largest country in Latin America and for a long time Washington's most important ally in the region, Brazil appeared to be wobbling away from the US orbit. This didn't just trouble the North Americans—it troubled much of Brazil's elite, too. Unlike in Indonesia, Washington's officials here did not have to adjust to a vastly different local culture and then plant the seeds of an anticommunist movement. In Brazil, they were able to work easily with conservative political forces that had emerged from Brazil's own history.

The Portuguese arrived in this part of South America around 1500, and like so many other places in the colonial world, it was named for one of its first raw material exports: brazil wood, or *pau brasil*.[4] This huge chunk of South America, twice the size of the European Union, technically ended up in Portuguese hands because of the 1494 Treaty of Tordesillas—or, rather, when the Pope drew an arbitrary line down a very badly drawn map to split the New World between Spain and Portugal. The indigenous population who fell into the newly designated Portuguese territories lived differently from those who lived in modern-day Mexico or Peru. There was no large, centrally governed empire like the Aztec or Inca, but smaller, more self-sufficient groups. In the very early years, Europeans made tentative alliances with these tribes, intermarrying and fighting and losing battles and forming new alliances and being captured only to escape and send (largely true, if sensational) accounts of cannibalism back to Europe. The most famous

European to relate this experience survived only by crying and begging for his life, leading the locals to believe he was too weak and pathetic to be worth eating. He became a best-selling author.[5] By the time the Europeans had subdued the native population, they decided that indigenous Brazilians, who were dying from disease and brutal enslavement, did not provide enough free labor for the extraction of natural resources for export.

So Brazil imported almost five million human beings from Africa, far more than the United States did, and equal to almost half of all slaves brought to the Americas. Just as in the US, enslavement in Brazil was unimaginably cruel. In addition to the whip, stocks, and iron collars studded with spikes to prevent escape, slave owners affixed iron masks, which prevented the slaves from committing suicide by shoving earth into their own mouths.[6]

When it came to independence from Europe, most other countries in Latin America threw Spain out in violent revolutions in the early nineteenth century. But in Brazil, the Portuguese royal family fled Napoleon's invading forces and set up shop in Rio de Janeiro in 1808, bringing the capital of the empire to the colonies. Thousands of Europeans did their best to set up a royal court in Rio, and they established a local monarchy, which ruled until 1889 and still has some (unofficial) influence today.

Soon after the liberation of African-descendant Brazilians, in 1888, the largest country in South America promptly embarked upon a policy of explicit *branqueamento*, or whitening. The idea was to bring in white immigrants, and to breed the African blood out of the population through "miscegenation." Newly freed slaves were intentionally left languishing in poverty, rather than paid to work in the new system. This approach was also what brought Ing Giok's Japanese classmates to São Paulo. Brazilians deemed the Japanese, which they categorized as the "whites of Asia," the most desirable Asian immigrants.[7] This racism remained public and paramount, with cultural organizations producing posters to "show" that a Japanese man and a Brazilian woman would produce "white" offspring.[8]

More conservative in outlook than its neighbors, Brazil looked more to Washington than to Spanish-speaking Latin America. From the fall of the monarchy to the middle of the twentieth century, Brazil enjoyed a "special relationship" with Washington, and would often play the role of conciliator between the US and Spanish-speaking Latin America. In 1940, Brazil became the first Latin American nation to sign a military staff agreement with US military officials in Washington. The State Department saw Brazil as the "key to South America," because of its size and mineral wealth. In 1949 the Escola Superior de Guerra (ESG) was founded, modeled after the US National War College, where some Brazilians had trained.[9]

Outside the military, this special relationship began to fall apart at the beginning of the Cold War. President Eurico Gaspar Dutra (in office 1946–51) did everything he could to join Washington's anti-Soviet campaign, including breaking off relations with Moscow and banning the Brazilian Communist Party (PCB), the strongest communist party in Latin America.[10] But President Dutra also believed that the United States was standing in the way of Brazil's economic development. The US, the only available source of capital for Brazil's huge public investment needs after World War II, refused to grant the loans Dutra's government requested, surprising Washington's wartime ally. The two countries also clashed over the cost of coffee, an extremely important Brazilian export. But the greatest source of friction between the two largest countries in the hemisphere was the question of US corporate involvement in the oil sector—Brazilian lawmakers wanted to favor local petroleum companies, while Washington insisted US firms be allowed to operate in the country. By 1949 Brazilians felt exasperated by apparent gringo indifference to Brazil's economic position, and in 1950 Dutra issued a public rebuke when he politely declined to assist the US in Korea.[11]

When Getúlio Vargas, a longtime force in Brazilian politics, returned to the presidency in 1951, relations with the US only worsened. He had been a dictator in the 1930s and '40s, but had reinvented himself as a democratically elected populist. Although Vargas had a history of fiercely repressing communism in his own country, and Brazil supported John Foster Dulles's cherished anticommunist declaration at the Caracas Conference just before the Guatemala coup, after another fight over aid he too concluded the US was opposed to Brazilian economic development, and announced the country would support colonial freedom struggles at the UN (by this point in the Cold War, this was an obvious affront to Washington's policy).[12] Vargas also proposed a tax on excess profits that would clearly affect foreign investors and then oversaw the creation of Petrobras, a state-owned oil monopoly. The reaction in the United States to all of this was predictably hostile.[13] The *New York Times* reported that "competent opinion" was that Brazil could never raise the money required to extract its own petroleum, so that effectively, "what the government did was to bury deep in the ground whatever oil reserves Brazil has."[14]

Not only for these reasons, the Escola Superior de Guerra began plotting to remove Vargas, with US support.[15] But it never happened. Soon after a decree to double the minimum wage caused outrage among Brazil's elite, everything came crashing down on its own.

Carlos Lacerda, the most prominent critic of President Vargas in Brazil, was attacked by gunmen while walking in Copacabana; he survived with a bullet wound to the foot, while a military officer accompanying him did not make it. It soon emerged that the attempted assassination may have been ordered by someone in the president's own bodyguard force. The military was definitely coming for Vargas now, and they were going to succeed. Rather than let that happen, Vargas wrote a final letter to the country, then shot himself in the chest on August 24, 1954, upturning politics forever from beyond the grave.

The victor of the election that followed in 1955, Juscelino Kubitschek, was a pro-US centrist and economic nationalist. Nonetheless, Washington viewed him with suspicion. During his campaign, the United States Information Service doubled its budget for "programs to educate Brazilians on the dangers of communism and communist-front organizations."[16] US officials also sought to expose ties between the banned PCB and the Soviet Union. The Communist Party endorsed Kubitschek, or "JK" for short (almost all Brazilian presidents get nicknames), causing him even more problems—despite the facts that the small PCB was illegal and JK disavowed its support.

As president, JK built things. He undertook an ambitious infrastructure program and built a new capital, Brasília, from scratch in the middle of the country. Still, the Eisenhower administration refused to agree to an important long-term assistance program for Brazil, specifically because they didn't want to boost Kubitschek's popularity.[17]

But it was the ascendance of JK's vice president, a young, left-leaning bohemian named João Goulart, often referred to simply by his childhood nickname, "Jango," that really concerned the North Americans. As the former labor minister for Vargas, Goulart had introduced the explosive bill to double the minimum wage in 1954. He was firmly a member of Brazil's elite political establishment, a millionaire landowner and devout Catholic. But Goulart's proposed reforms set off alarm bells in Washington. This was not little Cuba, they reasoned. This was one of the world's biggest countries. If Jango was not stopped, warned US Ambassador Lincoln Gordon, Brazil could become "the China of the 1960s."[18]

Gordon, a former professor at Harvard Business School, had worked on the Marshall Plan before absorbing Modernization Theory and helping design the Alliance for Progress.[19] He was an old friend of Richard Bissell, the Frank Wisner CIA recruit who had designed the plans to assassinate Lumumba and take Cuba at the Bay of Pigs.[20] When Gordon arrived in Brazil in 1962, he recognized quickly that hyper-megalopolis São Paulo was a lot like his native New York, in that it "had an elite class—the four hundred families that dominated the city's social and economic life—but also had a large class of immigrant families, like his own, striving to realize the American Dream."[21] The democracy Brazil set up after World War II was very limited. Striking was illegal. Because of literacy requirements, a majority of the population (mostly black, very poor Brazilians) was barred from voting; Jango and his supporters wanted to change this, just as a growing civil rights movement in the US was putting pressure on Washington to repeal racist voting restrictions there.

Goulart served as vice president under JK from 1955 to 1960. Then in 1960, he ran to serve as vice president again, this time under Jânio Quadros, a theatrical provincial politician backed by the right-leaning UDN party. Despite his conservative leanings, Quadros managed to alienate the Kennedy administration right off the bat. He admired neutralists like Nasser in Egypt and Nehru in India, but he didn't even want to go as far as to be neutral. Brazil would remain pro-West, he said, but the country also wanted to look more to the South, to become a leader of the Third World. He certainly did not want to turn resolutely East, but he did want to improve economic relations with the socialist world. For Kennedy, even this much was dangerous.[22]

This seemed like an obvious case of "Do what I say, not what I do." Quadros asked, "Why should the United States trade with Russia and her satellites but insist that Brazil trade only with the United States?"[23] He announced Brazil would participate in the upcoming conference of Non-Aligned Countries in Belgrade, the meeting that grew out of Sukarno's 1955 Bandung Conference. He never made it. Just months into his term, Quadros awarded Che Guevara the *Cruzeiro do Sul*, Brazil's highest award for foreigners. This was pragmatism, not ideology—he hoped Havana could help facilitate trade with socialist countries. Carlos Lacerda, now one of the country's most influential people, began denouncing Quadros everywhere he could. The president abruptly resigned. He expected that the military and widespread popular support would sweep him back into power. They didn't.[24]

Brazil sent another representative to the first meeting of the Non-Aligned Movement in Yugoslavia in September. A wildly diverse set of political leaders pledged to pursue peace and development while on a middle course between the poles of Washington and Moscow. But João "Jango" Goulart, who became president after Quadros resigned, had more pressing problems. Jango and his Brazilian Labor Party were always viewed with deep suspicion by the elite and the military, but he was considered acceptable as the number-two man to the union-busting Quadros. Jango as president, however, was seen as well-nigh unthinkable. Lacerda, some outlets in the (largely conservative) media, and part of the military hoped to block him from taking power at all. But on September 7, 1961, the grinning forty-three year old, impeccably dressed in a blue suit, arrived to be sworn in as president.

From day one, he had almost no political capital. His fatal mistake, considering the posture of the elite, the military, and the United States, was to seek to remedy this by shoring up support among previously neglected sectors of Brazil's population, rather than among its political insiders. This had never been done successfully before. Jango backed a set of reforms, called the "*reformas da base*," which would change Brazilian politics considerably. They would extend voting rights to all Brazilians, while unrolling a literacy program around the country. And Goulart backed land reform, despite the fact that he—like much of Brazil's political class—was actually a *latifundista*, or large landowner, himself. Even he knew this was a gamble. Sustaining this kind of a program meant relying on support from grassroots movements, unions, and the organized left.[25]

Goulart also alienated the military high command with reforms that would affect them more directly. He wasn't just proposing to extend the vote to illiterates—he also wanted to allow lower-ranking soldiers to cast ballots. Current law dictated that they could not do so while serving. The idea that he was appealing directly to the lower ranks made the high-ranking officers, who tended to be more conservative than their left-leaning subordinates, very suspicious. If he was ignoring their authority over the lower orders, they could convince themselves, perhaps he wanted to overturn their authority entirely. In Brazil, the threat of rebellion from below had terrified elites for five centuries, and they always responded—successfully—with violence.

It didn't take Kennedy's White House long to respond, either. Jango went to visit Washington in early 1962, and it seemed to go OK, though he failed to get any concessions on aid or trade. On July 30, however, Kennedy had a meeting with Ambassador Gordon, which was recorded. The two men agreed to spend millions on anti-Goulart plans for elections that year, and to prepare the ground for a military coup to, as Gordon put it, "push him out, if it comes to that."

Gordon said, "I think one of our important jobs is to strengthen the spine of the military. To make it clear, discreetly, that we are not necessarily hostile to any kind of military action whatsoever if it's clear that the military action is—"

"Against the left," Kennedy finished.[26]

Gordon: "He's giving the damn country to the—"

"Communists," said Kennedy.

"Exactly."

After Gordon's July meeting with JFK, CIA money began pouring into Brazil. The Agency sent agent Tim Hogan under "deep cover," and he began "organizing farmers and labor."[27] Kennedy's administration initiated a "counterinsurgency" assessment, authored by General William H. Draper Jr., which came to the conclusion that "every effort should be made" to provide US training for the local Army.[28] Years before this, Draper had come to the conclusion that Brazil was the perfect model for the use of the military to fight internal enemies and modernize economies in the Third World.[29] The White House also sent in Vernon Walters, a military attaché with deep ties to Brazil's military, to represent Washington publicly alongside Gordon.[30]

It did not matter that Jango actually sided with Kennedy when the US detected Soviet missiles in Cuba in 1962. Jango publicly backed the blockade of the small island and told Walters, in private, that he would understand if the North Americans bombed the place.[31] For Washington, he represented the threat of communism in their own hemisphere. Under Kennedy, US activity in Brazil was different from what had been done in Iran and Guatemala in the 1950s. There were no large, noisy interventions with Uncle Sam's hand quite obviously pulling the strings. The US carefully nurtured powerful anticommunist elements, and let them know they would have support if they were to act.

It was also a major departure from JFK's promises to the Third World, and from the original intent behind the Alliance for Progress. That program was now widely seen as an imperfect cover for traditional US policy in the region, not only because Washington continued intervening throughout the region. One of JFK's best biographers put it this way,

> How could he square professions of self-determination—a central principle of the Alliance—with the reality of secret American interventions in Cuba, Brazil, British Guiana, Peru, Haiti, the Dominican Republic, and every country that seemed vulnerable to left-wing subversion? (And that was just the beginning: A June National Security directive approved by the president had listed four additional Latin American countries "sufficiently threatened by Communist-inspired insurgency"—Ecuador, Colombia, Guatemala, and Venezuela. . . .)[32]

In Brazil, Goulart's most controversial proposal was land reform, as had been the case in Guatemala under Árbenz. Brazil's landed gentry were horrified by the policy; they withdrew from negotiations and put all their energy into taking down Jango instead. Inflation was already out of control, but things got much worse for the economy when all US aid dried up, and Brazil's international creditors stopped all further loans while Washington instead funneled cash to state governors committed to a *golpe de estado*, or coup, in Brazil.[33] Brazil's Congress caught one US-backed front channeling millions to opposition politicians, and Jango shut them down, but that didn't stop the ongoing, effective destabilization of his government.[34] With the US now effectively leading an international capital strike, Jango struggled to finance basic state functions. He certainly had no help from the men in Moscow; after the Cuban Missile Crisis, the Soviets did not want to cause any trouble in Washington's backyard.[35]

Then, Carlos Lacerda, the man who had played a role in the end of both the Vargas and Quadros presidencies, acted again. In October 1963 he gave an interview to Julian Hart, the Brazil correspondent for the *Los Angeles Times* (and therefore my own predecessor), in which he accused Jango of plotting a coup himself, calling him a *golpista* (Portuguese for putschist), and asked Washington to intervene.

Washington officials knew, as did everyone else, that if Jango was going down, it would be the military that would depose him. Just as in Indonesia, the Armed Forces in Brazil were the country's most reliably anticommunist force. But their allegiance to this ideology went far deeper than was the case in Indonesia. It was even deeper than the Cold War. In some ways the Americans could not hope for a better ally, and this perfect anticommunist partnership grew out of a powerful legend going back to 1935, when a younger President Vargas had used a sputtering left-wing revolt to crack down on communists and build a dictatorship.

The Legend of the *Intentona*

The Brazilian Communist Party was founded in 1922, largely by immigrants and former anarchists.[36] When they immediately joined Lenin's recently established Communist International, Moscow had little idea what to do with them. The Comintern classified Brazil as a large "semicolonial" country, in the same category as China, and put it on the back burner. At the time, the directive the Brazilians got from the Soviets was to form a united front with the national "bourgeoisie" against imperialism, without Communist leadership—in the same way that Mao was ordered to work with Chiang Kai-shek, with very mixed results.[37]

Brazil's Communist Party was mostly committed to that line. But it also operated in a country where military plotting was routine for every political tendency. Getúlio Vargas first took power in a military coup in 1930, and after he began taking cues from the fascist movements in Italy and Spain, a man named Luis Carlos Prestes, a charismatic communist lieutenant who had once attempted a failed left-populist revolt, founded the *Aliança Nacional Libertadora* (ANL).[38] The ANL was opposed to fascism and *integralismo*, which in Brazil was a rabidly anticommunist, kind of Catholic, local variant of fascism. The *Aliança* included many moderate supporters of Vargas who wanted to pull him back from the right, and also gained the backing of the Communist Party itself.

Moscow did not set up the ANL, nor did it order the National Liberation Alliance to act; indeed, the Soviets were worried the Brazilians were being reckless and adventurist. However, when Communist leaders in Moscow realized that Prestes might launch another rebellion, they didn't want to be left out. They sent a small advisory staff, including a German explosives specialist and Victor Allen Barron, a US citizen and communications expert who was tasked with communicating with Communist leadership back in Russia.[39]

Most of the civilians in the Communist Party and the ANL didn't know any preparations were underway for a rebellion. And it started on accident, up in Natal, in poor northeastern Brazil, after soldiers there became enraged by the dismissal of some colleagues. The Communist Party there asked the soldiers to wait, but to no avail. The rebellion exploded, and rebels actually took control of the city for a time, commandeering cars and robbing the banks. When the uprising reached Recife, also in the northeast, the government's response was a slaughter, as the military put down the uprising and executed the leftist rebels.

"It was brutal, tremendous repression! They killed left and right, crooked and straight. The life of a communist wasn't worth ten bits of raw honey," said Lieutenant Lamartine Coutinho, using an old Portuguese expression we might translate as "wasn't worth shit."

Then the final act came, on a small beach just around the bend from Copacabana in Rio de Janeiro. The attack began in the wee hours of the morning on November 27, 1935. Military troops launched a grenade toward the barracks, which blew up in front of a pillar. Then they opened fire.

"It was an ugly, horrible battle!" said one of the soldiers under attack that morning. "Shots all over the place!" But in the end, only two soldiers died in combat.

The ANL had recklessly wasted human lives, probably dozens across the country, and only succeeded in handing themselves over to the government, to be used as they pleased.[40]

As it happened, the story of a failed communist coup perfectly served the interests of the elites that were pushing for a rightward shift at the time. The powerful newspaper *O Globo* had already published an entirely false report, signed in June by owner Roberto Marinho, that communists had received orders to take over the country by "shooting all non-communist officials, preferably at the doors of their homes or even after invading their domiciles."[41]

The Vargas government used the real event, from then on somewhat incorrectly referred to as "*Intentona Comunista*," or Communist Uprising, to crack down on the left and his critics in general, and then as an excuse to consolidate dictatorial powers. Vargas declared a state of emergency, created the "Committee for the Repression of Communism," suspended individual liberties, and began to round up the country's leftists. Many of the *Intentona*'s leaders were executed, though the popular Prestes remained in jail. Authorities banned left-wing books.[42]

The tale of violent communist subversion served the needs of the right-wing elements in the military and government so effectively that they created another one. In 1937, a general "found" a document outlining the "Plano Cohen," a Jewish-communist plot (capitalizing on antisemitism on the fascist right) that included directives to invade the houses of wealthy Brazilians and rape them.[43] Vargas used this entirely fabricated plan to authorize a new military coup, promulgate a new constitution, and take control of a full-fledged dictatorship.[44]

The 1935 *Intentona* served as a foundational legend for the Armed Forces, and for the increasingly virulent anticommunist movement that overtook the military and society in general. Every year, on November 27, the military gathered in front of a memorial structure on *Praia Vermelha*, or "Red Beach," to commemorate the defense against the communist rebellion. And a powerful myth took shape. The military came to tell the story that November 1935 was not a conventional attack on military barracks. The tale became that communists snuck into the chambers of officers, and stabbed them to death while they slept.

This parable of unique communist evil was disproved many decades later by careful historical investigation. As historian Rodrigo Patto Sá Motta affirms, citing autopsy reports: "No one died from a stab wound that morning . . . after all, it would be curious to imagine professionals from the Brazilian Armed Forces—no matter what their political convictions—carrying out a military uprising using daggers!"[45]

Communists with knives drawn, ready to stab you in your sleep, became a common trope in Brazil's voluminous anticommunist material over the next few decades. In the press, you could also find illustrations indicating that communists were insects that could only be "exterminated" with liberty, the family, and morality. Communism was called a plague, a virus, or cancer, terms that were also hurled at communists at the time in nearby Argentina.[46] More often than not, communism was associated with pure evil or witchcraft, drawn with the use of demons or Satanic beasts, such as dragons, snakes, and goats. There was often the implication, or outright depiction, of sexual perversion and deviancy.[47]

Launching false accusations of communism could also be profitable. Police, soldiers, and low-level politicians would "find" evidence that a certain citizen was communist, earning more resources for their departments or, very often, generating direct bribes. The fascist political party, *Ação Inte-gralista Brasileira* (AIB), reportedly used classic extortion tactics on small businesses, but with an anticommunist twist. In the dark of night, party members would cover the walls of shops and homes with seemingly commu-nist graffiti. Then they'd show up a few days later, asking the owners to make donations to the AIB, to prove to the concerned citizens in the neighborhood that they weren't actually communists.[48]

In the 1950s and early 1960s, Brazil's military deepened its ties with Washington. The US maintained its largest service missions in Brazil, and Brazilian officers received extra appointments to train at Fort Leavenworth's command school, alongside all those soldiers from Indonesia.[49]

For Brazil's many right-wing elements, especially in the military, Jango's entire presidency was a mistake. But in 1961, Jango made a blunder that upset the military further. The announcement that Brazil would reopen relations with the Soviet Union came just days before the annual commemoration of the *Intentona*, and was seen as a provocation. Not long after, one of the coun-try's armed far-right groups, *Movimento Anticomunista* (MAC), covered Rio de Janeiro in graffiti, with slogans like "Death to the traitors," "Let us shoot, fellow Brazilians, Moscow's secular forces," and "War to the death for the PCB," the country's still-illegal Communist Party.[50] It is widely believed the MAC received funding from the CIA and carried out several bombings, as well as shooting up the National Student Union.[51]

Another anticommunist group, the Society for the Defense of Tradition, Family, and Property (TFP), founded in 1960 in São Paulo, sought to counter the decadent threat of international communism by forcing its youth brigades to cut their hair short, wear modest clothing, refrain from watching TV, and learn to fight karate.[52] TFP was international in its vision, and soon established chapters across Latin America, in South Africa, and in the United States.

As for the actual Brazilian Communist Party, it split in 1962. Under the leadership of Luis Carlos Prestes, still influential decades later, the PCB had gone along with Khrushchev's decision to move away from Stalinism, and remained committed to working peacefully within the boundaries of Bra-zilian democracy. A splinter group, more inspired by Mao and convinced of the need for outright revolution, rejected this "revisionism" and formed the almost-identically named *Partido Comunista do Brasil* (PCdoB). Under Jango's government, the PCB was actually much more moderate than other actors on the left at the time, since they didn't even support updating the constitution.[53]

All this anticommunist fire and brimstone was directed at opposing a president who was, at most, a liberal reformist. But Jango and his reforms were popular. If he had eventually succeeded in enabling more people to vote, the country would have changed in very noticeable ways for the elites. And these changes were supported by the country's small number of communists, who really did exist. If you were opposed to anything that communists approved of, and terrified of the consequences that social reform would have had in a country like Brazil, you could find many reasons to oppose Jango. If you accepted all the tenets of fanatical anticommunism as J. Edgar Hoover laid them out back in the 1940s—and the Brazilian elite and US government did—their opposition made sense.

The association between Jango and clandestine communism did not just lurk on the dark, right-wing fringes of Brazilian society. A January 1964 cartoon in *O Globo*, the newspaper published by what is still Brazil's most important media group, ran with the headline "The Literacy Campaign," referring to Jango's plan to teach more people to learn to read and write. On the right sat a dirty man in ragged clothes, his face the picture of ignorance. On the left, his teacher, pointing at him and cackling. Behind the instructor, protruding from his suit, is a long devil's tail, with a hammer and sickle stamped on its pointy tip.[54]

Three Down

In the fall of 1963, President John F. Kennedy ordered his ambassador in South Vietnam to facilitate the removal of President Diem. As an ally, Diem was now causing Washington more trouble than he was worth. The CIA passed the word along to a local general, and on November 1, 1963, Diem was kidnapped along with his brother, and they were both shot and stabbed in the back of an armored personnel carrier. Kennedy hadn't actually wanted Diem killed, but he knew that he was responsible for his death, and the assassination shook and badly depressed the young president.[55]

A few weeks later, Kennedy himself was murdered, while driving through Dallas. The men closest to him, knowing they had been actively trying to get rid of Castro, and were using methods that were far from innocent all over the world, scrambled to guess who had done it. Bobby Kennedy himself suspected the killing might have been the work of the CIA, the mob, or Castro, all of which would have meant he himself was partly responsible. Vice President Lyndon Johnson's first suspicion was that it was retaliation for Diem's murder.[56] Johnson did not even know the administration had been trying to kill Castro, and as he took over the presidency, he struggled to wrap his mind around the network of covert operations he would inherit.[57]

Lyndon Baines Johnson was a hardworking, all-American Christian from Texas. LBJ was liberal, probably more so than Kennedy, and regarded as the "Master of the Senate," where he had served as its incredibly powerful leader for six years.[58] But when it came to foreign policy, he was less experienced. He had none of Kennedy's appreciation for the historical battles between imperialism and national revolution in the Third World. According to biographer Doris Kearns Goodwin, who knew him well, Johnson held an all-too-common American belief that the rest of the world was basically just like the USA, but a bit behind. He held a "belief in the universal applicability of American values, the existence of a global consensus," she wrote. But LBJ didn't have the confidence in his own mastery of foreign policy to challenge the men left behind by Kennedy.[59] So he often neglected foreign affairs, deferring to the wisdom of these advisers.

In Brazil, covert operations were well underway. CIA agent Tim Hogan and military attaché Vernon Walters were already in the country and active. They were using both the military and economy against the president. The screws were tightening around Jango.

The influential daily *Jornal do Brasil* published an editorial, *"Basta!,"* which would serve as the rallying cry for the country's *golpistas*. "Before we arrive at Revolution, we say ENOUGH! We say that as long as there are organized, cohesive and disciplined Brazilian Armed Forces . . . ENOUGH! The time has come . . . we register the death of the false politics of class reconciliation carried out by the President's witchcraft and spells . . . national patience has its limits."[60] In late November, just days after Kennedy was killed, Jango attended the country's annual celebration of the defeat of that fabled *Intentona Comunista* on the Red Beach in Rio de Janeiro. His presence only served to annoy many of the country's most committed conservatives, who went as far as to boycott the ceremony and organize other anticommunist events nearby.

At that commemoration on November 27, 1963, Army General Jair Dantas Ribeiro gave a terse, ominous speech. "In the quiet of the night, driven by principles never understood, extremist groups took off on an inglorious endeavor," he began. "Without flag and without cause, without ideals and without a destination, the action of these adventurers found no echo in the heart of the nation, whose Christian structure is entirely immune to hate and extremism." Speaking with Jango in the audience, he continued:

> Those hateful terrorists of 1935, raising the communist shield that means only ruin and rancor, propagating humanitarian popular sentiments that, in reality, served only to hide subaltern proposals and thirst for power, murdering treacherously in the shadow of night, our armed brothers, wrote a black page in the History of Brazil. . . . We should not, however, suppress this story: that attempt remains an example for these pests, who want to install an anti-democratic regime. . . .
>
> For now and forever, the example of the Army and its vigilance will remain, and serve as a warning.[61]

For Ribeiro, the "pests" were communists. And military officers were already formulating their own theories as to Jango's intentions. Many were now convinced that in addition to giving low-level soldiers the vote, he would appeal directly to them, subverting the authority of the superior officers.

Brazil's right-wing forces began to spread the idea that it was actually Jango who planned his own, left-wing, coup. They charged that to get his reforms implemented, he would shut down the government, abolish Congress, or declare a new constitution. The country's major newspapers helped to disseminate this story. If this was true, the thinking went, a coup that removed him from power would actually save democracy. US Ambassador Lincoln Gordon shared this view. And since Jango was a weak president, Gordon speculated, he might be supplanted by even more radical—maybe communist—forces later if he wasn't stopped now.[62]

Behind the scenes, the Americans were coordinating with the military. In March, Gordon sent a cable back to Washington. He wrote: "My considered conclusion is that Goulart is now definitely engaged on campaign to seize dictatorial power, accepting the active collaboration of the Brazilian Communist Party, and of other radical left revolutionaries to this end. If he were to succeed it is more than likely that Brazil would come under full Communist control . . ."

The Americans had their eyes on a specific Brazilian replacement. Gordon continued:

> The most significant development is the crystallizing of a military resistance group under the leadership of Gen. Humberto Castello [sic] Branco, Army Chief of Staff. Castelo Branco is a highly competent, discreet, honest, and deeply respected officer. . . . Castelo Branco's preference would be to act only in case of obvious unconstitutional provocation, e.g., a Goulartist move to close Congress or to intervene in one of the opposition states (Guanabara or Sao Paulo being the most likely ones). He recognizes, however (as do I) that Goulart may avoid such obvious provocation, while continuing to move toward an irreversible fait accompli by means of manipulated strikes, financial undermining of the states, and an executive plebiscite—including voting by illiterates . . .[63]

Earlier in his life, Castelo Branco had trained at Fort Leavenworth in Kansas. There, he had met Vernon Walters, the military attaché Kennedy sent to Brazil. After they studied together in Kansas, Castelo Branco and Walters were roommates, living together in a small hotel in Italy.[64]

Given the circumstances that led to his inauguration, Jango had almost no support in Congress, and had few allies in Brazil's media, much of which was owned by a few powerful landowning families. In order to demonstrate public support for his reforms, he organized a series of street rallies. On March 13, 1964, Jango gathered with other left-leaning leaders to speak to nearly two hundred thousand people in front of *Central do Brasil*, the iconic train station in downtown Rio. A tense Jango took the stage, called again for land reform, and attacked right-wing false democrats for being "anti-people, anti-union, and anti-reform." He said, "Meeting with the people on the streets is not a threat to democracy. A threat to democracy is when you pounce on the people, exploiting their Christian beliefs; and the mystifications of an anticommunist industry—they are a threat to democracy." Cameras caught some attendees carrying signs with slogans like "Down with the *Latifundistas*," a photo of Fidel, and "Legalize the Communist Party"—more fuel for the right-wing conspiracists.[65]

The conservatives responded with their own rally. On March 19, just a few miles from the Tan family's new home in São Paulo, the "*Marcha da Família com Deus pela Liberdade*," or "March of the Family with God and for Liberty," brought almost five hundred thousand people to the streets. Most of them were from well-off, conservative families—though some forced their maids to come—and the presence of respectable women and children emboldened the scheming military officers. Ing Giok Tan and her family, living just miles away, were wary of these kinds of things, and stayed away. The US government did not. It supplied material and moral support to the march, which was already well grounded in homegrown Brazilian elite attitudes.[66]

Jango's final and fatal error, as far as the military was concerned, came just after that. A group of two thousand marines in Rio, supporters of the *reformas da base*, staged a little rebellion against their superiors, demanding better working conditions and a relaxation of their disciplinary code. The rebels showed the pro-mutiny, anti-imperial Soviet classic film *The Battleship Potemkin*, which did little to calm nerves back at military high command.[67] Jango's initial response—neither to support the uprising nor back an immediate crackdown—served as ultimate proof to the military that the president would support an uprising of low-level soldiers and subvert the military hierarchy. To make matters worse, he gave a talk to military police at the Brazil Automobile Club the next day. He didn't say anything radical, but by then it was considered a direct affront that he would even speak directly to sergeants and low-level officials.

The coup against Jango began on March 31, 1964, and many of the plotters were motivated by the belief that communists had built some kind of revolutionary plan around Goulart. This was entirely false, but it was also entirely consistent with the fanatical anticommunism of the time, all the way back to the McCarthy hearings and the mythology surrounding the *Intentona*. Wherever there were communists, no matter how limited in number, and no matter what their stated declarations, they must have a secret, nefarious plot.

Within the mythology of Brazil's own anticommunism, this likely meant the communists had something deeply perverse planned. Many in the elite believed that communists practiced violence that they carried out with "Satanic pleasure," that it was their deep desire to murder the faithful en masse and deliver them to "Red Hell."[68]

Although the military high command and Washington had been plotting a coup for weeks, it started prematurely. A single outraged general, Olímpio Mourão Filho, the same man who had created the fake Jewish-communist conspiracy known as the Cohen Plan back in 1937, led a march of poorly equipped soldiers on Rio, where Jango was in residence. Goulart flew to Brasília, but when it became clear to him that the military high command was dead-set on removing him, he fled to Uruguay. Tanks rolled up and parked outside Congress. Invoking an "Institutional Act" with no legal basis, the military junta declared that the left-wing members of the *Congresso Nacional* had lost all their legal rights.[69]

As the coup began, the US State Department began an operation it dubbed Brother Sam, and made tankers, ammunition, and aircraft carriers available to the conspirators.[70] None of these were needed. The Brazilian Congress declared the presidency "vacant," in clear violation of the constitution. Then, after that first Institutional Act removed about forty of their left-wing colleagues from office, 361 of Brazil's remaining lawmakers voted to install General Castelo Branco as president. Almost all of Brazil's media supported the coup.[71] US assistance began to pour back in.[72]

With Jango gone, the military delivered a very different kind of speech at the 1964 memorial of the 1935 *Intentona*. General Pery Constant Beviláqua declared, "The fatherland is here! There it is in this beautiful flag! As we contemplate it, we feel your presence, you heroes of November 1935!"[73]

Ambassador Lincoln Gordon called the 1964 coup "the single most decisive victory for freedom in the mid-twentieth century."[74]

As Brazilian historian Marco Napolitano puts it, "Just as in a Hollywood film, there was a happy ending (for the plotters, that is). The communist bad guys and their sympathizers were deposed. The good guys were in power. And best of all: this was achieved without the United States needing to appear as a visible agent of the conspiracy."[75]

This was huge, and novel. In Iran (1953) and Guatemala (1954), Indonesia (1958) and Cuba (1961), anyone who was paying attention knew that Washington had been behind the regime change operations. These very obvious signs of US intervention had not only tainted Washington's image worldwide—they had undermined the efficacy of the states they installed when they were victorious. Guatemala's government fell apart quickly after the CIA-backed coup, as did the Shah's government in Iran, eventually.

This achievement in Brazil in 1964 was not only possible because of the new tactics JFK put in place to build alliances with the military. The United States also got lucky. And importantly, Brazil had its own, very deep anti-communist tradition, built on five centuries of fear of the black, the poor, and the violent and marginalized, and with its own, incredibly effective, myths and annual rituals.

Despite his support among the population, the legally elected Jango did not mount a counteroffensive. He likely believed that this, like other coups in Brazilian history, would be a minor reset to the system, and that he would be able to regroup and run in the next election. He was wrong. Brazil would not hold another democratic election for twenty-five years. Washington's commitment to military-led modernization remained strong during the Johnson administration, and Brazil was now one of the most important US allies in the Cold War. Indeed, Latin America's largest country would soon play a crucial role in flipping other countries into the Western camp.

6

The September 30th Movement

THE COUP IN LATIN AMERICA reverberated around the globe, and made its way to Indonesia. The mainstream press in Indonesia covered it; so did the communist *People's Daily*. A new English-language publication run out of Jakarta called the *Afro-Asian Journalist* said the Brazilian "military junta" helped to carry out a "US imperialist plot."[1] That article may have been translated by Francisca, who worked there now.

In the early 1960s, Francisca became more involved in politics than ever before. It wasn't just her—the country had moved to the left, and society in general was infused with revolutionary energy, after the bombings carried out by the US and as the campaign for West New Guinea heated up. But it was Francisca's exceptional language skills that brought her right into the center of world history.

After a decade working in the library, and with her children now in school, she began giving private English lessons to embassy staff from all around the world. She started off with the wife of the Hungarian chancellor; she ended up teaching Russian embassy staff too, and then an official from the Democratic Republic of Vietnam (usually called "North Vietnam" at the time in the West). She would give classes at the embassies or at the lavish residences of the ambassadors themselves, around central Jakarta and the upscale Senopati neighborhood, and more often than not she would get to chatting about international politics as they practiced. When Castro's government sent its first-ever ambassador to Indonesia, Benigno Arbesú Cadelo, he got lessons from Francisca too.

As a matter of course, all Francisca's new clients were from socialist countries. This was the social circle that she and her husband ran in. By this point, Zain was a relatively influential figure on the left.[2]

Sukarno, for his part, went to Havana to visit Fidel and Che. He selected a trusted friend from the days of the revolution, A. M. Hanafi, to serve as ambassador, and Indonesia and Cuba began working on a "tricontinental" conference, which would expand the 1955 "Afro-Asian" conference to include Latin America. The entire Third World united.

Sukarno was again talking about the unity of Marxism, Islam, and nationalism, and repackaged it into one of his trademark acronyms—NASAKOM, for *Nasionalisme*, *Agama* (Religion), and *Komunisme*. He talked of forming a NASAKOM cabinet, but the right wing of Indonesian politics blocked the Communists.[3] General Nasution, head of the Armed Forces and point man for Washington, told Ambassador Howard Jones in 1960 that the military would never allow the PKI to participate at the executive level of government.[4]

In reality the three political forces in the country were not nationalism, religion, and communism but rather the PKI, Sukarno, and the military. The president would use his personal influence to play rivals against each other, and maintain a delicate balance. Unlike in Brazil, fanatical anticommunism did not have widespread support in Indonesian society. Despite what military leaders said to Americans in private, they were not opposed to the left in general, and they often echoed Sukarno's revolutionary language in their literature and public statements. The entire country was essentially anti-imperialist, by definition.

In early 1963, the countries brought together by the Bandung Conference founded the Afro-Asian Journalist Association at a Jakarta conference. Francisca was asked to serve as an official interpreter at the meeting, and she stayed on as they founded the *Afro-Asian Journalist*, published by the Lumumba Foundation (named after murdered Congolese leader) in Jakarta. They kept her busy translating pieces from multiple languages and a wide range of countries. The *Afro-Asian Journalist* published what has been called "socialist cosmopolitan journalism," and viewed world struggles as one interconnected fight. The magazine was much more eclectic and liberal than many of the world's actually existing socialist publications; the editors valued cultural pluralism and artistic innovation, publishing anti-imperialist cartoons and features from a wide range of global contributors.[5]

This was an exciting job for Francisca—not only because she got to travel the world, meeting revolutionary leaders across Africa and Asia. It looked like the dreams she had nurtured since she was a little girl were on the way to being realized. At the end of 1963, Jakarta served as host for the GANEFO, or the "Games of the New Emerging Forces" (characteristically, Sukarno gave them an acronym). This was an Olympic Games for the Third World, and its slogan was "Onward! No Retreat!" The games originally came about because of a fight that broke out when Indonesia excluded the Republic of China (Taiwan) and Israel from the 1962 Asian Games. The Western-led International Olympic Committee suspended Indonesia from its games in retribution, so he turned around to put on an anti-imperialist games, which the IOC didn't like one bit. But that's not what Francisca remembered about the "Games of the New Emerging Forces." She was struck, for life, by seeing an event organized entirely by people from the Third World, and by the athletic and cultural performances put on that week in Jakarta.

"For the first time in my life, I became aware that I didn't actually come from an uncultured or backwards people, and the other peoples of Africa and Asia weren't backwards either. I had always been told, and even thought, that we were very stupid Indonesians who didn't know what we were doing, trying to build a country without any education or resources," she said. She was now almost forty years old. "We played our own sports, put on our own dances. This was really an awakening for us. It felt like this was what the West had been trying so hard to keep down, for centuries, and it was finally revealed."

Even her husband's Communist Party felt more independent than ever before. In the 1960s, the PKI had increasingly moved closer to China's side in the Sino-Soviet split, partly because Beijing was more supportive of Indonesia in its territorial conflicts. But technically the PKI was still ideologically committed to the Soviet Union's anti-Stalinist line. These were the years in which Mao was sidelined as a result of the disastrous Great Leap Forward, launched in 1958. Suspicious that the Soviets were trying to hold him back, he ignored their agricultural advice and launched a wildly utopian farming program. Millions died in the resulting famine, and the other leaders of the Chinese Communist Party put the blame, rightfully, on Chairman Mao. He was forced to resign from party and national leadership, and starting in 1960 watched as Liu Shaoqi and Deng Xiaoping took control of the economy, reintroduced small-scale capitalism, and temporarily reduced Mao to an ideological figurehead.[6]

More importantly, the PKI didn't think it had to take orders from anybody.[7] It was now the third-largest communist party in the world, the largest outside China and the Soviet Union, and its strategy of nonviolent, direct engagement with the masses had led to impressive results. The PKI now had three million card-carrying members. The organizations affiliated with the party—including SOBSI (the Central All-Indonesian Workers Association), LEKRA (the People's Cultural Institution), BTI (Front of Indonesia), *Pemuda Rakyat* (People's Youth), and *Gerwani* (Women's Movement)—had at least twenty million members. This added up to nearly a quarter of Indonesia's population of one hundred million, including children, and nearly a third of the country's adult registered voters were PKI affiliates.[8] They operated openly, in every corner of the country. But at the national level, they relied almost entirely on Sukarno for their influence over policy. They had no other choice. As a means of achieving power, they had neither arms nor the ballot box; they had been peaceful since the expulsion of the Dutch, and deprived of elections by Guided Democracy (and the US-backed Army, which had been so alarmed that the communists kept winning).[9]

On the other side of the political divide, the military was allied with Muslim groups, and increasingly relied on the enthusiastic support of the United States. The Indonesian military had already radically increased its influence during the CIA's attempt to break up the country in 1958, and Kennedy and Johnson's "civic action program," or CAP, had delivered them the resources and training to emerge as a political and economic force to be reckoned with. The political lines were clear to anyone paying attention—communists and Sukarno on one side; Army and the West on the other.

And Sukarno no longer felt any shyness about taking on the West. His revolution had bested the CIA in 1958; he had gotten Kennedy and the Netherlands to back down on West New Guinea. With interventions in Brazil and escalating interventions in Vietnam apparently confirming his view of Washington as an imperialist aggressor, he felt he was on the right side of history. So he overestimated his strength, and took on the United Kingdom while problems grew at home.

Konfrontasi

Malaya, a colonial possession covering the Malaysian peninsula from the Thai border down to the tip of Singapore, was one of Britain's last and most important territories in Asia. When London finally decolonized the region and began to create the new country of Malaysia, Sukarno became adamantly opposed to the form it took. He believed that the English were employing imperial trickery to weaken revolutionary forces in Asia. He was mostly right. And Howard Jones knew it.[10]

The British did not want to create a country that was majority Chinese, since too much of Malaya's population, especially in Singapore, sympathized with communism for their liking. As a solution to this "problem," London added its possessions on the top half of the huge island of Borneo into what would become Malaysia, and excluded the island of Singapore. This move would combine the entirely distinct peoples of Sarawak, Borneo, and Sabah into the new Malaysia, which would dilute the proportion of ethnic Chinese to levels the British considered acceptable. The southern half of Borneo was part of Indonesia—so Indonesians would share a long border with British colonial territories shoehorned into Malaysia just to dilute the power of leftists. One very rough way to understand this is to imagine that, after revolution swept through the United States, King George III made Protestants in Northern Ireland citizens of Canada, allowing him to make sure loyalists to the crown would win elections in perpetuity north of the US border. This intentional dividing and mismatching of different peoples was employed by the British very famously in Africa and the Middle East, with consequences to this day. President Sukarno also distrusted Lee Kwan Yew, Singapore's first prime minister, because that small city-state had cooperated with the CIA in the 1958 attacks on Indonesia.

Jones knew what Britain was doing. But he was shocked by Sukarno's response. After a small rebellion in northern Borneo convinced him the locals were against becoming Malaysian, the president declared himself very openly, and very forcefully, opposed to the creation of Malaysia on these terms. Much to the chagrin of British authorities, Sukarno declared in early 1963 that the formation of Malaysia was "the product of the brain, the thinking, the goals, the effort, and the initiative of neocolonialism." Sukarno's confrontational approach had the enthusiastic support of the PKI, tentative support from the military, and likely the support of much of the population.[11] The episode came to be known as *Konfrontasi*—"confrontation" in both Indonesian and Malaysian—after Foreign Minister Subandrio coined the term.

He made those declarations just as his economic advisers went to Washington to negotiate with officials from the International Monetary Fund (IMF). Indonesia was suffering economically in the early 1960s, and locked in discussions with the US. There were two major issues. First, Sukarno had dedicated a huge portion of national resources since 1958 to the military, and to the pursuit of disputes over West New Guinea and now Malaysia. Second, Indonesia had begun to rewrite the regulations governing its oil industry after expelling the Dutch, greatly concerning US officials. The *New York Times* published an editorial warning that Sukarno was "inexorably addicted to nationalistic excess" and adding: "How he deals with the oil companies will be a major test of his intentions."[12]

The IMF demanded what amounted to a structural adjustment program in Indonesia, which dictated spending cuts, an increase in the production of raw materials for export, currency devaluation, monetary tightening, and an end to government subsidies.[13] Sukarno's ministers went along with the IMF's demands, and they had a swift, severe, and widespread impact on the population, which saw prices double, triple, or even quintuple overnight. The PKI denounced the measures as an attack on the poor, but the government pressed forward anyway, seemingly committed to securing the next aid package from Washington.

Konfrontasi threw all these delicate international negotiations into question. Indonesian troops began to engage in low-level, cat-and-mouse skirmishes at the Malaysian border on the island of Borneo. The US government was concerned about its alliance with the British, whose support it wanted to keep in Vietnam.

Sukarno badly overestimated the leverage he had in forcing the issue with the UK and the UN. Some of his moves alienated allies in the Non-Aligned Movement he had helped found.[14] Even many of his friends in other Third World nations believed he was making a mistake. But to him, Malaysia's expansion represented an existential threat to Indonesia's territorial integrity, and Sukarno was far from certain postcolonial independence would last. He had lived through numerous assassination attempts; he was watching war restart in Vietnam; and just a few years earlier, the United States had dropped bombs all over the country, in an attempt to break it up.

Indonesian leftists knew that the British had used their "Special Branch," or police intelligence, to capture, bribe, and infiltrate the Malaysian communist movement and make sure decolonization there happened as they planned.[15] With the UK carving up Malaysia in an obvious attempt to curb the forces of left-wing nationalism—of which Sukarno was perhaps the world's most famous proponent—just across a porous border in Indonesian Borneo, a little bit of unease and suspicion was probably inevitable.

US officials, however, could usually only see reactions like this as irrational paranoia, a view shared by Modernization Theorist Lucian Pye, who went as far as to see anti-Americanism in postcolonial states as a psychological pathology.[16]

As tensions rose on the international stage, things became more difficult for regular Indonesians. The economic crisis made it hard to acquire basic goods, and life became confusing for those not swept up in the politics of the dispute.

Magdalena

In the village of Purwokerto, Central Java, one quiet young woman began to feel the squeeze.[17]

Magdalena grew up in a troubled peasant family, always tossed back and forth as a result of marital strife, sickness, and poverty. Like most residents of Java (with the notable exception of the ethnic Chinese), she was Muslim, but she never got very deep into studies of the Quran. At school, she loved gamelan, the traditional Javanese music form, in which a small percussive orchestra plays meditative, meandering ensemble pieces, which can rise and fall slowly for hours. But she was pulled away from all of that fairly quickly. At thirteen, she dropped out to work as a maid in a nearby household. At fifteen, her mother fell ill, so she came back home and began to sell what they could to their neighbors for some money: bits of wood, salads, cooked meals, fried cassava, whatever they could to get by. And at the age of sixteen, as talk of *Konfrontasi* dominated conversation in the capital and the economy continued to flounder, that little business dried up.

She had never been to a big city, but word was it was easier to get a job in Jakarta. An aunt of hers, Le, had some connections in the capital and told her she could help her get set up there. So she got on the train, and rode for a full day, moving slowly westward on tracks originally put down by the Dutch a hundred years earlier, and arrived in Jakarta, all alone. As she passed by the National Monument, she marveled at its scale—about ten times as high as any building she'd ever seen.

They were right about the job prospects. Almost immediately, she started working at a T-shirt factory. Her new employer put her in a small, shared apartment attached to the company's office, with all the other girls. In the morning, she'd put on her uniform and wait. Just after six, she and all the other girls piled into a big truck, which took them from their little home in Jatinegara, East Jakarta, and rode through the morning to Duren Tiga in the South, as the city sped by. They worked from seven to four, and the pay wasn't bad. The men washed the cloth, and the women cut it into the right shapes. Someone else, somewhere else, put it all together.

Conditions were OK, Magdalena thought. And she learned, right away, that this was because of SOBSI, the trade union network affiliated with the PKI that had organized most of the workers in the country. She joined, like everyone else did, and after a few months got a minor administrative role in her local union, without many real duties. She came, cut the cloth, and went home.

That was her first, very minor, introduction to Indonesian politics. She barely understood the revolutionary slogans or ideological jargon coming through the radio at work. She remembers hearing the word "NASAKOM" once and not having the slightest clue what it meant. She hardly knew anything about the Communist Party, or if it had anything to do with her job. SOBSI was part of the gig, she knew that, and it helped out a lot.

"They would support us, they had our backs, and their strategy worked," she said. "It really worked. That's what we knew."

When she got off work, she was usually too tired to do much—and a bit too young and lonely to venture out into the big city. She kept her head down, and just observed. She didn't talk politics after work—she would lie around and make small talk with her best friend in Jakarta, Siti, maybe gossiping about boys, discussing which girls had boyfriends or husbands. Though she had always been single, she had learned early, growing up back home, that she was considered very pretty. Dating was something she might try later. For now, she was working on building some savings for a life that was just a little more secure.

The radio reports came and went, and she kept working. If she heard the words "Lyndon Johnson" at the end of 1963, she didn't know what they meant.

But John F. Kennedy's death meant a lot for Indonesia indeed.

The End of the Jones Method

Indonesia was one place where Lyndon Johnson took a different approach from his predecessor. He had a lot less time for Sukarno. Just three days before he died, Jack Kennedy had reiterated his clear, if slightly cynical, commitment to the strategy of ongoing engagement with Sukarno—the very strategy that Smiling Jones had long been advocating. He said, according to White House aide Michael Forrestal, that "Indonesia is a nation of 100 million with perhaps more resources than any other nation in Asia. . . . It doesn't make any sense for the U.S. to go out of our way to permanently alienate this large group of people sitting on these resources, unless there is some very, very, persuasive reason." *Konfrontasi* was not enough for Kennedy to abandon Sukarno and Jones.[18]

Johnson wasn't interested in direct engagement with Indonesia, and he didn't want to spend political capital pushing Asia policies that were unpopular in Congress. Kennedy had met Sukarno, understood Indonesia, and cared about the issue. JFK had agreed with Jones that a visit to Jakarta could have smoothed the whole thing over. Of course, the military counterinsurgency program Kennedy put in place was still underway. But Johnson was not going to fight any political battles for those one hundred million people and the resources under their feet.

Howard Jones remembers the shift, wistfully: "Regarding himself as the leader not only of the new Asian-African nations but all the 'new emerging forces,' I am sure [Sukarno] felt that an understanding, if not an alliance between himself and the man considered the leader of the Western world, was possible. He was being wooed by Khrushchev and Mao—why, then, should not the leader of the other world bloc be equally interested in working with him?"

Jones believed Sukarno would back off on Malaysia as long as that didn't mean national humiliation, and he had told Kennedy a presidential visit to

Indonesia was probably just what was needed. Kennedy agreed, and planned to come.[19] But a few months after JFK's death, Jones asked the newly sworn-in Johnson to sign an official determination that continued aid to Indonesia was in the US national interest. Johnson declined. "President Kennedy, I knew, would have signed the determination almost as a matter of routine. It was disappointing," Jones remembers. In December, Robert McNamara, one of the advisers left behind by Kennedy, began suggesting aggressive curtailment of aid. "Thus began a shift of emphasis in American policy to a harder line," the ambassador wrote.[20] This was also the end of the Smiling Jones approach to uniting the two countries, the strategy he had developed for nearly a decade.

Johnson did make a deal, with the British. In exchange for their support in Vietnam, where things were also beginning to escalate, Washington would back them on the creation of Malaysia.[21]

Sukarno noticed a shift in the way the world's most powerful country was treating him. He went so far as to speculate that JFK was killed in order to stop him from visiting Indonesia and cementing an alliance between Washington and Jakarta.[22]

The debate raged in Washington as to whether or not Indonesia deserved more assistance. And Sukarno was watching. In response to that discussion, the Indonesian president gave a speech in March 1964, just as Brazil's generals were putting the finishing touches on US-backed plots. Though he expressed gratitude for aid that was offered without political strings attached, one line, delivered in English, predictably made headlines—and traveled quickly back to Washington. When anyone offers aid that comes with political demands, he said that his message to them was: "Go to hell with your aid!"

As Jones put it, "He had really done it now."[23]

Whatever goodwill there was for Sukarno in Washington began to dissipate. Over the next few months all direct aid to the national government dried up completely. Crucially, one program continued. The US continued to pour money directly into the Armed Forces, and military advisers continued to work closely with Indonesian Army high command.

Sukarno became more publicly anti-American, and with more gusto than ever before. The Soviet Union had been entirely uninterested in backing *Konfrontasi*, so Indonesia formed closer ties with Asian socialist countries. Domestically, an anti-American campaign escalated, with the Communists often leading the charge. The government instituted a de facto ban on

American movies, even though Sukarno had always loved them. Protests erupted against American citizens and American businesses, though Jones himself maintained cordial relations with the government.[24]

Then there was another explosion, much closer than the one in Brazil, whose waves quickly crashed onto the shores of Java. In the Gulf of Tonkin, a US destroyer called *Maddox* was in Vietnamese waters, violating the international twelve-mile limit, attempting to intercept North Vietnamese communications. On August 2, three Vietnamese patrol boats approached the *Maddox*, and the US opened fire, killing four sailors. The Vietnamese shot back, and then fled. On August 3, Johnson said that patrols in the Gulf of Tonkin would continue, warning against "further unprovoked military action." On August 4, nothing happened. But US vessels thought something was happening, and they began "firing at their own shadows."[25] This second, nonexistent confrontation was used as pretext for the "Gulf of Tonkin Resolution," which gave Johnson the authority to start a full war in Vietnam.

Three days later, Sukarno defiantly established relations with Ho Chi Minh's government in the northern half of Vietnam. "I think your Asian policy is wrong," he told Howard Jones directly. "It is not popular with Asian people generally. It looks to them as if you are interfering with the affairs of Asian nations. . . . Why should you become involved?" Needless to say, this was a scandalous position in Washington. But most Indonesians agreed with Sukarno. To people like Francisca and Sakono and Magdalena, the Vietnamese were fighting for national independence.[26]

On August 17, Sukarno gave another fiery speech, and declared a "year of living dangerously." He spoke of a "Jakarta-Phnom Penh-Hanoi-Peking-Pyongyang axis . . . forged by the course of history" and subtly attacked Army generals for profiting off the state enterprises they controlled. A few months later, in angry retaliation for Malaysia's accession to the UN Security Council, Sukarno decided to pull Indonesia out of the UN in protest. He also accused the CIA of trying to kill him.[27]

Howard Jones made plans to leave Jakarta for Honolulu, where he would take over at the East-West Center at the University of Hawaii. As he made his final preparations, he continued to make last-minute pleas to the men who would take over for him, arguing that personal diplomacy with Sukarno offered the best chance for reversing the tide in Jakarta. But he knew that in this position he was isolated, quite literally on an island, and the water was coming up around him. The Howard Jones approach to Indonesia was over.

In his short resignation letter to President Johnson, he wrote, "Indonesia is a beautiful country with gentle, friendly people. I have great faith in the Indonesian people and believe they will ultimately work their way out of their present difficulties." He continued, "I am convinced that there is basic empathy between the people of America and Indonesia."[28]

As Jones prepared to leave the country, Foreign Minister Subandrio—the same man whom Jones unintentionally lied to back in 1958 about the CIA's role in the civil war—sent him a small, hand-written invitation. He wanted to dine with the ambassador and his wife one last time. They met on May 18 to say goodbye over a simple lunch. On the menu that day: *lumpia* (Indonesia's version of Chinese fried egg rolls), the customary white rice, sweet and sour *gurame* fish, shrimp cooked with lime and pepper, and fried pigeon.[29]

The sendoff Jones got from the US press was a little less gracious. After he announced his departure, the *Washington Post* affirmed, in a piece that gave ample space to critics of his tenure, that he was "Sukarno's pal," and called the man "almost angelically naive."[30] The *Los Angeles Times* was a bit more direct in a different version of the same story, and asked, in the headline, if Jones was a "patsy."[31]

Clandestine Operations

When Jones's diplomatic approach collapsed, both the US and the British governments escalated secret activities in Indonesia. Their full nature is still hidden to us, but they included "black operations" and preparations for psychological warfare. The British created the position of "director of political warfare" in Singapore in December 1964. The US government approved a secret plan on March 4, 1965, though the funding source and the amount of money provided remain classified. Most of the secret activities were probably carried out by CIA and MI6. Given the way these organizations operated, it is almost certain that operations also included placing untrue or provocative stories in the Indonesian and international press. They wanted to goad the Communists into taking action.

Since the early 1960s, both the American and British governments had believed, and discussed often, that the ideal situation would be a "premature PKI coup" that could provoke an Army response. It's possible that some version of this plan had been worked on secretly, under the cover of Kennedy's civic action program, since 1962.[32]

At one of the last meetings he held as ambassador, Howard Jones himself told State Department officials behind closed doors in the Philippines, "From our viewpoint, of course, an unsuccessful coup attempt by the PKI might be the most effective development to start a reversal of political trends in Indonesia."[33]

Some of the more conservative elements in Indonesia were dissatisfied with Sukarno's turn to the left. The most prominent of these was the Army, but they also included some Muslim groups. In some parts of the country, local landowners were in low-level conflict with the PKI. After the passage of a very moderate land reform package, the Communist Party took it upon itself to attempt to put pressure on landlords to respect the law, leading to some clashes, especially in East Java and Bali.[34]

Sukarno had been considering the creation of a new militia, a national "Fifth Force" composed of regular people, workers, and peasants, a kind of National Reserve that would exist alongside the regular soldiers. China had urged the Indonesians to create a people's militia because, as Zhou Enlai told Foreign Minister Subandrio, "the militarized masses are invincible." The Army was opposed to the idea, however, and Sukarno planned to talk about it with them soon.[35] As the CIA noted in May 1965, the PKI itself had "only limited potential for armed insurgency and would almost certainly not wish to provoke the military into open opposition."[36]

In August 1965, Sukarno fell ill and was treated by a Chinese doctor. He recommended the president reduce his workload and "exercise restraint in his sex life." Sukarno refused, and political insiders began to worry about what would happen if he died.[37] Aidit, the leader of the Communist Party, went to Beijing and had a meeting with Mao, and we have a partial transcript of their conversation:

Mao: I think the Indonesian right wing is determined to seize power. Are you determined, too?

Aidit: [Nods] If Sukarno dies, it would be a question of who gains the upper hand.

Mao: I suggest that you should not go abroad so often. You can let your deputy go abroad instead.

Aidit: For the right wing, they could take two possible kinds of actions. First, they could attack us. If they do so, we would have reasons to counterattack. Second, they could adopt a more moderate method by building a Nasakom government. . . . The Americans told Nasution that he should wait patiently; even if Sukarno dies [head of the Armed Forces, General Nasution] should be flexible rather than start a coup. He accepted the suggestion from the Americans.

The Chinese leader was much less trusting of the Indonesian military and its backers in Washington.

Mao responded, "That is unreliable. The current situation has changed."

Aidit then described a counterattack plan in which the Communists could establish a military committee, mixing left and center elements so as not to raise the "red flag" and invite immediate opposition. Mao shifted the conversation to his own experience with the Chinese Nationalist Party, perhaps to make a "suggestion that Aidit should be prepared for both peace talks and armed struggles," according to Taomo Zhou, the historian who recently unearthed this conversation.[38] Aidit, however, did not prepare his party for any armed struggle.

As 1965 went on, rumors that right-wing generals were conspiring with the CIA or some foreign power began to spread like wildfire in Jakarta. The Indonesian government found a letter, purportedly written by British Ambassador Andrew Gilchrist, stating "it would be as well to emphasize once more to our local army friends that the strictest caution, discipline and coordination are essential to the success of the enterprise." Sukarno summoned the military chiefs, demanding to know who these "army friends" were. The "Gilchrist document" could have been a forgery. It could have been real. Or it could have been planted by the British or Americans as a psyops trick, perhaps one of many, to provoke the left into action.[39]

Suspicions held by Sukarno and many in the Indonesian government intensified when they found out who was coming from Washington to replace Howard Jones. Newly minted Ambassador Marshall Green, they learned, had been in Seoul when Park Chung Hee took power in a military coup that destroyed the short-lived parliamentary Second Republic. Just as the Guatemalans had been suspicious of John Peurifoy's aggressive past when he was sent to interact with Jacobo Árbenz, Green's arrival was widely seen as a signal that Washington had abandoned the soft, diplomatic Howard Jones approach and was now fully committed to regime change.[40]

Like Kennedy before him, Johnson's administration considered Indonesia more important than Vietnam. "President Johnson has come increasingly to the conclusion that, at the end of the day, he would be ready for major war against Indonesia," said Secretary of State Dean Rusk to a British official.[41] A meeting of the National Security Council's secret 303 committee concluded that "the loss of a nation of 105 million to the 'Communist camp' would make a victory in Vietnam of little meaning."[42] Under Secretary of State George Ball and National Security Adviser McGeorge Bundy agreed that the loss of Indonesia would be "the biggest thing since the fall of China."[43]

In December 1964, Pakistan's ambassador to Paris, J. A. Rahim, sent a letter to his foreign minister, Zulfikar Ali Bhutto, reporting on a conversation he had with a Dutch intelligence officer working for NATO. He wrote that Western intelligence agencies were organizing a "premature communist coup." Indonesia, the NATO officer told him, "was ready to fall into the Western lap like a rotten apple."[44]

Francisca spent much of 1965 in Algeria, working on preparations for a conference that would bring the Afro-Asian Journalist Association together with journalists from Latin America. But a military coup deposed Ben Bella, Algeria's revolutionary socialist first president, and threw those plans into disarray. When she came home, in August 1965, she felt that things were different. Tense. The widespread rumors about an imminent right-wing coup were indeed everywhere. In her social circle, people were talking about the possibility of a right-wing Council of Generals working secretly to remove Sukarno or destroy the left.

At some point, a group of midlevel Army officers formed a group and decided to call it the *Gerakan 30 September* ("G30S" or "September 30th Movement") and came up with a plan. But unless you were closely following political developments in Jakarta, September 29, 1965, felt like another normal day for most people around the country. That includes members of the PKI and its affiliated organizations. Wayan Badra, the young son of a devout Hindu priest in Bali, woke up early in his tiny village, and walked to the ocean, then turned left at Seminyak Beach, to trod four kilometers across the empty sand to school in Kuta. Two of his teachers were Communist Party members, and all the students liked them. A few other teachers were from the nationalist PNI Party. Wayan Badra saw them all as Hindus, as the Balinese had been for almost two millennia, as well as allies in the construction of the new Indonesia. Sakono, the eager young left-leaning student from Central Java, who loved both Marxism and soccer, had grown up—well, turned nineteen, at least. He was now a member of the Communist-affiliated

People's Youth organization and feeling very proud that he had just qualified to work as a teacher. He sat around, waiting patiently to get word he could start working. Sutrisno, his curly-haired teacher and friend, continued organizing as a full Communist Party *kader*, or cadre, in their village. Magdalena, in Jakarta, caught the truck to work, cut cloth into T-shirt shapes for nine hours, then rode back home, past the towering National Monument, and flopped onto her bed.

Night Call

Very late at night on September 30, 1965—really, it was already the early hours of October 1—the *Gerakan 30 September* met at Halim Air Force Base, the same airport where Francisca and Zain had made their first modest home in a garage fourteen years earlier.

The leaders of the September 30th Movement were from the Armed Forces: Lieutenant Colonel Untung, for example, was a stocky military man who had attacked Dutch troops in the fight for West New Guinea; and Colonel Abdul Latief was a distinguished commander who had fought in the revolution against the Dutch in the 1940s.

They organized seven teams, made up of soldiers already under their official military command. Each had a similar mission. They would head to the homes of seven of the highest-ranking officers in the Armed Forces, arrest them, and bring them back. In the deep darkness of the morning, they set off toward the center of Jakarta in Army trucks.

They were partially successful. Six of the teams brought back their men, including Lieutenant General Achmad Yani, the commander of the Army. However, the most important target, General Nasution—the friend of Washington and Howard Jones since 1958—got away. As they started the raid on his home, Nasution jumped over the back wall of his house, in the upscale neighborhood of Menteng, and hid in the home of his friend, the Iraqi ambassador. The September 30th Movement brought back his military assistant instead. During the raid, his five-year-old daughter was shot and killed.

Some of the members of the September 30th Movement, mostly regular Army soldiers, went into town and occupied Independence Square, site of the towering National Monument that Magdalena passed when she first arrived in Jakarta. One of the movement's higher-ranking officers went to the Presidential Palace to inform Sukarno they had arrested generals who were plotting against him. He wasn't there. As he often did, he was sleeping at his third wife's house that night.

At 7:30 a.m., the residents of Jakarta heard a radio broadcast of "a statement obtained from Lieutenant Colonel Untung, the commander of the September 30th Movement." The voice told the people of the capital that the movement was formed to prevent a "counterrevolutionary coup" being planned by the Council of Generals, a group that "harbored evil designs against the republic and Indonesia and President Sukarno." The movement had arrested them to protect Sukarno, and more news would be forthcoming.

At around 9:00 a.m., Sukarno finally arrived at Halim Air Force Base to meet with the representative who had tried to find him several hours earlier.

For reasons we still don't fully understand, all six of the captured generals were dead by the time he arrived, their bodies at the bottom of an abandoned well near Halim Air Force Base. We don't know if President Sukarno, or even the member of the September 30th Movement designated to meet him, knew this at the time.

The September 30th Movement's leaders were from the Army. Neither the Air Force nor the Navy nor the police command were involved. However, when the leaders of the Air Force were informed of the movement and its success, they cheered. They believed that an internal military action, loyal to President Sukarno, had prevented a right-wing plot. Reportedly, Sukarno himself was surprised by the nature of the radio announcement, but he was willing to wait and see what had happened and how the situation would develop before taking a position.

Aidit, the leader of the Indonesian Communist Party, and some members of the People's Youth also arrived at Halim Air Force Base at some point on October 1. They were in a different building, and unable to communicate directly with the leaders of the Army rebellion. The movement had cut off telephone lines in the city, and they didn't have walkie-talkies or radios. Nor did they have tanks, the standard equipment for coup plotters at the time.[45]

The confusion lasted for no longer than one day: within twelve hours, the movement was crushed, and the Army, now led by right-wing General Suharto, was in direct control of the country.

More than fifty years later, we still don't have a complete understanding of who planned the *Gerakan 30 September,* or what the real purpose of the night raid was. What we have is a range of credible theories.

One possible version of the story, put forward by historian John Roosa, is that Aidit helped to plan the raid through a Communist intermediary within the military. Because his conversations with the Army were secret and indirect, both sides (Aidit and the movement) ended up signing off on a plan that was badly conceived and doomed to failure. They intended to quietly arrest the generals—as had long been customary in Indonesia, since before Sukarno himself had been kidnapped in 1945—and present them to the president as traitors. Their deaths, in this version, would have been the result of incompetence and panic. This is probably the most "conservative" of the credible accounts, the account that presents the strongest case against the PKI. Aidit would have only told a tiny group of people in the party—not even the Central Committee nor the Politburo. In this version, Aidit and a tiny group of high-level Communists would have been guilty of contributing to the accidental deaths of those generals, and they would have been provoked into doing so by those US and UK misinformation campaigns, which were explicitly designed to make them believe they had no choice but to act.[46]

This story doesn't convince everyone.[47] Why, some ask, would Aidit take armed or violent action against the Army when the Communist Party's position was so well established with Sukarno in office? Aidit knew very well that the PKI's influence was entirely based on soft power, and that the military had all the weapons. And how is it that trained military men charged with arresting their sleeping superior officers would *accidentally* end up killing all of them and throwing them in a well?

There are a number of competing theories. Benedict Anderson, perhaps the most famous Indonesia expert of the twentieth century, and scholar Ruth McVey presented an account in 1966, in which the movement was largely what it says it was—an internal Army movement that the PKI did not help organize.[48] As a result, Anderson was kicked out of Indonesia for twenty-six years. Just before his death in 2015, he said he still believed this to be the case.[49]

Then there are the entirely plausible assertions that General Suharto, the man who rose to power after the dust settled, planned or infiltrated the movement, perhaps with foreign assistance, to engineer his rise to power. He was, after all, close to the leaders of the rebellion. Suharto had a history of conflict with Nasution and Yani, and was the only high-ranking, openly right-leaning Army official not targeted by the movement. Former Foreign Minister Subandrio, the same man who had to listen to Howard Jones deny that the CIA was bombing the country back in 1958, presents a credible insider's account, in which Suharto was notified in advance by his friends leading the September 30th Movement; he pledged his support to them, but instead planned to hold back and use the rebellion as a pretext to seize power.[50] G30S leader Latief also said, afterward, that Suharto was informed of the plans in advance.[51]

We know there was a conspiracy. Unless the CIA and other organizations such as the Indonesian military release what they have, we can only theorize as to its true nature based on the available evidence.[52] But the next part of the story is not in doubt.

After the events of October 1, General Suharto seized control of the country, and told a set of deliberate, carefully prepared lies. These lies became official dogma in one of the world's largest countries for decades.

Propaganda *Bersendjata*

On October 1, 1965, most Indonesians had no idea who General Suharto was. But the CIA did. As early as September 1964, the CIA listed Suharto in a secret cable as one of the Army generals it considered to be "friendly" to US interests and anticommunist.[53] The cable also put forward the idea of an anticommunist military-civilian coalition that could gain power in a succession struggle.

Suharto, a laconic forty-four-year-old major general from Central Java, was serving as head of the Army's Strategic Command, or KOSTRAD. Suharto had studied under a man named Suwarto, a close friend of RAND Corporation consultant Guy Pauker and one of the Indonesian officers most responsible for implementing military-led Modernization Theory, "a state within a state," and US-allied counterinsurgency operations.[54] Suharto had a checkered past within the Indonesian military. He had been caught smuggling in the late 1950s, and was fired by Nasution himself. According to Subandrio, Suharto's flagrant corruption so angered Yani and Nasution that Yani personally gave him a beating, and Nasution almost put him on trial.[55] During *Konfrontasi*, Suharto had made sure that troops along the border with Malaysia were understaffed and underequipped, using his power to minimize Indonesia's conflict with the UK (and the US) at the time.[56]

Curiously, General Suharto took command of the Armed Forces on October 1, not Nasution—the highest-ranking officer in the country—after Washington's longtime friend was lucky enough to survive the events of the previous night. This was such an unexpected role reversal that it took several key actors weeks to understand that Suharto was actually in charge.

Everything Suharto did in October suggests that he was executing an anticommunist counterattack plan that had been developed in advance, not simply reacting to events.

On the morning of October 1, Suharto arrived at KOSTRAD, which for some reason had not been targeted or neutralized by the September 30th Movement, even though it sat directly across from Independence Square, which they occupied that morning. At an emergency meeting in the early morning, he took over as commander of the Armed Forces. In the afternoon, he told the troops at Independence Square to disperse and put an end to the rebellion or he would attack. He retook central Jakarta without firing a single shot, and went on the radio himself to declare the September 30th Movement had been defeated. President Sukarno ordered another major general, Pranoto, to meet him at Halim Air Force Base and assume temporary command of the Armed Forces. Contradicting a direct order from his commander in chief, Suharto forbid Pranoto to go, and gave Sukarno himself an order: leave the airport. Sukarno did so, and fled to a presidential palace outside the city. Suharto then easily took control of the airport, and then the entire country, ignoring Sukarno when he saw fit.

Once in command, Suharto ordered that all media be shut down, with the exception of the military outlets he now controlled. Curiously, *Harian Rakyat*—the Communist Party newspaper where Zain had worked for more than a decade—published a front-page editorial endorsing the September 30th Movement on October 2, a full day after the coup had failed and the offices were reportedly occupied by the military. The fact that it was the only nonmilitary paper to come out that day might indicate that the Army published it so as to incriminate the party, or it may indicate that the party thought there would be nothing incriminating about going forward with a piece offering support for an internal Army movement with, at that time, the seemingly laudable goal of stopping a right-wing coup.[57] Theories abound. Author Martin Aleida, who was working at the paper at the time, says the editorial's prose was markedly different from the style employed by Njoto, the PKI member who usually wrote these sorts of things.[58] The cover page of the paper that day featured a cartoon, drawn in usual *People's Daily* style, with the September 30th Movement depicted as a fist punching the "Council of Generals," drawn as a man who falls back, revealing a hat with "CIA" written on it. Francisca simply remembers that Zain continued working that day as usual, until *Harian Rakyat* was shut down.

After that, Suharto controlled all mass communications. He accused the PKI of shocking crimes, using deliberate and incendiary falsehoods to whip up hatred against the left across the country.

The military spread the story that the PKI was the mastermind of a failed communist coup. Suharto and his men claimed that the Indonesian Communist Party had brought the generals back to Halim Air Force Base and begun a depraved, demonic ritual. They said members of *Gerwani*, the Women's Movement, danced naked while the women mutilated and tortured the generals, cutting off their genitals and gouging out their eyes, before murdering them. They claimed that the PKI had long lists of people they planned to kill, and mass graves already prepared.[59] They said China had secretly delivered arms to People's Youth Brigades.[60] The Army paper, *Angkatan Bersendjata* (*Armed Forces*), printed photos of the dead generals' bodies, reporting they had been "cruelly and viciously slaughtered" in acts of torture that were "an affront to humanity."[61]

As the first news of these developments came in, US Under Secretary of State George Ball reportedly called CIA Director Richard Helms to ask if they "were in a position where [they] can categorically deny this involvement of CIA operations in the Indonesia situation." Helms said yes.[62] Ambassador Green was probably not expecting anything to happen on October 1, and all the State Department documents now public indicate the embassy was confused by the events for the first few days of October. It's unclear whether, as was the case with Howard Jones seven years previously, information was being kept from the new ambassador.

Soon after the initial confusion, the US government assisted Suharto in the crucial early phase of spreading propaganda and establishing his anticommunist narrative. Washington quickly and covertly supplied vital mobile communications equipment to the military, a now-declassified October 14 cable indicates.[63] This was also a tacit admission, very early, that the US government recognized the Army, not Sukarno, as the true leader of the country, even though Sukarno was still legally the president.

The Western press did its part too. Voice of America, the BBC, and Radio Australia broadcast reports that emphasized Indonesian military propaganda points, as part of a psychological warfare campaign to demonize the PKI. These broadcasts reached inside the country in Bahasa Indonesia as well, and Indonesians remember thinking that the credibility of Suharto's narrative was more trustworthy because they heard respected international outlets saying the same thing.[64]

Every part of the story the Indonesian Army told is a lie. No *Gerwani* women participated in any killings on October 1.[65] More than three decades later, Benedict Anderson was able to prove not only that the account of the torture of the generals was false, but that Suharto knew it was all false in early October. He himself ordered an autopsy that showed all the men were shot except one, who may have been stabbed with a bayonet in a fight at his home.[66]

But by 1987, when Anderson's proof was published, not much of that discovery mattered anymore. The story of a demonic communist plot to take over the country by mutilating good, God-fearing military men in the dark of night had become something like part of the national religion under the Suharto dictatorship. Not long after he took over, Suharto erected a monument to the men killed that night, just like the Brazilians erected a monument at Red Beach in Rio de Janeiro celebrating their fallen heroes. The two structures are even similar—at both, steps lead up to a white marble slab, with a bronze figure, or figures, of the military victims standing in front. Just as with the *Intentona Comunista* in Brazil, Indonesians celebrated the anniversary of the event each year as a kind of anticommunist national ritual. But the Indonesian monument is bigger. And Suharto took this propaganda a bit further than statues and annual speeches—he ordered the production of a gruesome, three-hour film depicting his version of events, which was broadcast on September 30 each year on public television. The Army still screens it.

The story spread by Suharto hits on some of the darkest fears and prejudices held by Indonesians, and indeed men in general—around the world. A surprise night raid on your home. Slow torture with blades. The inversion of gender roles, the literal assault on strong men's reproductive organs carried out by demonic, sexually depraved communist women. It's the stuff of a well-written, reactionary horror film, and few people believe Suharto came up with it himself.

The similarities with the Brazilian legend of the *Intentona Comunista* are striking. Just a year after a coup in the most important nation in Latin America was inspired partly by a legend about communist soldiers stabbing generals to death in their sleep, General Suharto tells the most important nation in Southeast Asia that communists and left-wing soldiers whisked generals away from their homes in the dead of night to be murdered slowly with knives, and then both Washington-aligned anticommunist military dictatorships celebrated the anniversary of those rebellions in very much the same way for decades.

Historian Bradley Simpson at the National Security Archives in Washington, DC, notes, "Though we lack access to many of the classified US and British materials, it is highly likely that a key element of US and British covert operations in this period involved the creation of 'black' propaganda inside Indonesia," with the goal of demonizing the PKI.[67]

There are many ways Suharto's propaganda team could have taken "inspiration" from Brazilian anticommunist legend. Maybe some US official handed Suharto the idea or helped craft his narrative for him. Thousands of Brazilian and Indonesian military officers studied at Leavenworth over the same period of time, and maybe someone talked about the *Intentona* there. Perhaps Indonesian officials simply grabbed at, and hyper-amplified, anticommunist tropes that were floating out there in the global consciousness, in the international anticommunist movement that was already large, well-organized, and interconnected. By then, there was already the Anti-Bolshevik Bloc of Nations, made up largely of far-right Eastern Europeans; there was the Asian People's Anticommunist League, a kind of counter-Bandung group led by Taiwan and South Korea; and there was the Mexican-led Inter-American Confederation for the Defense of the Continent. Because of the intervention of a Brazilian anticommunist, all three groups had met in Mexico City in 1958, and had stayed in contact afterward.[68] Even regular North Americans knew about those old, absurd references to "reds under the bed." Or perhaps it's just a coincidence.

Suharto managed to give official legitimacy to a wildly anticommunist narrative, an absurdly fanatical and exaggerated version of global right-wing ideology. This was an astonishing turnaround from just weeks earlier. But Sukarno was still technically the president, and there were still a whole lot of people in the country who were communists, or broadly tolerant of communists. Over the next six months, the Army took care of both problems.

7

Extermination

THEY SAY THAT TIME FEELS like it slows down in revolutionary or historic moments. And we know that in moments of trauma or violence, time can nearly come to a stop. When eyewitnesses and victims talk about the six months after September 30, 1965, they speak differently. Elderly men and women who talk about other parts of their lives in terms of years, or decades, begin to talk about weeks, specific dates, hours, and minutes.

The now-public US government communications reporting on the same events are also very specific about dates. In deference to the manner that these two very different types of voices can now speak to us, what follows is a selected timeline of these months.

October 5

Jakarta—October 5 is Armed Forces Day in Indonesia. In the capital, the Army usually holds a parade. In 1965, it held a state funeral for the fallen generals and a demonstration of the military's new dominance.

Sukarno refrained from attending, out of fear for his safety. The president now had to publicly back the new military leadership or appear to support the defeated and discredited, indeed apparently demonic, September 30th Movement.

Defense Minister Nasution gave an impassioned speech condemning the treachery of the communist rebellion and recognizing Suharto's leadership.

Around the archipelago, local chapters of the Indonesian Communist Party participated in the festivities as they always would, proudly waving their hammer-and-sickle flags alongside the military celebrations.[1]

Washington, DC—The State Department received a cable from the US embassy in Jakarta on October 5, signed by Ambassador Marshall Green.

Green outlined the situation in Indonesia:

Following guidelines may supply part of the answer to what our posture should be:

A. Avoid overt involvement as power struggle unfolds.

B. Covertly, however, indicate clearly to key people in army such as Nasution and Suharto our desire to be of assistance where we can, while at same time conveying to them our assumption that we should avoid appearance of involvement or interference in any way.

C. Maintain and if possible extend our contact with military.

D. Avoid moves that might be interpreted as note of nonconfidence in army (such as precipately [sic] moving out our dependents or cutting staff).

E. Spread the story of PKI's guilt, treachery and brutality (this priority effort is perhaps most needed immediate assistance we can give army if we can find way to do it without identifying it as solely or largely US effort).

The new ambassador sent another, more direct summary of what lay before Washington in Indonesia that same day. He wrote, "The Army now has the opportunity to move against Communist Party if it moves quickly," he wrote.

"It's now or never."[2]

October 7

Banda Aceh—The Province of Aceh, at the top of the large, rich island of Sumatra, has a history of both communism and fervent Muslim faith. Indeed, they often overlapped in the days when Indonesia had a flowering of Islamic communism, and most PKI members in the region were devout believers.[3] Aceh, hot and dense and dark green, is the westernmost point of Indonesia, with Malaysia to its east across the Straits of Malacca. The Armed Forces had organized a number of civilians there as part of Sukarno's *Konfrontasi* with that young nation. According to interviews with Acehnese peoples at the time, the PKI did not have a bad reputation, even among very conservative Muslims, until the anticommunist propaganda started arriving after October 1.[4]

Aceh's military commander in 1965 was Ishak Djuarsa, an avid anticommunist who had studied at Fort Leavenworth in Kansas.[5] On October 7, he left the capital, Banda Aceh, for a whirlwind tour of the province, giving speeches to quickly assembled crowds.

"The PKI are *kafir* [infidels]," he announced, according to eyewitness reports. "I will destroy them down to their roots! If in the village you find members of the PKI but do not kill them, it will be you who we punish!"

Djuarsa led the crowd in a chant. "Crush the PKI!" "Crush the PKI!" "Crush the PKI!"

Locals in Central Aceh understood, they recall, that they were being instructed to help kill the communists, or be killed themselves.[6]

It is believed the mass murder started that day, on the island of Sumatra. Some of the killings were "spontaneous," carried out by civilians acting on their own after receiving orders like this. But that was not the rule. The military and police started arresting a huge number of people. Many leftists turned themselves in, thinking it was the safe and prudent thing to do.

The military put to use civilian structures it had created during the anti-Malaysia campaign. During *Konfrontasi*, the military had built up paramilitary organizations that could be used to implement martial law and repress the communists.[7]

The phrase used by Djuarsa, "down to the roots," had already been used once before, at midnight on October 1, by Mokoginta, another commander in Sumatra who had studied at Leavenworth. These words would become a constant, public refrain of the mass murder program.[8]

October 8

The Army newspaper *Angkatan Bersendjata* published a cartoon of a man striking a tree trunk with an axe. On the tree is written "G30S," the

Indonesian-language acronym for the September 30th Movement, and the roots spell "PKI," the Communist Party. The caption reads: "Exterminate them down to the roots."[9]

Internally, however, the Indonesian Army had a different name. It called this *Operasi Penumpasan*—Operation Annihilation.[10]

October 19

Jakarta—Magdalena barely noticed that there had been a bit of political chaos in early October in the capital. She certainly didn't know things back in Central Java, where she grew up, were much worse than they were in Jakarta.

Her grandmother had fallen ill, so she got time off from her job at the T-shirt factory and took a train back to her village to visit her. Health problems had plagued her family her whole life. By the time she arrived, her grandmother had already passed. The plan was to attend the funeral and spend a week, maybe two, grieving with the family, then get back to work in Jakarta. She went to bed in her childhood home in Purwokerto.

October 20

Washington, DC—The State Department received a cable from Ambassador Marshall Green. Green reported that the PKI had suffered "some damage to its organizational strength through arrest, harassment and, in some cases, execution of PKI cadres." He continued: "If army repression of PKI continues and army refuses to give up its position of power to Sukarno, PKI strength can be cut back. In long run, however, army repression of PKI will not be successful unless it is willing to attack communism as such."

Green concluded: "Army has nevertheless been working hard at destroying PKI and I, for one, have increasing respect for its determination and organization in carrying out this crucial assignment."[11]

Purwokerto, Central Java—In the early afternoon, two police officers arrived at Magdalena's family home, less than twenty-four hours after her arrival.

"You're coming with us. We need some information from you," they told her.

The entire house erupted, crying, screaming. Magdalena's family had heard some people were arrested recently in the neighborhood, but they didn't know she was a member of a SOBSI union in Jakarta, and neither they nor Magdalena knew that could ever be a problem in the first place.

At the police station, officers began to yell at her, interrogating her. They told her they knew she was a member of the *Gerwani*, the Women's Movement affiliated with the Communist Party. She wasn't. She didn't know what to say to them, except that she wasn't. According to the mythology spread by Indonesia's new command, this meant she was part of the group that danced naked while mutilating the military high command's genitals. She was in Jakarta, they said. Maybe she was even at the slaughter. She didn't know anything about this, she told them.

These interrogations started, and stopped, and started again, for seven days. Then the officers took her to another police station, in Semarang. As soon as she arrived, she collapsed. She was sick, or overwhelmed. She was dizzy all over. She was seventeen years old.

She's not sure how long she was at the second police station before two police officers raped her. She was *Gerwani*, in the minds of the police, which meant that she was not a human being, and not a woman, but a sexually depraved murderer. An enemy of Indonesia and Islam. A witch. These men were in charge of her now.

October 22

Washington—The State Department received detailed reports of the extent and nature of the Army operations as killings began in Java. A "Moslem Youth Leader" reported that "assistants" were accompanying troops on sweeps that led to killings.[12]

National Security Adviser McGeorge Bundy wrote to President Johnson that events in Indonesia since September 30 "are so far a striking vindication of U.S. policy towards that nation in recent years."[13]

The same day, Ambassador Marshall Green sent a cable to the State Department: "As yet, there is no indication Army incapable . . . we agree that it would be virtually impossible to keep secret any direct USG [US Government] assistance . . . if assistance were given and it became known, we question whether army would be helped rather than hurt. . . . We suspect that if military authorities ever really needed our help in this matter they would let us know."[14]

Two weeks later, the White House authorized the CIA station in Bangkok to provide small arms to its military contact in Central Java "for use against the PKI" alongside medical supplies that would come in from the CIA station in Bangkok.[15]

But after seven years of close cooperation with Washington, the military was already well equipped. You also don't need very advanced weaponry to arrest civilians who provide almost no resistance. What officials in the embassy and the CIA decided the Army really did need, however, was information. Working with CIA analysts, embassy political officer Robert Martens prepared lists with the names of thousands of communists and suspected communists, and handed them over to the Army, so that these people could be murdered and "checked off" the list.

As far as we know, this was at least the third time in history that US officials had supplied lists of communists and alleged communists to allies, so that they could round them up and kill them. The first was in Guatemala in 1954, the second was in Iraq in 1963, and now, on a much larger scale, was Indonesia 1965.

"It really was a big help to the army," said Martens, who was a member of the US embassy's political section. "I probably have a lot of blood on my hands, but that's not all bad."[16]

October 25

Purbalingga, Central Java—Sakono woke up early, and rode his bicycle six kilometers toward the local police station. He arrived, walked in, and signed his name on a little piece of paper. The officers were casual about the whole thing, and basically polite. This was routine by now.

When Sakono first heard about the September 30th Movement, he was sympathetic. As he understood it from radio reports, it was an internal Army movement that stopped a coup against his childhood hero, President Sukarno. But then news became a bit more confused. The People's Daily no longer arrived in his village. His local chapter of the People's Youth organization didn't give him any answers either, so he just kept waiting to start his job as a schoolteacher, desperate for scraps of news from Jakarta, as he had been since he was a teen.

As the narrative around the events shifted, with only military and foreign media reporting on them, Sakono knew that the left was under some suspicion, but he didn't really consider it a big deal. He got word that everyone in a communist-affiliated organization had to check in regularly with the police.

Though he had never dealt with law enforcement before, he didn't mind this much. He didn't have a lot to do, and he wasn't worried. Whatever had happened in Jakarta didn't affect his plans. He figured he would be the best revolutionary he could be as a teacher. "When education moves forward, the country moves forward," he thought. He continued waiting, helping out his family with the crops, just passing the time.

October 29

Galena, Maryland—Frank Wisner found one of his sons' shotguns while staying at the family farm, and used it to kill himself.[17]

November 2

Purbalingga, Central Java—Sakono checked in with the police once more. Once more, he walked out of the station, then got on his bike and rode back to his village. When he got home, around two in the afternoon, a pair of police officers were waiting for him. One of them was holding a letter. They told him the letter meant he had to go with them. "This is of the utmost importance," the police officer said. "You need to face this now."

So he went with them.

When Sakono entered prison, he felt just fine. He had done nothing wrong, so he figured he would just do some interviews, provide some information, and clear his name. He wasn't a full member of the PKI himself, but had been variously, and proudly, involved with the Communist Party since he was very young, so he immediately ran into a lot of old friends. There was Sutrisno, the party cadre who had given him classes in Marxism-Leninism when he was younger. Suhada, his short, slightly chubby older friend who always wore sunglasses, was there too. He was in the Party Central Committee, a funny guy who always gave amazing speeches.

It was practically a reunion. The mood was light, almost festive. They began singing revolutionary songs together—not even in defiance of the police, but just in a kind of joyful solidarity.

> *Move forward undaunted*
> *Defend what is right*
> *Forward, together,*
> *Of course, we win*
> *Move forward, move forward*
> *All together, all together*

That night, while everyone was sleeping, they took away twelve of the prisoners. They took away Sutrisno. They took away Suhada. They took away his friends Kamdi and Sumarno and Suharjo.

They never came back. No one ate breakfast the next morning. There was no more singing. No more cheer. No one talked. This couldn't be happening. It went against everything Sakono had learned, and believed, his entire life. The military and the police were defenders of the revolution. Indonesia had a system of law and order, of fair trial, of evidence and justice. He had barely seen any violence in the nineteen years since he was born.

"I'm not a rebel! I've never held a weapon! I would never rebel against my country! I never did anything wrong in my whole life!" Sakono shouted, over and over, but silently inside his own mind, as his body quivered, terrified he would be in the next group to be taken away.

What had happened to his friends? Sakono heard rumors, as did everyone in the region. They were taking some people to the Serayu River in the middle of the night. They tied up their hands and threw them into the water. Or maybe they shot them first. Or maybe they stabbed them. That there were mass killings became obvious. There were so many bodies piling up that they were blocking rivers, and unleashing a horrible stench across the country. But as to who was killed, and where and how, all the survivors had were rumors.

This was a new characteristic of the mass violence. People weren't killed in the streets, making it very clear to families that they were gone. They weren't officially executed. They were arrested and then *disappeared* in the middle of the night. Loved ones often had no idea if their relatives were still alive, making them even more paralyzed with fear. If they complained, or rebelled, could that be what cost their imprisoned loved ones their lives? Might they be taken too? Even in the face of overwhelming evidence that mass murder is occurring, the human instinct is to hold out hope that your son, or your daughter, might still be saved. This freezes people, and makes populations much more quiescent—easier to exterminate and easier to control. Historians who study violence in Asia believe this was the first time forced "disappearances" had been used.

Who murdered them? Just as in Aceh, military and police took captives to special locations at night and killed them. But very often it was not the actual uniformed officers who pulled the trigger or plunged the machete into human flesh.

The country's largest Muslim organization had a youth wing and an armed wing, the *Ansor* and *Banser*. These were acronyms, but the founder of the *Banser* said that he wanted the word to sound like *Panzer*, Hitler's famous tanks. He also said he had been studying *Mein Kampf*, starting in 1964, in order to learn how to deal with the Communists.[18] These groups participated in the killings in Central and East Java. In Aceh, the military press-ganged and threatened suspicious civilians, politically suspect individuals or outcasts, into carrying out the murders. Afterward, they would often down alcohol to numb themselves to what they had just done.[19] Whatever happened, whoever it was, almost all of Sakono's friends were gone now, and corpses were piling up everywhere.

November 6

Washington, DC—The State Department received a cable from Jakarta. The US embassy passed on some more reports of Army progress. The message ended precisely as follows:

E. Army info bureau also reported that para-comandos (RPKAD) in armoured vehicles entering city of Surakarta (no date given) were blocked in village at outskirts by nine "witches" from PKI women's affiliate

GERWANI, who insulted them and refused to let them pass. After asking them quietly to give way, and firing into air, para-comandos were "forced by their intransigence to terminate breathing of these nine GERWANI witches."

3. Miscellanous [sic]: Beginning what we believe will be major fad, Bandung renamed part of its main street "General Yani Boulevard" yesterday. It's good he has an easily pronounceable name.

Green[20]

November 22

Boyolali—The Armed Forces found, arrested, and executed D. N. Aidit, the leader of the Indonesian Communist Party in Boyolali, Central Java, on the morning of November 22. Aidit had been on the run since he realized that the military was after him.

The military told the world Aidit confessed to plans to take over the country, and this account was later published in *Newsweek*. After the issue came out, a cable from the embassy told the State Department that embassy staff knew it was "impossible to believe that Aidit made such a statement" because according to the military's version, he allegedly referenced a fake document, one they knew "was obviously being disseminated as part of an anti-Communist 'black propaganda' operation."[21]

December 13

Jakarta—Francisca kept working in the days after October 1, 1965. Zain stopped working after *The People's Daily* was closed down by the military. But Francisca kept going to the Afro-Asian Journalist Association office every day, and the staff continued working on preparations for their next edition, and for the Tricontinental Conference planned for Havana in 1966. Despite everything that was happening, Sukarno and a senior Communist Party leader, Nyoto, had managed to convene a conference in Jakarta in protest of US military bases around the world, and Francisca had helped *Afro-Asian Journalist* cover it in October.[22]

But Francisca knew people were being arrested all around the capital. Some of her colleagues, especially the journalists, stopped showing up for work. Still there was almost no reliable information as to what was going on. Everyone was keeping to themselves. No one knew whom they could trust. Every night, Francisca took the car straight back from the office, to her home with Zain in Menteng. She had lived two months like this, as the world of left-wing intellectuals in Jakarta was getting smaller and smaller.

At four in the morning on December 13, three men knocked on their door, and took them both away. Francisca and Zain went peacefully, into police custody. The officers told Francisca she was only being brought in for questioning, and that she would be home very soon, then loaded her and Zain into a Land Rover and drove to Independence Square. The kids were left alone in the house.

Soon after they got there, the men took Zain into a different room. Francisca saw a man begin to undo his belt as he entered another door. She was left with a military officer in an interrogation room. He pulled out a gun and put it on the table in front of her. She lost contact with her senses. She was certain she was going to die.

Somehow, she made it through. The interrogation was over. It might have lasted an hour, or several. She was in a daze. They brought her to the office of the military doctor, the one who treated the wives of the officers. Why was she there? Maybe to be killed in a different way? Then they brought Zain in. It became apparent he was there to say goodbye. It was also apparent he had been tortured. She could see cigarette burns up and down his arms. How many, she didn't know. Too hard to count. Then he was gone, and she was alone in the doctor's office.

She languished there for eight days. At night, she would sleep on a kind of a bench, seemingly an examination table that gynecologists used. She didn't eat, and she lost maybe fifteen pounds. She didn't know. She didn't know anything. During the daytime, the doctors would ignore her as they worked, seemingly unsure why she was there, but knowing she was some sort of a communist, and therefore undeserving of treatment.

But a patient, another woman, probably a soldier's wife, noticed her.

Francisca was sobbing uncontrollably. She didn't know where her children were. She didn't know if Damaiati or Kandida or Anthony, or her youngest, Benjamino, were OK. For days, the police had ignored her tears.

But this woman saw her, and asked her what was wrong. Francisca tried to tell her.

"You have children?" the woman asked.

"I have four!" Francisca said, and broke down again.

She turned to the doctor and shouted, "Why are you not taking care of this woman!"

The doctor gave in, and granted just a little of her humanity back. He must have called someone, because Francisca was transferred to the military office. It turned out the police had processed her incorrectly, and they forgot about her. Now she was taken to the women's prison. Still no contact with her family. At the women's prison she met a younger girl, only nineteen, a country girl pregnant with her first child. She looked up to Francisca, an older mother, now thirty-nine years old. The young woman was sobbing uncontrollably, and told Francisca her husband had already been killed.

December 16

Washington, DC—US officials were in close contact with the military, making it clear to them that direct assistance could resume if the PKI were destroyed, Sukarno was removed, and attacks on US investments halted. Aid flows were also conditional on Indonesia's willingness to adopt IMF- and US-approved economic plans.[23]

All Army leaders seemed to want to know, according to a State Department cable in December, was "how much is it worth it to us that PKI be smashed."[24] It was worth a lot.

But US officials were also very alarmed that the military government-in-waiting had not yet reversed Sukarno's plans to take over US oil companies, by far their most important economic concern at the time. They "bluntly and repeatedly warned the emerging Indonesian leadership" that if nationalization went forward, support from Washington would be withheld, and their grip on power was at stake, according to historian Bradley Simpson's analysis of the declassified communications. The White House enlisted Australian and Japanese officials in the fight.[25] They won.

On December 16, a telegram from Jakarta to the State Department described the victory. Suharto arrived at a high-level meeting by helicopter, strode into the room, and "made it crystal clear to all assembled that the military would not stand for precipitous moves against oil companies." Then he walked out.[26]

January 1, 1966

Bali—The violence arrived on the island of Bali in December. It's almost like it started at Indonesia's westernmost tip and moved east across the main population centers, through Central Java, to East Java, and then to Bali. Like the movement of the sun, only precisely in reverse.

The slaughter in Bali was probably the worst in all of Indonesia. As the new year began, the island convulsed with violence.

Agung Alit was just a little boy, but he knew they were looking for his father. His father, Raka, knew it too. So instead of sleeping at home, he went to sleep in the nearby Hindu temple. Agung stayed at home. As he slept, men came to their home night after night, rummaging around, demanding to know where Raka was. Finally they got him. Agung was awoken, and his family told him his father was gone. They weren't sure when he would be back.

The people of Bali knew something was very suspicious about the outbreak of violence. People were being killed with big machetes. Machetes are not native to the island. Balinese people use the *klewang*, a thinner, local blade. Someone must have brought the heavy weapons in from another island. And, as elsewhere, locals were participating in the killing. Agung heard that it was actually a neighbor, a man known by the family, who took away his father.

The machetes arrived around the same time that military anticommunist propaganda campaigns, nationally coordinated, arrived in Bali. One rumor declared that *Gerwani* women had plans to sell their bodies in order to buy weapons for a communist revolt, and to castrate the soldiers they seduced. Propaganda teams toured rural areas, spreading stories like this, driving home the message that the people must "be on the side of the G30S or stand behind the government in crushing the G30S. There is no such thing as a neutral position."[27]

Some killings were carried out by members of the PNI, the nationalist party Sukarno had founded long ago, as well as local paramilitary gangs that had already been opposing the government's national land reform program.[28]

Young Wayan Badra, the thirteen-year-old son of the Hindu priest in the Seminyak neighborhood, noticed that the two nice communist teachers at his school went away and never came back. Then he heard what was happening on the beaches. They were bringing people from the city to the east to kill them on the sand. It was public property there, and empty at night. The bodies were abandoned there. Some families came to recover them. Others were gathered by Badra's village, to be given anonymous funeral rites and cremated by his father.

For Balinese Hindus, the loss of a family member's body is a deep spiritual tragedy of infinite consequence. So a few years after the violence ended, Agung went with his family to find his father's body, and give him an honorable funeral and cremation. They walked four kilometers to the site where someone told them they could find his remains. They found a field of bodies.

They began looking through bones, picking up skulls.

Someone shouted, "This is Mr. Raka!"

But no, that skull didn't look right. Maybe the hair was wrong. Maybe that one? They kept sorting through decomposing bodies, desperately, for minutes, before someone realized it was impossible, crazy. There were just "too many skulls, too many skeletons."

They walked back home for an hour, processing the knowledge they would never lay him to rest, and sickened by the vast sea of humanity they had just entered.

In total, at least 5 percent of the population of Bali was killed—that is, eighty thousand people, probably the highest proportion in the country.[29]

The Balinese had been especially strong supporters of Sukarno's multifaith political project, because it gave Hindus more freedom in a Muslim-majority country.[30] A severe economic crisis in the early 1960s made the communists' promises of redistribution more attractive to some—and more threatening to others. The PNI killed Suteja, the governor, and members of his family, and spread the myth that he actually chose to *nyupat*, or volunteered to be executed and be reincarnated as a better person. Some Balinese were indeed asked if they wanted to *nyupat* or not. But those who said no were killed anyway, rendering the question meaningless.[31] They were executed, murdered one by one, over just a few months, for affiliation with an unarmed political party that had been entirely legal and mainstream just weeks earlier.

A little bit later, the first tourist hotel went up on the very beach, Seminyak, that had been used as a killing field.

January 14

Washington, DC—The State Department received a detailed assessment of the Indonesian situation from Ambassador Marshall Green:

> Prior to October 1, 1965, Indonesia was for all practical purposes an Asian communist state. . . .
>
> Events of the past several months have had three major effects on Indonesia's power structures and policies:
>
> 1. The PKI has ceased for the foreseeable future to be an important power element. Effective action by the Army and its Muslim allies has totally disrupted the party's organizational apparatus. Most Politburo and Central Committee members have been killed or arrested, and estimates of the number of party members killed range up to several hundred thousand. . . .

The memo listed the plan for the US response:

> 1. Ensure that our actions and statements do nothing to shore up Sukarno and his henchmen. . . .
>
> F. Without becoming directly involved, promote arrangements between the [Government of Indonesia] and the American oil companies. . . .
>
> H. Within the limits of prudence, give open or covert advice and assistance to responsible and competent anti-communist groups for worthwhile activities.[32]

March 11

Bogor—As the killings went on, State Department officials repeatedly expressed frustration that Suharto had not yet taken full control and formally deposed President Sukarno. Since October, Sukarno had been largely relegated to the palace in the city of Bogor and stripped of most of his powers, but he still had his official title and some influence.

Sukarno's reaction to the killings was both resignation and desperation. Though he wasn't getting full reports from around the country, he knew violence was taking place, and seemed overwhelmed by the avalanche of anticommunist propaganda. He told one group of officers and journalists, "Over and over it's the same thing . . . razors, razors, razors, razors, razors, a grave for a thousand people, a grave for a thousand people . . . over and over again, the same thing!"[33] He urged restraint, entirely ineffectively, as Suharto's forces literally hacked away at the number of people on the left wing of Indonesian politics.

Over the period of the killings, the economic situation deteriorated, reducing further what remained of Sukarno's power. According to Subandrio, his former foreign minister, Suharto intentionally engineered hyperinflation by working with businessmen to restrict the supply of basic goods like rice, sugar, and cooking oil.[34] Suharto encouraged anticommunist student groups, often drawn from the same schools Benny had attended just years earlier, to protest those high prices. The US government was intentionally destabilizing the economy.[35]

As student protests raged around him, Sukarno called top government officials to the Jakarta Presidential Palace on March 10 in an attempt to retain control. Instead, paratroopers loyal to Suharto, led by General Sarwo Edhie, surrounded him the next day.

Sukarno jumped onto a helicopter to flee, Subandrio running behind him barefoot, and rushed back to Bogor. But there, Sukarno was forced to sign a letter handing over executive power to Suharto.[36]

There are still controversies about this letter, the so-called *Supersemar*. No one has ever seen the original.

Regardless, Suharto used it as permission to take over immediately, and completely. In his first acts, he officially banned what was left of the Communist Party, then arrested much of Sukarno's cabinet, including Subandrio. The United States immediately opened the economic floodgates. The stranglehold on the economy was loosened, and US firms began exploring opportunities for profit. Within days of the transfer of power, representatives from the US mining company Freeport were in the jungles of West New

Guinea, and quickly found a mountain filled with valuable minerals. Ertsberg, as it is now called, is the largest gold mine on the planet.[37]

March 17

Washington, DC—Incoming cable from Jakarta:

"1. Several American correspondents here have sought our comments on 'reports from [Jakarta]' which we have traced to high-level British sources in Singapore. AP correspondent John Cantwell (protect source) told Congen flatly that British are planting stories."

The reporter knew he had been receiving misinformation as part of a campaign to strengthen Suharto. He didn't mind. The memo continues:

"Correspondent complained that, although he was reasonably certain British were feeding him false or misleading information, their stories were so spectacular he had no choice but to file them."[38]

Date Unknown

After many months, Francisca walked out of prison. Her father found a way to use his money and influence to pay for her release. Disoriented, she had no idea what day it was.

Broadly speaking, the violence in Jakarta was not as intense as it was in places like North Sumatra, Central and East Java, and Bali. Perhaps because those were the main centers of mass support for the PKI and for Sukarno himself, and perhaps because they couldn't treat leftists in the capital— surrounded by press and elites and diplomats—the same way they were treating regular people, far from the city. But the world Francisca discovered upon her release was still devastating.

Her house had been covered with violent graffiti, smeared with "G30S," the September 30th Movement. She was able to see her kids, finally. They were OK. But she found out that her oldest daughter had been taken out of class one day by the military, loaded onto a truck, and taken to Independence Square, where she was forced to line up and chant, "Down with Sukarno! Down with Sukarno!"

She knew that this chant was aimed at her father and mother, who had disappeared, for being on what was now considered the wrong side of history.

None of Francisca's friends would talk to her anymore. In fact, no one was talking to anyone. Gone were the days of literary discussions and language classes with progressive intellectuals from around the world. There was a new rule of conduct.

"You shouldn't trust anybody," she recalled. "They were using people from every type of organization to snitch on their former colleagues. So many people just can't stand the abuse. They break down, and betray their friends in their own organization. The less you know the better it is."

Zain was not there. He never emerged from prison.

A Gleam of Light

Most of the Western press repeated the narrative being peddled by the new Indonesian government, which Washington was enthusiastically welcoming onto the world stage. That story went, more or less, that some spontaneous violence erupted when regular people found out about what the communists had done, or been planning. These articles said that the natives had "run amok" and engaged in bloodshed. Because the word "amok" originated in Malay (the language that formed the basis for both Indonesian and Malaysian), this made it easier for Western journalists to employ Orientalist stereotypes about Asians as primitive, backward, and violent people, and blame the violence on a putative sudden, irrational outburst.[39]

On April 13, 1966, C. L. Sulzberger penned a piece, one of many in this genre, with the headline "When a Nation Runs Amok" for the *New York Times*. As Sulzberger described it, the killings occurred in "violent Asia, where life is cheap." He reproduced the lie that Communist Party members had killed the generals on October 1, and that *Gerwani* women slashed and tortured them. He went on to affirm that "Indonesians are gentle . . . but hidden behind their smiles is that strange Malay streak, that inner, frenzied blood-lust which has given to other languages one of their few Malay words: *amok*."[40]

The Malay, and now Indonesian, concept of *amok* actually referred to a traditional form of ritual suicide, even if the anglicization now refers to wild violence more generally.[41] But there's no reason to believe that the mass violence of 1965–66 has its roots in native culture. No one has any evidence of mass murder of this kind happening in Indonesian history, except for when foreigners were involved.[42]

This story of inexplicable, vaguely tribal violence—so easy for American readers to digest—was entirely false. This was organized state violence with a clear purpose. The main obstacles to a complete military takeover were eliminated by a coordinated program of extermination—the intentional mass murder of innocent civilians. The generals were able to take power after state terror sufficiently weakened their political opponents, who had no weapons, only public sympathy. They didn't resist their own annihilation because they had no idea what was coming.[43]

In total, it is estimated that between five hundred thousand and one million people were slaughtered, and one million more were herded into concentration camps. Sarwo Edhie, the man who ambushed Sukarno in March, once bragged that the military had killed three million people.[44] There's a reason we have to settle for estimates. Because, for more than fifty years, the Indonesian government has resisted any attempt to go out and record what happened, and no one around the world has much cared to ask, either. Millions more people were indirect victims of the massacres, but no one came around to inquire how many loved ones they had lost.

Their silence was the point of the violence. The Armed Forces did not oversee the extermination of every single communist, alleged communist, and potential communist sympathizer in the country. That would have been nearly impossible, because around a quarter of the country was affiliated somehow with the PKI. Once the killings took hold, it became incredibly hard to find anyone who would admit to any association with the PKI.

Around 15 percent of the prisoners taken were women.[45] They were subjected to especially cruel, gendered violence, which sprung directly from the propaganda spread by Suharto with Western help. Sumiyati, the *Gerwani* member who lived near Sakono in her teens, fled the police for two months before turning herself in. She was made to drink the urine of her captors. Other women had their breasts cut off, or their genitals mutilated, and rape and sexual slavery were widespread.[46] There has been some debate as to whether the Indonesian mass killings can be categorized as "genocide," but that is largely an argument about the meaning of the term, not about what happened.[47] In the overwhelming majority of cases, people were killed for their political beliefs or for being accused of having the wrong political beliefs. It's also true that some murderers used the chaos to settle personal scores, and that thousands were killed because of their race. This was especially true for the ethnic Chinese population. But the vast majority of real leftists were no more deserving of any punishment than those who were inaccurately accused of being associated with the Communist Party.

Except for a tiny number of people possibly involved in the planning of the disastrous September 30th Movement, almost everyone killed and imprisoned was entirely innocent of any crime. Magdalena, an apolitical teenage member of a communist-affiliated union, was innocent. Sakono, an active member of the People's Youth and enthusiastic Marxist, was innocent. His teachers and friends, card-carrying party members all, were innocent. Agung's father in Bali was innocent. Sumiyati and the other members of her *Gerwani* chapter, innocent. Sakono's childhood friends and Magdalena's union comrades didn't deserve to be killed. They didn't even deserve a small fine. They didn't do anything wrong at all.

They were sentenced to annihilation, and almost everyone around them was sentenced to a lifetime of guilt, trauma, and being told they had sinned unforgivably because of their association with the earnest hopes of left-wing politics. Declassified documents from Eastern Europe indicate that Zain, Francisca's husband, was a member of the Party's Central Committee.[48] Even in the case of someone like him, at the very top of the Communist Party, there's no evidence Zain was guilty of anything at all. In addition to the crime of extermination, an International People's Tribunal assembled later in the Netherlands found the Indonesian military guilty of a number of crimes against humanity, including torture, unjustified and long-term detainment in cruel conditions, forced labor amounting to enslavement, and systematic sexual violence. The judges found that all this was carried out for political purposes—to destroy the Communist Party and then "prop up a violent, dictatorial regime"—with the assistance of the United States, the UK, and Australia.[49]

It wasn't only US government officials who handed over kill lists to the Army. Managers of US-owned plantations furnished them with the names of "troublesome" communists and union organizers, who were then murdered.[50]

The prime responsibility for the massacres and concentration camps lies with the Indonesian military. We still do not know if the method employed—disappearance and mass extermination—was planned well before October 1965, perhaps inspired by other cases around the world, or planned under foreign direction, or if it emerged as a solution as events unfolded. But Washington shares guilt for every death. The United States was part and parcel of the operation at every stage, starting well before the killing started, until the last body dropped and the last political prisoner emerged from jail, decades later, tortured, scarred, and bewildered. At several points that we know of—and perhaps some we don't—Washington was the prime mover, and provided crucial pressure for the operation to move forward or expand.

US strategy since the 1950s had been to try to find a way to destroy the Indonesian Communist Party, not because it was seizing power undemocratically, but because it was popular. In line with Frank Wisner's early strategy of covert direct confrontation, the US government launched secret attacks and murdered civilians in 1958 in the attempt to break up the country, and failed. So American officials adopted Howard Jones's more subtle on-the-ground insights, turning to a strategy of building deep connections with the Armed Forces and building an anticommunist military state within a state. John F. Kennedy's active engagement with the Third World and especially its military, under the guidance of Modernization Theory, provided the structure to expand the power of this operation in Indonesia. When Washington parted ways with Jones and his strategy of working directly with Sukarno, it instructed its secret and not-so-secret agents to destabilize the country and create conflict. When the conflict came, and when the opportunity arose, the US government helped spread the propaganda that made the killing possible, and engaged in constant conversations with the Army to make sure the military officers had everything they needed, from weapons to kill lists. The US embassy constantly prodded the military to adopt a stronger position and take over the government, knowing full well that the method being employed to make this possible was to round up hundreds of thousands of people around the country, stab or strangle them, and throw their corpses into rivers. The Indonesian military officers understood very well that the more people they killed, the weaker the left would be, and the happier Washington would be.

Up to a million Indonesians, maybe more, were killed as part of Washington's global anticommunist crusade. The US government expended significant resources over years engineering the conditions for a violent clash, and then, when the violence broke out, assisted and guided its longtime partners to carry out the mass murder of civilians as a means of achieving US geopolitical goals.

And in the end, US officials got what they wanted. It was a huge victory.

As historian John Roosa puts it, "Almost overnight the Indonesian government went from being a fierce voice for cold war neutrality and anti-imperialism to a quiet, compliant partner of the US world order."[51]

This was something for almost everyone in the US government and elite media circles to celebrate, given the thinking that was dominant at the time. James Reston, a liberal columnist at the *New York Times*, published a piece under the headline "A Gleam of Light in Asia." He noted, correctly, that "There was a great deal more contact between the anti-Communist forces in that country and at least one very high official in Washington before and during the Indonesian massacre than is generally realized . . . it is doubtful if the coup would have ever been attempted without the American show of strength in Vietnam or been sustained without the clandestine aid it has received indirectly from here." Reston said that the "savage transformation of Indonesia from a pro-Chinese policy under Sukarno to a defiantly anti-Communist policy under General Suharto is, of course, the most important" of a number of "hopeful political developments in Asia" that he saw as outweighing Washington's more widely publicized setbacks in Vietnam.[52]

Reston knew Washington's foreign policy establishment very well. Back in the 1950s, he was a frequent guest at Frank Wisner's raucous Sunday night dinner parties in Georgetown.[53] In his final days, before he took his life, it's not clear how much attention Wisner was paying to the news, or if he even knew what happened in Indonesia at all.

For writers like Reston, this was an obvious victory for US geopolitical interests as Washington understood them at the time. And for hardened anticommunists around the world, the method behind this "savage transformation" would soon be seen as an inspiration, a playbook. But how could the international press, and the State Department, remain entirely untroubled by the fact that this was achieved through the mass murder of unarmed civilians? Howard Federspiel, at the State Department, summed up the answer perfectly. "No one cared," he recalled, "as long as they were Communists, that they were being butchered."[54]

8

Around the World

INDONESIA DID INDEED BECOME A "quiet, compliant partner" of the United States, which explains why so many Americans today have barely heard about the country. But at the time, things were very different.

The annihilation of the world's third-largest communist party, the fall of the founder of the Third World movement, and the rise of a fanatically anticommunist military dictatorship violently rocked Indonesia, setting off a tsunami that reached almost every corner of the globe.

In the long term, the shape of the global economy changed forever. And the scale of the anticommunist victory and ruthless efficiency of the method employed inspired extermination programs named after the Indonesian capital. But first, that giant bloody wave wrought short-term consequences as it crashed onto shores around the world.

Vietnam

US strategy in Southeast Asia was dictated to a large degree by the logic of the "domino theory," which posits that as one country in Asia "fell" to communism, so could the rest of the region. This theory is well remembered to this day. What is completely forgotten is that Indonesia was by far the biggest domino. When influential officials in Washington realized how decisive their victory was in Jakarta, they came to a conclusion. They could afford to lose the battle in Vietnam, because the war was already won.

The fall of the PKI "greatly reduced America's stakes in Vietnam" is the way that Robert McNamara put it, summarizing the 1966 opinion of George F. Kennan, who invented the Cold War containment strategy. "Fewer dominoes now existed, and they seemed much less likely to fall."[1]

Later, McNamara himself looked back on his own pro-war views on Vietnam in 1965 and concluded, regretfully, that he and other high-level officials "took no account of the centuries-old hostility between China and Vietnam . . . or of the setbacks to China's political power caused by recent events" in Indonesia.[2] By 1967, when McNamara recommended against escalating the war, he "pointed to the Communists' defeat in Indonesia and the Cultural Revolution then roiling China, arguing that these events showed the trend in Asia now ran in our favor."[3]

In the end, McNamara was right. Officials in Washington lost the Vietnam War, but they still got, eventually, the version of Southeast Asia that they always wanted.

Then there were the actual people of Vietnam. Southeast Asia's second-largest communist party (until the Indonesian communists had been destroyed, when it became the largest), like much of the socialist world, responded to the events of October 1 with hesitation at first. The official organ of the party, *The People*, didn't comment on events in Indonesia until October 7, when the paper published a message from Ho Chi Minh to President Sukarno. It avoided the question of commenting on the September 30th Movement entirely.

"We are very delighted to hear that the President is well. We wish that you and the Indonesian people are able to continue with your revolution."

Then, on October 9 and October 18, *The People* published two headlines: "Forces in Indonesia, supported by the imperialist US, have for months planned a coup against President Sukarno," read the first one; the second read, "Imperialist US and their cohorts are provoking an anti-communist campaign in Indonesia."[4]

Of course, as Washington's military engagement ramped up, Hanoi was hardly in a position to do anything about Indonesia. The Vietnamese communists did eventually win against the Americans, but at tremendous cost. Three million Vietnamese people were killed in that war, and two million of them were civilians.[5] Many more were killed in Cambodia and Laos. In

Indochina, Washington's anticommunist crusade erased human life on a truly colossal scale, with no appreciable positive results.

The dynamics of the Vietnam War have been very well documented—especially compared to the attention paid to Indonesia.[6] But one aspect often escapes attention, and it's a program with echoes of Guatemala in 1953, Iraq in 1963, and Indonesia in 1965.

The US military launched the Phoenix Program with the assistance of Australia and the South Vietnamese government in 1968. The goal was to "neutralize" the enemy's administration through persuasion or assassination. This meant murdering civilians, not waging war. The military drew up blacklists and went hunting for its targets. Operation Phoenix killed tens of thousands of bureaucrats and unarmed people.[7]

One man working in the operation was already a veteran of Washington's anticommunist operations. A Cuban exile named Felix Rodriguez fought at the Bay of Pigs invasion; then, he joined the CIA and led the operation that hunted down and executed Che Guevara in Bolivia in 1967; when finished there, he went to Vietnam to work in the super-secret Phoenix Program.[8]

The Soviet Union

The Soviet Union reacted to the fall of Sukarno and the destruction of the PKI with mostly quiet resignation. On the one hand, by this point in the Sino-Soviet split, Moscow was not eager to see Beijing's outspoken ally succeed. On the other hand, Leonid Brezhnev, general secretary since October 1964, was hoping to win the PKI and Aidit back over to the Soviet side. After all, the Indonesian Communists were still "revisionists" according to Beijing, and Aidit—who never liked Khrushchev much—had tried to make a fresh start with Brezhnev.[9]

It appears that officials in Moscow, like most everyone else, were caught off guard by the events of October 1, and adopted a "wait and see" approach. On October 10, Soviet leaders sent and published a letter to Sukarno, wishing him "sincere wishes of great success." After learning about the mass extermination program, *Pravda* asked in February 1966, "What for and according to what right are tens of thousands of people being killed?" The official Communist paper reported that "rightist political circles are trying to eliminate the communist party and at the same time 'eradicate' the ideology of Communism in Indonesia." They compared the slaughter to the "White Terror" unleashed in Russia in 1917.[10]

However, the Soviets did not actually take any decisive international action. Relations worsened between the two countries as Suharto consolidated power, of course, and the Soviets slowly wound down aid to Indonesia and its military. But there were no fierce denunciations at the UN or threats of retaliation.[11] Harsh comments made by the consul general of East Germany, to the effect that "the PKI has seriously failed in connection with the incidents of 30 September," may indicate that privately, some major officials in the Soviet orbit believed the Indonesians had it coming.[12] At least, they found justification for staying out of the way as communists were annihilated, as they often had before.

But there were a lot of Indonesians living in the Soviet Union in 1965. Many of them were students at Patrice Lumumba University, set up in the early 1960s to educate visitors from the Third World. Since independence, Indonesian students had been sent all over the world to study, but as Sukarno moved to the left in the 1960s, opportunities in socialist countries increased relative to spots in the West.

So Gde Arka and Yarna Mansur, a young Indonesian couple from Bali and Sumatra, respectively, jumped at the opportunity to head to Moscow in 1963. They got a little bit of ideological training before they took off—mostly so they could spread the good news about Indonesia's revolution to the other students—but they weren't communists. They would have happily gone to England or the Netherlands to study if they could.[13]

They found Moscow cold, but also quite rich and developed. Everyone had health care, free education, the things Indonesians believed they deserved but hadn't received yet. Russian wasn't so hard—they'd been learning and switching between languages far more complex than that since childhood—so they were speaking and studying in the local tongue before long, alongside students from everywhere: Latin America, the Middle East, Japan, Cambodia, Thailand, India, Sri Lanka, Iran, and Iraq.

After October 1, 1965, news of events back home became disjointed. They tuned in to reports from Soviet Radio, the BBC, and Radio Australia. None of it made sense. Worse, they were cut off from contact with their families back home. Things got even more confusing when the Indonesian embassy called them in to sign some declarations.

First, they were asked to sign something condemning the murder of the six generals. They did happily. But then later, they were asked to sign a form declaring allegiance to the new Suharto government. They hesitated; this didn't make much sense. They barely knew who this Suharto man was. This demand for allegiance split the sizable student population in Moscow. Some signed. Gde and Yarna did not. They figured, and hoped, that Sukarno, the president who had actually sent them abroad, would sort things out and return to power.

This didn't happen. Because they didn't sign, they had their passports revoked and lost their citizenship—which is to say, they lost their country. The same thing happened to thousands of Indonesians around the world, all of whom became stateless, condemned to seek assistance from the place where they were stuck or wander across borders—without a passport—until they could find a government that would take them.[14] They could not communicate with their families in Indonesia. They were marked as communists, and as a result were fully and truly outcasts.

Gde's uncle was killed in the anticommunist violence back in Bali. He was tortured, forced to watch his friends murdered in front of him, and then stabbed to death. Gde would only hear this full story when he was able to return to Indonesia thirty years later.

Guatemala

Almost a decade after the CIA-engineered coup, Central America's largest country was not doing well. Washington still had a Cold War ally in power there, and Guatemala was still tightly integrated with the US economy, but things had not exactly turned out as US officials had hoped.

For the rest of the 1950s, CIA agents watched the country sink back into "feudal repression" with some measure of regret.[15] Then the Bay of Pigs invasion indirectly triggered a civil war, which would last for more than three decades.

In November 1960, a group of junior officers led a small rebellion against President Miguel Ydígoras Fuentes, who had won an entirely fraudulent election after the general hand-picked by Washington in 1954 was assassinated. The junior officers were very broadly left-leaning, and shocked by the regime's levels of corruption and incompetence. But the spark for the revolt was the fact that the president had granted a base for CIA-backed Cuban exiles to prepare for their invasion of Cuba without asking them. The Cuban exiles were wealthy and reckless, driving impressive cars around the country.[16] This was not only an insult to the military and its hierarchy; it was theft, because the president pocketed all the money the US paid him.

The revolt failed. But some of the officers formed a guerrilla group, the *Movimiento Revolucionario 13 de Noviembre* (MR-13), to openly rebel against the government. Another officer formed a rival group, *Fuerzas Armadas Rebeldes* (FAR), and began collaborating with the underground Communist Party (PGT), which had been nonviolent since its founding.[17]

By 1964, the United States and its local military partners, frustrated by their inability to contain the rebellion, changed tactics. They began a series of counterinsurgency actions in Eastern Guatemala. They were assisted by a right-wing terror organization called the White Hand (*La Mano Blanca*), but victory was elusive. Totally undemocratic and governing a society that offered regular people no chance for advancement, the state had a very hard time establishing legitimacy. Its leaders pursued a different solution. They brought in two Americans from Southeast Asia, as violence continued to roil Indonesia.

In September 1965, a man named John Gordon Mein was appointed US ambassador to Guatemala. He had served as first secretary of the embassy in Indonesia before Howard Jones began his ambassadorial post, and then alongside Jones as the director of the Office of Southwest Pacific Affairs in the State Department. Soon after, Mein requested the services of John P. Longan, a former Border Patrol officer in the US who had worked with the CIA, in Thailand and elsewhere.[18] Longan had worked for the same Bangkok office that had authorized the supply of weapons to the Indonesian military during the killings.[19]

Soon after Longan arrived from Venezuela, he formed death squads. Within three months they carried out Operation Cleanup, or *Operación Limpieza*, which kidnapped, tortured, and executed thirty prominent left-wing figures in March 1966, just as Sukarno was stepping down in Indonesia. They didn't just kill them, though—they kidnapped and then disappeared them, murdering them without informing anyone what had happened.

It's believed the events of 1965–66 in Indonesia were the first time Asia suffered from disappearances as a tactic of state terror.[20] In 1965, two men with direct knowledge of US activities in Indonesia arrived in Guatemala City. Historians who study violence in Latin America believe that 1966 in Guatemala was the first time the region suffered from disappearances as a tactic of state terror.[21]

The People's Republic of China

October 1 is a special date on the Communist Chinese calendar. It's National Day, the celebration of the founding of the People's Republic of China, which turned sixteen years old in 1965. When Mao, Zhou Enlai, and Deng Xiaoping gave speeches that day in Tiananmen Square, some Indonesian students and leftists were in the crowd.[22] At a banquet afterward, the Indonesians were the largest foreign delegation.[23]

As Suharto consolidated control over a new regime in Indonesia, anticommunists used the coincidence of that date to make bad faith accusations that China had somehow engineered the September 30th Movement. Beijing had neither the ability nor the intention to change Indonesia's government; instead, Chinese officials were profoundly confused as to what was happening.[24] At first, they believed a genuine right-wing coup had been stopped; then they thought that Sukarno would regain control of the country and continue to govern with the PKI supporting him; then they were alarmed that Sukarno was unwilling or unable to stop the Army from raiding the homes of Chinese embassy staff in Jakarta.

In December, when Mao learned of D. N. Aidit's death, he composed a poem:

> *Sparse branches stood in front of my windows in winter, smiling before hundreds of flowers*
> *Regretfully those smiles withered when spring came*
> *There is no need to grieve over the withered*
> *To each flower there is a season to wither, as well a season to blossom*
> *There will be more flowers in the coming year.*[25]

Apparently, as late as December, Mao thought the leftists would rise once more in Indonesia. Instead, they were being slaughtered, and anticommunist protesters and student groups increasingly targeted the Chinese embassy.

In February, more than a thousand right-wing youth attacked the building, and staff did their best to defend themselves with beer bottles, light bulbs, and kung fu. Taiwan's anticommunist, anti-Beijing government provided resources and training to these groups as they carried out more assaults. In total, the embassy was attacked more than forty times.

Reports of the clashes made their way back to China, and became part of the official discourse of the budding Cultural Revolution. Suharto's dictatorship and the Cultural Revolution emerged in synchrony, says Taomu Zhou, the scholar who best knows Chinese documentation on Indonesia in the period. "These two significant and stormy processes in Cold War Asia were mutually reinforcing," she writes—and the conflict with Indonesia "greatly contributed to the growing sociopolitical mobilization during the early stages of the Cultural Revolution." Heroic resistance to the brutality of the likes of Suharto became one of the Red Guards' favored themes.[26]

First, enraged Chinese youth petitioned to put up posters to attack "Indonesian reactionaries." Then, the image of a Chinese diplomat who was injured in an embassy attack in Jakarta became a media sensation across the country. Six hundred thousand Red Guards protested in front of Indonesia's embassy in Beijing. As ethnic Chinese refugees fleeing the violence in Indonesia arrived in China, they joined the Indonesian students and leftists already stranded there.[27] Their stories of the horrors in their homeland became iconic during the Cultural Revolution, used as potent symbols of the dangers of right-wing violence and the need to heroically resist imperialism.

At an event with some of these refugees, in front of a crowd waving the Little Red Book, Foreign Minister Chen Yi declared, "The Chinese people, armed with Mao Zedong thought, cannot be humiliated; the overseas nationals of strong socialist China can never be persecuted!" He continued, "The savage Indonesian reactionaries will ultimately face the harsh judgment of history."[28]

The Cultural Revolution was built around the idea that hidden bourgeois elements could infiltrate and threaten a left-wing movement. The events in Indonesia in 1965–66 served as self-evident justification for this narrative. Just weeks previously, the world's largest unarmed communist party had held considerable influence in the huge country across the South China Sea. Mao and Zhou Enlai had encouraged the Indonesian leftists to arm the people.[29] It did not. Then overnight, hidden right-wing elements emerged to kill them all and turn a left-leaning anti-imperialist nation into an ally of Washington. It would be the perfect propaganda tale to invent, if it were not all true.

The United States

US government officials were almost uniformly celebratory of the massacres in Indonesia, even as their scope and brutality became clear. Ironically, one dissenting voice on this topic came from the man with a reputation for pushing for the most violent and reckless covert operations in the early 1960s.

In January 1966, Senator Bobby Kennedy said, "We have spoken out against the inhuman slaughters perpetrated by the Nazis and the Communists. But will we speak out also against the inhuman slaughter in Indonesia, where over 100,000 alleged Communists have not been perpetrators but victims?" No other prominent US politician condemned the massacre. By this time, RFK was in the habit of speaking out forcefully in ways that others wouldn't.[30] It's unclear whether he knew that the Johnson administration was actively assisting with the massacre at that point. Maybe RFK had a kind of conversion about the nature of black ops after his brother's death. Maybe it was politics. But we know that whatever it was, Washington did not stop helping to carry out Operation Annihilation.

The US economic elite heard a very different message. Indonesia was open for business. In 1967, the first year of Suharto's fully consolidated rule, General Electric, American Express, Caterpillar, and Goodyear Tire all came to explore the new opportunities available to them in Indonesia. Star-Kist foods arrived to see about fishing in Indonesian waters, and of course, defense contractors Raytheon and Lockheed popped over, too.

James Linen, president of Time-Life, went a step further. He contacted both the embassy and Suharto himself, expressing interest in putting on a major business conference focusing on Indonesian opportunities. Ambassador Green said "this seemed to him an excellent idea," because "a number of American companies, particularly in the extractive industries, were already in Djakarta."*[31]

---

* The capital was spelled "Djakarta" until Indonesian orthography was updated in 1972. This book uses modern spelling except in the case of direct quotes.

Linen wrote to Suharto: "I had the privilege of visiting your country last fall and was most favorably impressed with the progressive developments that have been taking place. It occurred to me that an international investment conference . . . could be a most productive undertaking."

Suharto agreed. They began preparations for a swanky get-together in Geneva that fall.

At least one million Indonesians were still in concentration camps, comprising one of the largest populations of political detainees anywhere in the world. They were subject to starvation, forced labor, physical and psychological torture, and attempts at anticommunist re-education.[32] The families of up to another million victims were reeling from the disappearance of their loved ones, without explanation and often without confirmation they were even dead. Bodies were strewn about the country. Sakono was imprisoned. Magdalena was imprisoned, and badly confused. Francisca was in the process of giving up on her husband and finding a way to escape the country and keep the rest of her family safe.

Judging by the materials prepared after the conference, titled "To Aid in the Rebuilding of a Nation," the meeting in Geneva was a roaring success. Under Secretary of State George Ball was there. New Foreign Minister Adam Malik, a longtime Washington favorite in Indonesia, gave a speech emphasizing the importance of the military as "the only credible political power in Indonesia." And David Rockefeller made some very encouraging final remarks: "I have talked with a good many people over the course of the last couple days and I think I have found universal enthusiasm."[33]

Cambodia

Like Sukarno, Prince Norodom Sihanouk had attempted to maintain his neutrality in the Cold War since Cambodia's participation in the Bandung Conference in 1955, but his relationship with Washington became increasingly strained from years of CIA plotting and the escalation of the Vietnam War.

At the same time a man, born Saloth Sâr but known now to the world as Pol Pot, was leading a very small group of idiosyncratic Marxists camped out near the Vietnamese border. His group, then called the Workers Party of Kampuchea, had almost no public support, and alternately collaborated and quarreled with the more experienced—and much busier—Vietnamese Communists to his east. Pol Pot had ignored directives from both the Soviet

Union and the Vietnamese to keep peace with Sihanouk's government, and his group was organizing a rural rebellion.[34]

Pol Pot and his followers were also paying very close attention to Indonesia. They studied the collapse of the PKI, and concluded that its strategy of aligning with Sukarno and winning mass democratic support had only led to disaster. As a result, he vowed that his movement would not meet the same fate at the hands of reactionaries, and resolved that power for his group would be achieved and maintained through arms and violence. The PKI had no arms, and trusted far too much in democratic niceties; that was its downfall, the secretive leader of the "Khmer Rouge" concluded. He would be different.[35]

Ghana

If sub-Saharan Africa had a Sukarno, it was likely Ghana's Kwame Nkrumah. Born to a poor family in what was then called the "Gold Coast"—as usual in the Third World, it was named for a precious commodity by its British colonizers—and educated at the historically black Lincoln University in Pennsylvania, he saw firsthand how virulent racism defined black life in the United States.[36] At first, authorities in London viewed him as a threat, then briefly saw him as useful, until he was a problem again.

In 1957, he helped create Ghana, the first independent nation in Sub-Saharan, "black" Africa.[37] He was a socialist, and opposed to Western imperialism; he wanted to change the rules of the world economy to favor formerly colonized peoples; and by the 1960s he rivaled Sukarno on the world stage as the man who most loudly railed against "neocolonialism."

In his 1965 book, *Neocolonialism: The Last Stage of Imperialism*, he wrote that "neo-colonialism is the worst form of imperialism." According to Nkrumah, the new way of the world was that "foreign capital is used for the exploitation, rather than for the development of the less developed parts of the world," and that imperial powers no longer even had to admit what they were doing—not even to themselves.[38]

In 1966, while the US was still assisting in the extermination of Indonesia's leftists, Nkrumah was deposed in a military coup backed by the United States and Britain. The role of the CIA is still unclear; it is established, however, that the coup plotters had trained in the United Kingdom. Nkrumah took refuge in Guinea, then led by Third World movement ally Ahmed Sékou Touré.

By the end of the 1960s, it was safe to say that the Third World movement was in disarray, if not destroyed. The "Bandung Spirit" had become a ghost. The leaders of the progressive wing of the postcolonial movement were gone: Nehru had died in 1964; Sukarno was languishing in Indonesia as his allies bled out, waiting to die soon himself; Ghana's Nkrumah and Burma's U Nu had been deposed in military coups. Many of Iraq's leftists were already dead, and US-backed Saddam Hussein would finish them off soon; Egypt's Nasser had been weakened by the collapse of the United Arab Republic following a coup in Damascus, whose leaders in turn purged the Syrian Communist Party.

Living in Guinea, Nkrumah came to a new conclusion about the nature of neocolonialism. Given the state of the world, and considering the success of Western imperialism, the only path to revolution was protracted guerrilla struggle.[39]

As Vijay Prashad, director of the Tricontinental Institute, put it, "The destruction of the Left had an enormous impact on the Third World. The most conservative, even reactionary social classes attained dominance over the political platform created in Bandung. As an adjunct to the military regimes, the political forces that emerged rejected the ecumenical anticolonial nationalism of the Left and the liberals for a cruel cultural nationalism that emphasized racialism, religion, and hierarchy."[40] Or, in the words of German historian Christian Gerlach, speaking about the body that had probably been the best global forum for advancing the Third World movement: by 1971, "a murderer like [Indonesian Foreign Minister] Adam Malik could even become President of the UN General Assembly."[41]

Chile

In 1964, the Christian Democratic Party easily won presidential elections in Chile, one of Latin America's most stable and prosperous nations. The Christian Democrats were the party favored by Washington—and the CIA—and they received very significant help from Uncle Sam.

The Agency pumped $3 million into that election. That came out to almost a dollar per vote for Eduardo Frei, more than Lyndon Johnson spent in his own 1964 campaign.[42] In addition to funds, the CIA also delivered a crude "scare campaign" to the Chilean people.[43] The Agency made extensive use of the press, radio, films, pamphlets, and posters, and painted the walls of the cities. One red-baiting radio ad featured the sound of a machine gun operated by murderous communists, followed by a woman declaring, "They have killed my child!" There were up to twenty radio spots of this kind per day.[44]

The CIA also distributed disinformation and "black propaganda," falsely attributing materials to the Communist Party.[45]

Chile had been a stable democracy since 1932, and Frei was no dictator. He initiated a modest land reform program, made efforts to bring regular people into the educational system, and made taxation a bit more progressive. This long, thin country on South America's cold Pacific coast was nothing like Guatemala, where the generals ruled through terror, or even most of its neighbors closer to home, which were periodically rocked by military coups. It was Latin America, yes; inequality was rampant, and the racial hierarchy was obvious to any visitor, but many middle-class Chileans remember the 1960s as a pleasant time. Supporters of the second-place finisher that year—Salvador Allende—and other leftists in the country believed that a move toward socialism could happen Chilean-style, without much fuss or trouble, and help the country to develop on more equal terms. But the virulence of the 1964 campaign had been a shock.

Carmen Hertz was nineteen, studying at the University of Chile, and she and her friends understood very well how strongly Washington opposed Allende and his assorted allies. Growing up in a strict, well-off, and conservative home, with afternoon tea more reminiscent of the England of *Mary Poppins* than the mountains of Cuba, she arrived at college in braids, and sixteen years old.[46] She had been sympathetic to the right-leaning Liberal Party while living at home, but a growing social consciousness pushed her to the left, and her personality had always been a bit radical and confrontational.

There were two left-wing groups active around her at the time. On the one side was the Communist Party (PCCh). Its members were more conservative, in every sense of the word. Short hair, moral rectitude, and discipline were their identifying characteristics. They represented one of the more important communist parties in the world, one with its mass base in the working class, tightly disciplined and maintaining good relations with Moscow. They followed the Soviet line on Latin America at the time, and so insisted that the left should participate in elections and work within the democratic system, bourgeois or not, that Chile had.

The other group, *Movimiento de Izquierda Revolucionaria* (MIR), was new, and very much a creation of the 1960s. Its members were more bohemian. And they looked not to boring old Brezhnev but to Che Guevara, inspired by his model of guerrilla warfare and the lessons he learned in Guatemala in 1954. They thought the road to democratic socialism was a trap, and they worried they would be swallowed up by reactionary forces before they could get halfway there. They told the Communists, no, the only way is armed resistance.

Both sides noticed what had happened in Indonesia. Orlando Millas, a Communist Party official, had visited Jakarta recently, and spoke at length with Aidit about their worries that Washington was planning something against them.[47] Both leftist groups, the PCCh and the MIR, were horrified to hear about a massacre on a scale they considered impossible in Latin America. The leftists at Carmen's university were united in thinking that the future belonged to them, and that they would win soon. But it was the members of MIR who seized upon the violence in Indonesia to make their point about tactics.

Carmen remembers her radical friends saying, "You see what happens if you leave yourselves vulnerable?"

In 1966, the MIR newspaper, *Punto Final*, published a text attributed to philosopher Bertrand Russell. "I fear that the horror of the killings in Indonesia was only possible because in the West we are so saturated with racism that the death of Asians, even in the hundreds of thousands, doesn't impress us. Blacks in North America know it well," the article continued. "Knowing the same thing, the peoples of the world should take the path of open struggle."[48] *Punto Final* also published a guide to CIA activities in Indonesia, the Congo, Vietnam, and Brazil.[49] The paper got some details wrong; but just as was the case when *Harian Rakyat* covered Guatemala in 1954, Chile's leftwing press described events in Indonesia more accurately than the mainstream US press at the time.

While she studied at the University of Chile, Carmen was more sympathetic to the MIR than to the Communist Party, though she had a verbal sparring partner in Carlos Berger, a wild soccer fan who had been a disciplined, polite Communist Party member since he was fourteen. He was a man of incredible integrity, she realized—that is, in the old-school Communist way. He was totally devoted to the cause, to moral living. Nothing was for himself—everything was for a bigger cause.

The events in Indonesia would be a point in the MIR's favor in those ideological debates, Carmen thought. The violence did seem to support the MIR position, just as the 1954 coup in Guatemala had been proof for Che that peaceful revolution wasn't possible. Still, the Communist Party remained unconvinced; it wasn't the 1950s anymore, and this was mature Chile, the thinking went, not Central America or a little island in the Caribbean. Allende himself had become more radical after he heard about what happened in Guatemala in 1954.[50] But like Carlos and the Communist Party, he believed in Chile's institutions.

Thailand

In 1965, Benny was living in Bangkok. After finishing his studies so close to all those generals in Kansas, he went on to get his PhD in economics at the University of Texas, and then landed a job with the United Nations.

Thailand was a reliably pro-Western country, so that was where the regional UN headquarters were located. It was also where the CIA was based in the region, and the KGB had some agents there too. Both groups kept asking Benny out for food or drinks, perhaps trying to get information from him, or to feel him out as a possible asset. Benny would go, and just engage in small talk, entirely bemused by the whole thing.[51]

The CIA man who kept asking Benny to lunch was named Allan Fuehrer, which was hilarious to Benny and his UN colleagues, because, well, that's literally what Hitler was called. What made Benny laugh even more was that the CIA and the KGB men seemed not to know what his job was or what he could do for them. He was on the economics side of UN activities, and had nothing to do with the political work, so they would be wasting their time even if he had any interest in helping them. Which he did not.

Benny also watched as Bangkok slowly began to turn into a destination for sex tourism—American soldiers would visit for their "rest and recreation" breaks from the war in Vietnam. The steady inflow of GIs transformed parts of the city into a kind of factory row for prostitution.

Benny overheard those men talking about what they were doing back in Vietnam. There was a bar, Rendezvous, where the pilots would come and get drunk, and they'd just let it rip. "I dropped a load of fucking bombs on that village," they'd say, as soon as they fell into the chairs. The world didn't quite know yet, but Benny knew just from hanging out at Rendezvous that some-thing very disturbing was beginning to take place to his east. The pilots were clearly describing indiscriminate bombing and the massacre of civilians.

Benny first heard about the September 30th Movement on Radio Aus-tralia, which means—as he would find out only later—he actually heard a version broadcast by a station actively assisting in a psychological warfare campaign against the PKI. He was sitting in the garden with his wife, who was pregnant with their second child.

Later, a man from the embassy came to ask him some questions. Did he know anything about Jakarta? What did he think? He didn't know anything, he said. He really didn't.

As things worsened back home, Indonesians all around the world were being forced to declare their allegiances, and Benny's Chinese heritage made the new government doubly suspicious. His wife was also part of an Indo-nesian women's group, a semicompulsory organization of Indonesian wives and UN workers living abroad who supported Sukarno's causes, such as his conflict with Malaysia.

Benny was called in to the embassy for interrogation. The question was very simple.

"Who are your best friends in Jakarta?"

Benny had to be strategic now. He had always been opposed to com-munism, but never anti-Sukarno. He figured he knew exactly what to say to these interrogators. He gave them the names of rich, well-connected Catholic Indonesians who were forming an anticommunist nucleus around Suharto. He knew them from his days at the expensive private school he had attended, and figured they would vouch for him.

It worked. He was allowed to get back to work at the UN. But in 1968, a military attaché in Bangkok contacted Benny with a friendly warning. The name he was born with, Hong Lan Oei, was too Chinese. Suharto had sev-ered relations with China and banned all Chinese-language materials in In-donesia. Even Chinese characters were banned. The government had passed legislation strongly recommending that Chinese Indonesians drop names of Chinese origin. Benny had gotten away with keeping his own name on his passport for a while, because he was outside the country and working at the UN. But he had two options. Either he would drop his family name, or he would be subjected to periodic harassment and interrogation.

Like so many Indonesians of Chinese descent, he picked a Javanese-sounding last name. From then on, he was officially Benny Widyono.

In 1967, Southeast Asian nations came together in Bangkok to launch a new organization, called ASEAN. Previously, only the Philippines, the Federation of Malaya, and Thailand—all Western-facing conservative powers—made up a group called the Association of Southeast Asia. But now, with Suharto in power in Indonesia, the region's largest country and young Singapore joined them to form the Association of Southeast Asian Nations. A few things united them—authoritarian developmentalism, close ties with Washington, and, most importantly, anticommunism.[52]

In the 1970s, Thailand's government would kill thousands of people in its own anticommunist purge.[53]

Cuba

In 1963, President Sukarno had sent his old friend A. M. Hanafi to Havana, to serve as Indonesia's first ambassador to Cuba in the age of Fidel Castro. He wasn't a communist, but he was a committed revolutionary, loyal to the president since the days of the struggle against the Dutch back in the 1940s. He got along well with Fidel and Che, and his family settled into a luxurious neighborhood on the Caribbean coast.

His daughter, Nury, was seventeen.[54] She was impressed. Havana was more modern, more elegant than Jakarta. She was amazed to see that some of the grand houses in her neighborhood were filled with young students. "How lucky!" she thought. She couldn't believe that youngsters like her would be allowed to live here, and spend all day just studying like this. She only found out later, as she began her own studies in Cuba, that this part of the city had served as the "*bordel* of the United States," a vacation paradise for playboys and mafia types, and that the houses had been reclaimed by the revolution. That explained a lot.

As a child back in Jakarta, she had intimately felt the effects of political conflict. One of the attempts to assassinate Sukarno—maybe carried out by the Islamists? By the CIA? Who knew?—consisted of throwing a grenade into Nury's school, in the downtown neighborhood of Cikini, as he was visiting one day. Things felt a lot calmer in Cuba, at least in her corner of town.

Her father, now Ambassador Hanafi, was planning the Tricontinental Conference, an ambitious expansion of the Bandung project, set for January 1966. Then, while he was away for business, Nury heard about the events in Jakarta of October 1, 1965. Hanafi didn't return as planned. Nury and her family only got patches of information, before learning that he had gone to visit Sukarno at the palace in Bogor. Suharto, now effectively in power, made Hanafi an offer in an attempt to get him to join his new government. He refused, saying that Sukarno had posted him to Cuba as ambassador, and that was the mission he was going to carry out.

At least, that's what he told Nury and the family when he arrived back in Havana. Not long after, his job disappeared, because the embassy in Havana disappeared. He and his whole family lost their Indonesian passports.

Fidel, of course, understood. He and Che had built their entire revolution on the premise that Washington could strike to destroy Third World governments at any time, and he had survived countless attempts on his own life. He was hardly surprised that the ambassador and his family were stranded in Havana by the forces of imperialism. Even though Hanafi had lost his job and diplomatic protection, Fidel stepped in, gave them a nice house in the exclusive neighborhood of Cubanacán, and found Hanafi a job giving lectures on Asian history and the Indonesian revolution.

The Tricontinental Conference, officially called the Solidarity Conference of the Peoples of Africa, Asia, and Latin America, did take place in Havana in January 1966, without the participation of the country that spearheaded the Third World movement. In attendance, however, was Salvador Allende, the Chilean socialist and supporter of the Third World movement, who had been the presidential runner-up to Frei in the 1964 election.[55]

Nury lost contact with her family and all her friends back in Jakarta; she and her father were considered communists now, and it was dangerous for anyone from their old life to speak with them. She settled into a life in Havana.

Taiwan

The Republic of China, the state set up by Chiang Kai-shek's Nationalists in Taiwan, still insisted on its claim to mainland China and had long been home to active anticommunist crusaders. The small dictatorship run from

Taipei paid close attention to the massacre in Indonesia, sponsoring attacks on the Chinese embassy in Jakarta as a way to weaken both Sukarno and Mao's regime in Beijing.[56]

In 1966, Taiwan and South Korea—still run by Park Chung Hee, the dictator installed with the help of Marshall Green before Green took over for Howard Jones as US ambassador in Indonesia—came together to found the World Anti-Communist League (WACL).[57] Congressman Walter Judd and US religious figures flew out to attend the first meeting.[58] The new global organization, built on a structure provided by the existing Asian People's Anticommunist League, brought together moderate conservatives as well as far-right radical groups that had carried out atrocities for Hitler in World War II in countries like Romania and Croatia.[59] It would go on to hold yearly conferences around the world, allowing its members to exchange support, intelligence, and tips for the rest of the Cold War, and was now—alongside the Brazil-founded Tradition, Family, and Property organization—one of two such anticommunist organizations with global reach.

The WACL also began to recruit students for the Political Warfare Cadres Academy, in the Beitou district in Taipei. Like military academies set up by the United States, the Beitou school began to train soldiers for the global anticommunist struggle.

Hawaii

In 1965, just after he retired from the State Department and left Indonesia, former Ambassador Howard Jones took over as chancellor at the East-West Center at the University of Hawaii. He kept in contact with the embassy and watched as the situation deteriorated rapidly, but had no more control over events.

There at the East-West Center in Honolulu, a young Indonesian employee of the Armed Forces named Lolo Soetoro met and fell in love with an American anthropologist. He wasn't a soldier, but he worked for the military's topographical service, and had won a grant to study geography in Hawaii. He was a short, handsome man, from a big Javanese family that had felt the violence of colonialism. In Indonesia's revolutionary war, the Dutch killed his father and brother, then burned their house down.

In March 1965, Lolo married Ann Dunham, and became the stepfather to her son from a previous marriage with a Kenyan economics student. But then in 1966, as Suharto solidified his control over the country, Lolo was abruptly summoned back home, just like so many other Indonesians around the world. He obeyed, and over the next few months, Ann and her five-year-old son made preparations to go live with him as well.

Barack Obama's memories of life as a young boy in Jakarta from 1967 to 1971, published in his book *Dreams from My Father*, provide a vivid picture of life in the capital as Suharto's government, and the US State Department, attempted to move on from the violence they had just finished inflicting on the country.

The rule was silence. At first, neither young Barry, as he was then known, nor Ann knew why Lolo had come back, or the nature of his work. Barack Obama remembers that soon after they arrived, they were driving, and his mother used the word "Sukarno" in a sentence.

"Who's Sukarno?" Barry yelled from the backseat.

Lolo ignored the question.

He was working in West Papua, surveying the area that Sukarno had won from the Dutch with Kennedy's help just a few years before. Lolo would go on trips, Obama remembers, and come back with wild animals for his adventurous young stepson to admire.

But Ann and Barry both noticed that Lolo had changed since Hawaii: "It was as if he had pulled into some dark hidden place, out of reach, taking with him the brightest part of himself. On some nights, she would hear him up after everyone else had gone to bed, wandering through the house with a bottle of imported whiskey, nursing his secrets."

To busy herself, and fight the loneliness, Ann got a job at the embassy Howard Jones had left two years earlier. It was there she realized how ugly, and racist, the old white men working for her government could be. They'd insult the locals, until they realized she was married to one, and try to walk their comments back. She realized that some of these men, the occasional supposed "economist or journalist," would mysteriously disappear for months at a time, and it was never clear what these secretive men were really doing.

It was also there that she found out, very slowly, what had happened just before they arrived. "Over lunch or casual conversation, they would share with her things she couldn't learn in the published news reports," Obama wrote.

Innuendo, half-whispered asides; that's how she found out that we had arrived in [Jakarta] less than a year after one of the more brutal and swift campaigns of suppression in modern times. The idea frightened her, the notion that history could be swallowed up so completely, the same way the rich and loamy earth could soak up the rivers of blood that had once coursed through the streets; the way people could continue about their business beneath giant posters of the new president as if nothing had happened . . .

The more she found out, the more she asked Lolo, and the more frustrated she became as he refused to answer. Finally, one of his cousins explained the situation, and told her to try to be understanding.

"You shouldn't be too hard on Lolo," the cousin said. "Such times are best forgotten."

They grew further apart as he took a new job, working for Unocal, the US energy company. She didn't want to go to his company dinner parties, where Texas oilmen bragged about bribing officials and their wives complained about the quality of the Indonesian help. It became clear to her, and to him, that they were American, and privileged in a way Lolo was not, and that as a result he was bound to a life that maybe they did not want. Ann could speak out, knowing she would never lose her American citizenship or the comforts back home. But Lolo was constantly forced into painful moral dilemmas; people in his world were forced either to stay silent and try to get ahead in life, or to speak up and face the risk of poverty, starvation, even death. She couldn't stay there anymore.

Once, before they returned to Hawaii, Barry had the idea of asking Lolo if he had ever seen a man killed:

He glanced down, surprised by the question.

"Have you," I asked again.

"Yes," he said.

"Was it bloody?"

"Yes."

I thought for a moment. "Why was the man killed? The one you saw?"

"Because he was weak."

"That's all?"

Lolo shrugged and rolled his pant leg back down. "That's usually enough. Men take advantage of weakness in other men. They're just like countries in that way. The strong man takes the weak man's land. He makes the weak man work in his fields. If the weak man's woman is pretty, the strong man will take her." He paused to take another sip of water, then asked, "Which would you rather be?"[60]

9

Jakarta Is Coming

Paradigm Shift

The governments established in Brazil in 1964 and in Indonesia in 1965 were not Washington's perfectly obedient servants. They remained nationalist, in a way, and pushed back, at times, against the United States. Nor were they "neoliberal" in the sense that word is used today. The state remained significantly involved in the economy and attempted to guide national "development." They were simply capitalist—well, a certain type of capitalist—authoritarian regimes, well integrated into the expanding Western system.

But they sure had a lot in common, and these two anticommunist dictatorships were the best allies that Washington's foreign interventions had ever created. Things worked out so well that the US government and its allies began to use them as a model. Brazil, the largest country in Latin America, began working with the gringos to fight communism and create copycat regimes in its neighborhood. Indonesia, the largest country in Southeast Asia, would use anticommunism as an excuse to expand its influence eastward with Washington's approval, and the leader of Southeast Asia's second-largest country soon used a script similar to Suharto's in order to consolidate his own right-wing dictatorship.

Both military dictatorships, Brazilian and Indonesian, would quibble with Washington over this or that economic issue or foreign policy decision, but the big questions were settled. They were in the Western camp, and fiercely opposed to communist expansion. They were porous to international investment, and happy to export raw materials to rich countries under the existing terms governing the international economy. They certainly were not trying to rewrite the rules of the global economy, or use the power of a unified Third World to shift influence back to the majority of the world's peoples, to those who had been structurally disadvantaged by centuries of colonialism. They took advice from Western advisers and US-trained economists. In Indonesia, this was the "Berkeley Mafia," a set of economists trained at the University of California who worked with Suharto.[1] In Brazil, the coup was aided by the conspiring and propagandizing of the US-funded *Instituto de Pesquisas e Estudos Sociais* (Research and Social Studies Institute), which remained active under the dictatorship until 1972.

Both regimes were strongly influenced by Modernization Theory. And both countries began to experience economic growth. That was almost entirely sucked up by a small elite, but the GDP growth counted to foreign investors, and they could be sold as success stories. And in both cases, the countries had stable governments made up of local rulers who could trace their legitimacy to some Brazilian or Indonesian past, rather than appearing to their populations and the world as the obvious imposition of Washington.

In the long term, this was all much better than what had been created in Guatemala or Iran in the 1950s. Guatemala had plunged into a brutal civil war. Iran's government alienated its neighbors and much of the population, and this would explode very dramatically in Washington's face in the next decade.

Both Indonesia and Brazil were anticommunist dictatorships, and this doesn't only have consequences on the international stage. Internally, when anticommunism is the ruling ideology, almost the national religion, any legitimate complaint from below can easily be dismissed as communist. Anything that would be an obvious inconvenience to the small clique of rich families that run the country can be easily categorized as dangerous revolution, and cast aside. This includes any whiff of socialism or social democracy, any land reform, and any regulation that would reduce monopoly power and allow for more efficient development and market competition. It includes unions and any normal demands for workers' rights.

No one seriously pretended Brazil or Indonesia was a democracy. But this is not how capitalism is supposed to work, either—this arrangement may be just as far from the system that economics textbooks describe as Soviet society was from the sketches of socialism provided by Karl Marx. In capitalism, feudal lords are not supposed to be running much of the country as their own personal fiefdoms. Market inefficiencies—like massive corruption—are supposed to disappear as the result of competition. There is supposed to be a give-and-take between the various elements in the economy. There is supposed to be space for new and innovative firms to emerge, challenge entrenched interests, and diversify national production. But in the system set up in Brazil and Indonesia, the logic of survival required people to attach themselves to a corrupt, rapacious, and wasteful apparatus at the top of society or risk falling down into the abyss themselves, and become a poorly paid worker in the extraction machine.

Young Barack Obama had seen what this dynamic did to his stepfather. "Guilt is a luxury only foreigners can afford," Lolo told Barack's mother. Lolo did understand. "She didn't know what it is like to lose everything, to wake up and feel her belly eating itself . . . without absolute concentration, one could easily slip, tumble backward."[2]

There's a term that broadly describes this kind of economic arrangement. The people of Indonesia and Brazil lived under "crony capitalism."

This was a very different reality from that of Washington's European, capitalist allies. Francisca and her family arrived in Holland in 1968, and saw immediately how different Western Europe's dynamic, successful societies were from the Suharto regime.

The Communist Party had won a few seats in the most recent Dutch election, and participated in Parliament. In France and Italy, the communist parties aligned with Moscow were still major players. The PCF—*Parti Communiste Français*—got more than 20 percent of the vote in 1967 and formed parliamentary opposition with the Socialists and Radicals.[3] The Italian Communists had gotten second place in the previous election, and held solid chunks of the country as their loyal base. In West Germany, there was no influential communist party. But the main center-left party, the second-place Social Democrats, was founded as a Marxist party while Marx was still alive, and its leaders had chosen a more moderate path than the Leninists because of their success working within capitalist democracy.

The last time Francisca had seen Western Europe, just after the war, it was very different. Back in the 1940s, access to meat and butter was strictly limited, and everyone was scrambling to rebuild their lives. In the 1960s it was just, rich and relaxed. The region's economies had been rebuilt along more American lines thanks to the Marshall Plan. But these were not fanatically anticommunist nations when it came to their own affairs. Certainly not as much as the US, and nowhere near as much as Indonesia or Brazil. Even though the supposed Red Menace was just a few miles to the east, ready to swallow them up, Western Europeans were far less afraid of it than the United States, sitting half a world away.

It was very clear to Francisca why Europeans were allowed to experiment with social democracy and even communist politics, while her country had been taken away from her forever.

"Racism, very simply. White Europeans are offered tolerance and sympathetic treatment, while we are not."

When Frank Wisner and Howard Jones were working to re-engineer West Germany's financial system after World War II, the US government wiped out all public and private debt as they created the new deutsche mark. One shudders to think how a major Third World leader perceived as anti-American or "communist" would have been treated if his country tried the same thing after a war of independence.

In Western Europe's capitalist democracies, moderate and radical left-wing parties alike served as constant critics of the economic order from within the system without ever taking it over entirely. Of course, the CIA was still active in Europe, scheming in ways we still don't really understand. The Operation Gladio "stay-behind" networks that grew out of Wisner's early days continued into the 1980s. But when European governments shifted too far right for citizens, voters shifted to the parties on the left, and vice versa, and that was allowed.

Why did Cold War Washington let Western Europe "get away" with all this light socialism when similar policy orientations led to violent intervention in the Third World? Was it only that, as Francisca said, Americans simply trusted their European cousins—who were white, and therefore responsible—to handle the task of managing democracy? A complementary explanation might be that these countries, some still overseeing remnants of colonial empire, were incredibly rich and powerful. They were much harder to push around, even if Washington had wanted to, and—perhaps more importantly—they sat at the top of the world economy. They were being fully integrated into the US-led system, and so there was much less of a risk they would try to radically reshape the global order, because it had served them quite well.

There was no opposition allowed in Brazil or Indonesia, however, which meant that elites could get away with everything. Venality and violence ruled the day in Jakarta and Brasília. With a population too terrified to speak up, corruption exploded. In the early days of the Suharto regime, US oil executives bragged that they were taking advantage of exactly those dynamics as they dined in front of Barack Obama's mother. His government, along with the US-backed Mobutu regime in the Congo, would go on to set world-historical records for corruption.[4] Of course, the regime that Suharto set up was founded on mass violence. And by the late 1960s, Indonesia was operating a system of US-supported concentration camps comparable to the worst years of the Soviet Union.[5]

But Brazil slid toward state terror slowly. When General Castelo Branco took over in 1964, he had the backing of large portions of the old political order, but it slowly became clear that his real base of support was in the barracks and the boardrooms. In order to survive, he couldn't turn his back on the reactionary forces in the military or on the business class—both of which were making demands that required more forceful, long-term dictatorship to fulfill. But he could afford to alienate the more moderate forces that supported the 1964 coup believing there would be new elections soon. The generals and the capitalists, who wanted radical anticommunism and steady profits, were the only thing propping up the government now that democracy was gone, and politics was reduced to its most base elements. The nice liberals and the democrats could be ignored.

So they were. Over the next few years, a series of "Institutional Acts" consolidated power in the hands of the generals and brought back indirect elections, meaning that Congress simply selected the president. Again, the Soviet-aligned Communist Party took a very moderate line compared to the other forces on the left. The Brazilian Communist Party (PCB) called for a united coalition of all the country's forces that were now opposed to the dictatorship, including those that had initially supported the 1964 coup, to press for "democratic freedoms." Asking for anything more, including any kind of socialism in the short term, was irresponsible and reckless, "adventurism and petty bourgeois haste," according to the Brazilian Communists.[6]

It was groups of soldiers and students who looked to Che Guevara and Havana, rather than Brezhnev and Moscow, that took more radical actions in 1965–1968 and spooked the regime.[7] The PCB remained nonviolent. Right-wing extremists did not; they carried out a series of bombings, which were blamed on the left, with the goal of prolonging and radicalizing the military dictatorship.[8]

The generals proclaimed AI-5, or Institutional Act Number Five, in December 1968, giving the military leaders even more power, imposing censorship, and suspending constitutionally guaranteed rights in the name of "national security." Thus began the Brazilian *anos de chumbo*, or "years of lead," which meant torture and murder. The worst years of Brazil's dictatorship were largely overseen by Emílio Garrastazu Médici, a hard-line *gaúcho* general who took over the presidency in 1969.[9]

In the first years of the military dictatorship, students, artists, and intellectuals could still protest the regime, and violent repression was reserved for union leaders and the organized left. In the *anos de chumbo*, from 1969 to 1974, all that changed. Anyone could be suspected of being a "subversive" and taken off to a basement in São Paulo or Rio de Janeiro for rounds of torture that might end in death. In addition to their constant contact with the US government, soldiers learned techniques that the French had developed in Algeria, like the use of electric shocks.[10]

Médici's forces largely concentrated their efforts on suspected members of Brazil's small urban guerrilla movements, often young Marxists drawn from the educated middle classes who hoped to overthrow the dictatorship. In 1970, they arrested a young woman of Bulgarian descent. Dilma Rousseff later testified that they tortured her for weeks, hanging her upside down from a stick in a technique known as the "parrot's perch," beating teeth out of her head, and applying electric shocks.[11]

The military also put down a small rural rebellion, in the Araguaia River Basin, organized by the Maoist PCdoB, the new communist party that had split off from the PCB in 1962 and took inspiration from both Che Guevara and the communists in the Chinese Civil War.[12]

Brazil's military suppressed its internal opposition with relative ease, and never turned to mass violence on the scale employed in Indonesia or other Latin American countries. But the terror was very real. Paulo Coelho, now a famous author, remembers clearly what happened to those who fell on the wrong side of the law. It happened to him. A group of armed men broke into his apartment, he recalls:

They start going through drawers and cabinets—but I don't know what they're looking for, I'm just a rock songwriter. One of them, more gentle, asks that I accompany them "just to clarify some things." The neighbor sees all this and warns my family, who immediately panic. Everyone knew what Brazil was living at the time, even if it wasn't covered in the newspapers. . . .

On the way, the taxi is blocked by two cars—a man with a gun in his hand exits from one of the cars and pulls me out. I fall to the ground, and feel the barrel of the gun in the back of my neck. I look at a hotel in front of me and think, "I can't die so soon." I fall into a kind of catatonic state: I don't feel afraid, I don't feel anything. I know the stories of other friends who have disappeared; I will disappear, and the last thing I will see is a hotel. The man picks me up, puts me on the floor of his car and tells me to put on a hood.

The car drives around for maybe half an hour. They must be choosing a place to execute me—but I still don't feel anything, I've accepted my destiny. The car stops. I'm dragged out and beaten as I'm pushed down what appears to be a corridor. I scream, but I know no one is listening, because they are also screaming. Terrorist, they say. You deserve to die. You're fighting against your country. You're going to die slowly, but you're going to suffer a lot first. Paradoxically, my instinct for survival begins to kick in little by little.

I'm taken to the torture room with a raised floor. I stumble on it because I can't see anything: I ask them not to push me, but I get punched in the back and fall down. They tell me to take off my clothes. The interrogation begins with questions I don't know how to answer. They ask me to betray people I have never heard of. They say I don't want to cooperate, throw water on the floor and put something on my feet—then I see from underneath the hood that it is a machine with electrodes that are then attached to my genitals.

Now I understand that, in addition to the blows I can't see coming (and therefore can't even contract my body to cushion the impact of), I'm about to get electric shocks. I tell them they don't have to do this—I'll confess whatever they want me to confess, I'll sign whatever they want me to sign. But they are not satisfied. Then, in desperation, I begin to scratch my skin, tearing off pieces of myself. The torturers must have been frightened when they saw me covered in my own blood; they leave me alone. They say I can take off the hood when I hear the door slam. I take it off and see that I'm in a soundproof room, with bullet holes on the walls. That explains the raised floor.[13]

The modern defenders of Brazil's dictatorship protest that the generals "only" killed hundreds of people. But it was not through internal suppression that Brazil had the biggest impact on the mass murder programs that shaped the world we occupy today. In the early 1970s, under Médici, Brazil began intervening across South America, creating brutal regimes in its own neighborhood that also served Washington's interests.

As Tanya Harmer, the historian who has looked most closely at this short, influential but often-forgotten period, notes:

> The Brazilian dictatorship's body count is relatively low when compared to Chile or Argentina, but it was abroad that it had the most devastating impact on the intensification of the Cold War both through its example, its interference in other countries' domestic politics, and its support for counter-revolutionary coups. Brazil's experience in and after 1964 was a game changer that shaped the way in which the ideological battles of the 1970s were conceptualized and fought thereafter.

Brazil helped establish violent anticommunist regimes in Bolivia and Uruguay. By 1976, much of South America was a "killing zone" of US-backed regimes on its borders, which had employed Brazil as its "prototype."[14] But Brasília's most notable right-wing foreign intervention took place over on the west coast of South America, in pacific Chile.

Allende Arrives, Barely

In 1970, Salvador Allende ran for office again in Chile, and again the CIA financed a scare campaign. Henry Kissinger, national security advisor to

President Richard Nixon, approved the use of hundreds of thousands of dollars for a political warfare mission. "I don't see why we need to stand by and watch a country go communist due to the irresponsibility of its own people," Kissinger said.[15] The Agency fed propaganda to prominent reporters, and got a story on the cover of *Time* that was heavily influenced by its materials. In Chile, the CIA relied heavily on *El Mercurio*, a right-wing paper that received Agency funding, and paid for posters, pamphlets, and messages painted on walls across the city.[16]

The efforts failed. Allende's *Unidad Popular* coalition won by a slim margin. A few days later, *El Mercurio* published a large special on Brazil. One headline read: "Brazil—Tomorrow Is Today."[17] Over the next few months, the Brazilian military began plotting ways to help roll back socialism in Chile.

Allende was both a socialist and an urbane member of Santiago's elite. He was a Marxist intellectual who enjoyed sipping red wine in silk tweed jackets. He admired Fidel Castro and considered him a close friend, but he thought the Chilean road to socialism could be very different. He'd work within the system, and take advantage of a Cold War truce between Washington and Moscow, which he thought opened up space for *la vía Chilena*, the peaceful "Chilean way" to socialism.

When Richard Nixon was elected, he had sought "détente" with the Soviet Union, and as a result the two superpowers pretended to ignore ideological disagreements with each other. But as it turned out, the truce didn't apply to the Third World.[18]

The chaos and violence in Chile was not caused by President Salvador Allende, or the failures of his democratic socialist project. US-backed right-wing terrorism began before he even took office.

Under Chilean law, Congress had to ratify Allende's election, since he had not won an outright majority. Under Chilean custom, this was a formality. Nixon viewed it differently; he ordered the head of the CIA to find a way to stop Allende from taking over. Richard Helms emerged from the meeting with Nixon's orders written on a notepad:

> *1 in 10 chance perhaps, but save Chile! . . .*
> *$10,000,000 available, more if necessary . . .*
> *best men we have*
> *make the economy scream*[19]

While Allende was waiting to take office in 1970, the CIA opened up activities on two "tracks" in Chile. Track One was political warfare, economic pressure, propaganda, and diplomatic maneuvers. CIA agents tried to bribe Chilean politicians and terrify the population. If all that failed, they would "condemn Chile to utmost deprivation and poverty," Ambassador Edward Korry told Kissinger, hopefully "forcing Allende to adopt the harsh features of a police state."[20] They wanted Allende to abandon democracy. Track Two was a military coup. The CIA began conspiring with right-wing military officers, and funding a group of radicals that would grow into *Pátria y Libertad*, an anticommunist terrorist group known for its hideous geometric spider logo and sympathies with fascism.[21]

Like Frank Wisner's early forays into Eastern Europe, or the 1958 bombing of Indonesia, the 1970 CIA operation in Chile ended in total disaster.

René Schneider, commander in chief of Chile's Armed Forces, was a *constitucionalista*, which meant that he believed the military should never overstep its constitutional role. Allende had won the election, so he should be president. Schneider was strongly opposed to a military coup that would stop that from happening. His stance on this was so uncompromising that it became known as the "Schneider Doctrine." It also meant, as far as the CIA and its right-wing conspirators were concerned, he had to go. On October 25, 1970, a group of armed men tried to kidnap him, and killed him in the process. The plan was to blame the whole thing on left-wing Allende supporters, and therefore provide the justification for an anticommunist military coup.[22]

For placid, democratic Chile, this was a moment of unimaginable national trauma.[23] Terrorists had murdered the head of the Armed Forces in the attempt to subvert an election.

Things did not go exactly according to CIA plan. Schneider probably wasn't supposed to be killed. Maybe the wrong group carried out the wrong plan at the wrong time. At first, the Agency didn't even know which of their local partners had done it.[24] Most importantly, everyone in Chile found out who was really behind it. Instead of blaming the left, they correctly held right-wing terrorists responsible, and Chile's military rallied even more enthusiastically around the *constitucionalista* position. Allende was going to be president.

But it's hard to avoid the nagging question: what if they had succeeded? What if they convincingly blamed some radical leftists, supporters of Allende, for carrying out a violent kidnapping, even when such an action was entirely unnecessary for them to take power? Would we still believe today that it was true? Would there be an anticommunist monument to Schneider in the center of Santiago, like the one in Jakarta?

Instead, this was one of the CIA's notorious failures. Nixon was furious. Allende took over as president on November 3, 1970. For Chile's young leftists, it was a moment of unimaginable euphoria. Carmen Hertz was aligned with the MIR, the younger, more radical contingent of Chilean leftists who did not officially believe in electoral politics. But she voted for Allende anyway, as so many of her friends did.

"It was fantastic. Like everyone else, we flooded the streets" when Allende's victory was announced, Carmen remembers. "When we finally came home we were full of hope and joy, even spiritual ecstasy."[25]

They had done it. And they would do it. Carmen remembers: "I was convinced—just like everyone I hung out with—that we were going to change the world."

Allende was a believer in the Third World movement, and many of his supporters believed that global revolution was imminent, and would be led by the Global South. Not long after Allende took power, Chile joined the Non-Aligned Movement and became increasingly active in Third World organizations.[26]

Fidel advised Allende against picking a fight with Washington, as did economist Orlando Letelier, a member of the so-called "elegant left" working at the Inter-American Development Bank. Castro also told Allende not to "ignite" continental revolution or incite the Yankees unnecessarily by being "too revolutionary"; for that reason, he did not attend Allende's inauguration.[27] Fidel knew it was best not to provoke the gringos.

As in Guatemala, it was clear what Washington really considered a threat in Chile. It was not an alliance with the Soviet Union—indeed, Allende went to Moscow and came back largely empty-handed.

The Soviets continued to view Latin America as Washington's sphere of influence, and they maintained their long-held orthodox view that revolution should progress gradually in the Western Hemisphere.[28] Allende had opposed aggressive Soviet moves in the international arena, and had condemned the 1956 invasion of Hungary and Moscow's 1968 intervention in Czechoslovakia.[29]

Washington was not worried that Chile's economy would be destroyed under irresponsible left-wing mismanagement either, or even that Allende would harm US business interests. What scared the most powerful nation in the world was the prospect that Allende's democratic socialism would succeed.

Just days after Allende was elected, President Nixon convened his National Security Council. Nixon said:

> Our main concern in Chile is . . . that [Allende] can consolidate himself, and the picture projected to the world will be his success. . . . If we let the potential leaders in South America think they can move like Chile and have it both ways, we will be in trouble. I want to work on this and on military relations—put in more money. On the economic side we want to give him cold Turkey [sic]. . . . We'll be very cool and very correct, but doing these other things which will be a real message to Allende and others. . . . No impression should be permitted in Latin America that they can get away with this.[30]

After Allende took office, the White House pushed for closer relations with Brazil as a way to counterbalance the perceived threat from Chile. Brazil was, at times, even more ferociously opposed to Allende than the United States. Brazil urged the US to get more involved in South American affairs, because they were working for the same goals.

In 1971, the year that Brazil's military began to "disappear" its own dissidents, Médici's dictatorship helped to overthrow the government in Bolivia and install right-wing General Hugo Banzer as dictator. Evidence indicates Brasília and Washington both supplied money and assistance for the August coup.

A few months later, Uruguay had an election. It appeared the left-leaning *Frente Amplio* coalition might win, so Brazil moved troops to the border and covertly interfered with the vote. Authorities handed the victory to the incumbent, right-leaning Colorado Party.[31]

At the very end of 1971, Médici met with Nixon in Washington. The Brazilian leader told the president his dictatorship was in contact with Chilean military officers and working to overthrow Allende. He told Nixon, "We should not lose sight of the situation in Latin America, which could blow up at any time." Médici said that Brazil could assist organizing a "million" Cuban exiles to fight back against Castro, and urged more action in South America. This was not because he thought the Russians were plotting something. Exactly the opposite. Médici was recorded as saying that "he did not believe that the Soviets or the Chinese were interested in giving any assistance to these countries' communist movements; they felt that communism would come all by itself because of the misery and poverty in these countries."

The problem for both men, in other words, was not an international communist conspiracy. The problem was that they thought the Soviets and Chinese might be right. The impoverished people in Brazil's neighboring countries might choose "communism" all by themselves, and they had to be stopped.

Nixon was very impressed with Médici. He privately told Secretary of State William Rogers that he wished Médici were "running the whole continent." Then, before the general left the United States, Nixon made a toast at a farewell banquet. He proclaimed: "Where Brazil goes, Latin America will follow."[32]

The same year, back in the United States, former Ambassador Howard P. Jones published his memoir on Indonesia, *The Possible Dream*, reflecting on the failures of US policy in Asia. It didn't make much of a splash. At the same time, the world was living through another anticommunist massacre. The Communist Party of Sudan, the largest of the remaining Bandung-era communist parties (in the 1960s, it was in third place, behind the parties in Indonesia and Iraq, both of which had since been annihilated), attempted a coup against a new regime that was trying to destroy it. When the coup failed, the Gaafar Nimeiry government liquidated the opposition: the order was to "destroy anyone who claims there is a Sudanese Communist Party." This didn't make much of a splash in the West, either.[33]

Operation Jakarta

As the Brazilian government collaborated with right-wing forces in Chile, the word "Jakarta" was put to new use. In both countries, the capital of Indonesia now had the same meaning.

Operação Jacarta, or "The Jakarta Operation," was the name of a secret part of an extermination plan, according to the documentation compiled by Brazil's Truth Commission. Testimony gathered after the fall of the dictatorship indicates *Operação Jacarta* may have been part of *Operação Radar*, which was aimed at destroying the structure of the Brazilian Communist Party. The goal of *Operação Jacarta* was the physical elimination of communists. It called for mass murder, just as in Indonesia. Before the Jakarta Operation, the dictatorship had aimed its violence at open rebellions. *Operação Jacarta* was a hidden plan to expand state terror to Communist Party members operating openly with civil society groups or in the media.[34]

The Brazilian public would not hear the words *Operação Jacarta* until three years later. But in Chile, the word "Jakarta" made a very public arrival.

Around Santiago, especially in the eastern part of the city—up in the hills, where the well-to-do people lived—someone began to plaster a message on the walls. It took a few forms.

"*Yakarta viene.*"

"*Jakarta se acerca.*"

That is: "Jakarta is Coming."

Or sometimes, simply, "Jakarta."

The events in Indonesia had been a part of right-wing discourse for years. Most significantly, Juraj Domic Kuscenic, a Croatian anticommunist who wrote in right-wing outlets like *El Mercurio* and had maintained close contact with *Pátria y Libertad* since 1970, had made frequent references to it since the 1960s.[35]

The first record of "Jakarta" appearing as a threat was in a January 1972 edition of *El Rebelde*, the official MIR newspaper. The cover asked, "What is Djakarta?" and on the inside showed a photo of the word slapped onto a wall. In a small article, "*La Via Indonesia de Los Fascistas Chilenos*," the paper attempted to explain what the message meant. The Indonesian Communist Party had played an active role in an "independent, progressive" state, and then—overnight—all that was left of its members was a "sea of blood."[36] At this point, not all of the left knew the Indonesian story, and the idea of a wave of violence here seemed far-fetched.

The second article on Jakarta came out in February 1972 in *Ramona*, a Communist Party youth magazine. It claimed that the right wing had adopted something called "Plan Djakarta," and said it had gotten the plan from David Rockefeller or Agustín Edwards (the owner of *El Mercurio*). "The Chilean extreme right wants to repeat that massacre," the article explained. "What does that mean concretely? The terrorists have a plan which consists of killing the entire Central Committee of the Communist Party, the top of the Socialist Party, the national directors of CUT, the *Central Unitaria de Trabajadores de Chile* union organization, leaders of social movements, and all prominent figures on the Left." The article was published on February 22, signed by Carlos Berger, the Communist Party member who had argued with Carmen Hertz about left-wing tactics and the meaning of the Indonesian massacre when she was back at the University of Chile.[37] Carlos and Carmen Hertz were now married.

Wall painting was a popular political device in Santiago in the early 1970s. On the left, volunteer collectives painted murals with elaborate images created by young artists inspired both by famous international muralists, such as Diego Rivera in Mexico, and by Chile's indigenous Mapuche culture. On the right, money pouring in from Washington or supplied by local elites was used to contract professional painters, who were both more efficient and less talented, because they were used to plastering simple advertising messages. Patricio "Pato" Madera, a founding member of the left-wing Ramona Parra Brigade of muralists, recognized the "Jakarta" graffiti as the handiwork of the same class of hired hands who had been painting right-wing slogans in recurring terror campaigns since 1964. But this was an escalation. It was a mass death threat.[38]

In addition to painting walls, they also sent out postcards. They arrived at the homes of officials in the left-wing government and Communist Party members.

Sometime in 1972, Carmen Hertz and her husband got one. The paper was thin and flimsy. On top, it said "Jakarta is Coming." On the bottom was the geometric spider, the *Pátria y Libertad* logo.

The terror campaign worked. Carmen and Carlos lived a life of twenty-four-hour anxiety. They were on permanent "maximum alert." All around them were sabotage, threats, and aggression. Only in her twenties, Carmen had been hired to work as a lawyer in the Allende government's land reform program, and had seen just how violent the opposition could be. In addition to party activities and journalism, Carlos helped with public relations at the Finance Ministry. They both suspected that Washington was intentionally wrecking the economy. And mindful of domestic threats, the two of them often slept at work. They would only stay at home now and then, and never for too many days in a row. In the streets, they'd often exchange words with members of *Tradición, Família y Propriedad* (TFP), the Chilean chapter of the anticommunist group founded in 1960 in Brazil. In Santiago, TFP youth would wear medieval-style tunics, and were often protesting in the streets, ready to yell at Carmen. But when she got the postcard—"*Yakarta se acerca*"—she felt even more in imminent danger.

After she read it, Carmen heard a loud pounding on her door. And then shouting: "*Comunista!*" She yelled back. She took her newborn baby, Germán, in her arms, grabbed a pistol hidden in the house, and ran to the street, pointing it back and forth wildly. She shot it into the sky. She only realized later, as her heart stopped pounding so loudly, that she was still holding on to Germán as she fired. She couldn't sleep at home that night, so she tried to flag down a bus to get to Carlos's childhood home. None came, so she walked down the chilly streets of Santiago, with the baby gripped tightly against her body.

The rifts in Chilean society split Carmen's own family down the middle. She knew that her mother, whom she loved, may have been more sympathetic to those right-wingers than she was to her own daughter. It was always patient Carlos who tried to mend their relationship, who always insisted on visiting Germán's grandmother, and tried to laugh and calm them down as they inevitably fought.[39]

But Carmen and Carlos thought history was on their side. They were at battle, yes—but they were playing by the rules, they had the people behind them, and so they thought they would win. They also believed the country was suffering from foreign sabotage, and on this count they were certainly right. The CIA, working with its far-right partners, was trying to ruin the economy, and doing its best to make it look like it was Allende's fault.

The most obvious problem for Allende's government was probably a nationwide strike in October 1972. Truckers—who were indirectly receiving funding from Washington—brought transportation to a halt, meaning regular people were left without basic supplies. Once the strike started, the CIA did its best to keep it going.[40]

It was not just economic sabotage, however. "Track two never really ended," said one CIA officer, meaning that since 1970, the Agency had never stopped looking for ways to organize a coup. The officer's notes from the time record Kissinger asking, "Since Allende is holding himself out as a moderate, why not support extremists?"[41]

The thing about destabilizing a country is you don't need surgical precision. A pretty big hammer works. Soon Chile was in chaos, and as a result

Allende was forced to skip his much-anticipated trip to the Conference of the Non-Aligned Movement in Algeria.[42]

But there were still two major problems. First, Allende would be in power for at least another three years, and the left still had plenty of support among the public. Still, the same circumstance had not stopped the coup in Brazil. The second problem, the real obstacle, was that Carlos Prats, the man who took over as head of the Armed Forces after René Schneider, was also a *constitucionalista*. He saw that there was an economic crisis, and that conservatives were clamoring for a military coup. But he was loyal to the Schneider Doctrine, and to democracy, so he refused to step outside of his legal role. Allende remained in power.

At the end of 1972, the world gained another anticommunist dictatorship. Since 1970, students had been protesting the government of Ferdinand Marcos in the Philippines, both for his blatant corruption and his government's collaboration with the US war in Vietnam. The Philippines was the site of Washington's largest experiment with direct colonial rule, and its independence had been carefully managed to keep Manila in the Western camp, ever since the CIA had defeated the left-nationalist *Huks* using terror and psychological warfare in 1954. US bases in the Philippines were used in 1958 when the CIA attempted to break up Indonesia. The right-wing Marcos, re-elected under slightly suspicious circumstances in 1968, and his wife, Imelda, were close friends of California Governor Ronald Reagan, who attended the gala opening of Imelda's lavish, multimillion-dollar Cultural Center.[43]

Some of the anti-Marcos students were followers of Communist José Maria "Joma" Sison, a Maoist literature professor inspired by Lumumba, Castro, and Western New Left intellectuals. Sison studied in Indonesia before the fall of Sukarno and came to the conclusion in 1965–66, just like Pol Pot, that the unarmed PKI had left itself too vulnerable. In 1968, he founded the Maoist Communist Party of the Philippines (CPP), which relied on guerrilla groups in the countryside rather than the open, mass party tactics the PKI employed. (Sison told me that what he saw in Indonesia in 1965 convinced him the CPP had to be armed and clandestine, and the party is active to this day.)[44]

But many of those anti-Marcos protesters were simply supporters of the centrist Liberal Party. Marcos himself was behind others. "Disorders must now be induced into a crisis so that stricter measures can be taken," he wrote. "A little more destruction and vandalism, and I can do anything."[45]

Marcos and his defense secretary, Juan Ponce Enrile, repeatedly warned of a communist threat. Then, on September 22, 1972, Enrile faked an attempt on his own life. He took a different car as gunmen lit up the car he was supposed to be in. He and Marcos, who helped plan the ruse, said God had saved him. Of course, they blamed the communists. They also claimed, on the same day, that all of this left them no choice but to declare martial law. Military units fanned out to arrest opposition leaders, the first of whom was the Liberal Party Senator Benigno Aquino Jr. Suharto already had an anticommunist ally in Marcos, but now he—and Washington—had a friendly authoritarian regime in Southeast Asia's second most-populous country. Marcos, with active US support, created his own version of crony capitalism with record-setting levels of corruption. He went on to kill thousands of people, often dumping their bodies in public in order to terrorize his enemies.[46]

Marineros Constitucionalistas

As 1973 started, Pedro Blaset was twenty-three, a working-class sailor in Chile's traditionally more upper-class, conservative Navy. He was lucky enough to hop on a cruiser trip to Switzerland for six months, and had missed much of the radicalization back home. In Europe, he and his shipmates were shocked at how liberally navies were organized in contrast to the strict, Prussian traditions in Chile. When he first entered the service, he was beaten, as a form of hazing. And when he and some friends celebrated Allende's victory in 1970, they were reprimanded. The deeply conservative naval officers, usually privately educated and self-consciously aristocratic, had not even liked the CIA-backed Eduardo Frei government much. As Blaset understood it, their main problem was that his modest reforms brought some members of the middle class into their elite schools, and their children were forced to study with their inferiors.

But when Pedro got back to Santiago in February 1973, things were different. The Navy was likely the most anticommunist branch of the military, and his colleagues weren't hiding their feelings. The high officers talked about their collaborations with the Brazilian embassy. They spoke about passing weapons to *Pátria y Libertad*. They savagely criticized Army leader Prats for his constitutionalist stance, especially after the left did well in the March elections. They began to talk, quite openly, about something called *"El Plan Yakarta."*

Pedro had heard tales about Jakarta before. Not long after he entered the Navy in 1966, sailors began trading horror stories from a particularly strange trip through Southeast Asia. They said they'd witnessed the carnage caused by an "extermination" program in the Indonesian capital. Stories about loose heads on spikes terrified the young sailors, as they took in tales of fantastical violence from a distant land.[47]

But when his superiors started talking about *El Plan Yakarta* in 1973, they were being very specific, and very serious. The plan was to kill around ten thousand people, the left and its core supporters, as a way of ensuring a stable transition to a right-wing government. Pedro and his friend Guillermo Castillo heard this being discussed on more than one boat.

"If we just put the Jakarta plan into place, kill ten or twenty thousand, then that's it," one officer said. "Then that's all the resistance and we win." Perhaps their superiors figured their underlings were on board with this kind of strategy, or at least respected the internal Navy hierarchy enough to keep quiet.

But this wasn't normal to low-ranking sailors. "Who are they talking about killing? Our families?" Pedro asked a few of his closest friends. "What happened to Chile while I was gone?"

They decided to meet up, form a small, clandestine *constitucionalista* group within the Navy, and talk about the situation. They figured their oath was to the country, not their immediate superiors, so they decided to pass a warning on to politicians.

They were discovered. Pedro and Guillermo were imprisoned by the Navy, and tortured repeatedly. They would not see the light of day until well after a Chilean version of *Plan Yakarta* was indeed put into effect.

Operação Jacarta. Yakarta Viene. Plan Yakarta. In both Spanish and Portuguese, in all three ways it was used, it's clear what "Jakarta" meant, and it's a far cry from what the word meant back in 1948, when the Truman administration was guided by the "Jakarta Axiom." Back then, "Jakarta" stood for independent Third World development that Washington need not view as a threat. Now "Jakarta" meant something very different. It meant anticommunist mass murder. It meant the state-organized extermination of civilians who opposed the construction of capitalist authoritarian regimes loyal to the United States. It meant forced disappearances and unrepentant state terror. And it would be employed far and wide in Latin America over the next two decades.

Operation Condor

In 1973, Allende fell. He died, and so did the Chilean dream of democratic socialism. In its place emerged a violent anticommunist regime that worked with Brazil and the United States to form an international extermination network. Their murderous terror was not only reserved for the left. They also unleashed it on former allies who got in the way.

In the months before September 11, 1973, Chile had a good deal in common with Brazil in 1964. Private-sector groups were funding opposition groups, pro-"tradition" and "family" groups were organizing protests, and the right-wing media was spreading fears of a putative left-wing plot. The CIA reported at the end of 1972 that Chilean opposition groups were receiving "economic assistance and weapons such as machine guns and hand-grenades" from Brazil's dictatorship.[48]

But the days after September 11, 1973, looked more like Indonesia in 1965, though on a smaller scale—at first. While Brazil's military government moved only slowly toward terror, General Augusto Pinochet's dictatorship began with an explosion of violence.

The first coup attempt came in June. The "Tanquetazo," as it was called, failed largely because Carlos Prats, leader of the Armed Forces, put down the military rebels allied with Pátria y Libertad. Prats was not going to oversee the Chilean Army while it betrayed its historic mission.

In the weeks that followed, left-wing publications began to report that Pátria y Libertad and other right-wing forces behind the coup had planned to activate Plan Yakarta if they had succeeded. It seems they had reason to be worried. One politician, Domingo Godoy Matte, from the right-wing National Party, actually stood up in Congress and declared that they—the Nationalists—"estarán aquí hasta que se produzca el Yakarta" ("will be here until Jakarta is produced").[49] This inspired a wave of shocked condemnations on the center and left, furious accusations across a range of publications that the right was openly planning "mass murder." The Socialist Party paper displayed a postcard that had been sent to its editorial director with the words "Jakarta is coming." The paper blamed the United States.[50]

Strangely, right-wing media began to run an inverted version of the "Jakarta" terror meme. *El Mercurio*, the CIA-funded paper, reproduced the story that communists had massacred generals in Indonesia, and could do so in Chile, too.[51]

In 1970, Castro had warned Allende against provoking Washington. It was too late for that now. As right-wing terror and coup-plotting built up around the Chilean president, Castro advised him to start taking a harder line. He said Allende gave too much freedom to the opposition, and was too unwilling to use violence to advance his revolution. He warned that a confrontation between "socialism and fascism" loomed on the horizon and if Chile's left didn't take his advice, they would not survive it.[52] But Allende's *Unidad Popular* government remained committed to democratic socialism.

In July, right-wing terrorists killed another military official, Arturo Araya, Allende's aide-de-camp, as he stood on the balcony of his home.[53]

By August, Carlos Prats had realized there was too much pressure on him. Powerful elements in the military wanted a coup. So did much of the elite, as evidenced by the groups of military wives protesting outside his home.[54]

And it seemed the right-wing terrorists running wild would rather kill General Prats than let Allende finish his term. All three of those groups had the backing of the most powerful government in history. But Prats wasn't going to give them their coup. On August 23, he handed in his resignation, and got ready to take off for Buenos Aires.

He was replaced by Augusto Pinochet, an unremarkable, laconic general who had been loyal to Prats and had shown no particular inclination toward a coup just a few weeks earlier. After the failed June *Tanquetazo*, Pinochet had told a meeting of coup plotters that he did not want to "talk about politics, because that is against the constitution."

On September 9, Carlos Altamirano, the leader of the Socialist Party, gave a speech at the National Stadium in Santiago. He read a letter delivered to the government by the group of *constitucionalista* sailors, like Pedro Blaset and Guillermo Castillo, attempting to warn them about plots for a coup in August.

"For us it was vital to avoid that great massacre that they planned to commit against the people between August 8 and 10," he read from the letter.

"Our bosses explained to us that for this or that reason the Marxist government should be overthrown, and the people should be washed of its Marxist leaders. For them, every left-wing leader would get, without a doubt, the Jakarta Plan."[55] By then, it would have been clear to most left-wing Chileans what "the Jakarta Plan" meant. By then, it was also clear to almost everyone that a coup was imminent. Altamirano's speech was more of an homage to the sailors' bravery than a news flash.

Two days later, on September 11, Salvador Allende knew what was coming. He barricaded himself in La Moneda Presidential Palace, and gave a final radio address to his supporters.

> Surely, this will be my last opportunity to speak to you. The Air Force is now already bombing the antennas. . . .
>
> I will pay with my life for my loyalty to the people. And I tell you all that I am certain that the seed we have planted in the conscience in thousands and thousands of Chileans cannot held back forever. . . .
>
> *Viva Chile! Viva el pueblo! Viva los trabajadores!* [Long live Chile! Long live the people! Long live the workers!]
>
> These are my last words, and I am sure my sacrifice will not be in vain.

He took his machine gun (Fidel Castro had given him one as a gift), slung it over his shoulder, and put on an Army helmet. As the Chilean Air Force bombarded the presidential palace and strafed poor communities they thought might want to defend the president, Allende shot himself in the head.[56]

That night, the new military junta made it exceedingly clear which ideology had propelled their violent rise to power. In a televised address to the nation, General Jorge Gustavo Leigh, one of its four members, said, "After three years of supporting the Marxist cancer . . . we consider ourselves obligated, in the sacred interest of our country, to accept the sad and painful mission we have undertaken. . . . [We] are ready to fight against Marxism, and willing to eradicate it to the very end."[57]

The murder and disappearances started right away.

Fanatical anticommunism, once more, was the founding ideology for a new, murderous regime in the Global South. Internationally, the junta would be a close ally of the United States. But locally, they didn't want to emulate the US. They wanted to emulate Brazil.[58] The junta began establishing a dictatorship and justifying their own existence.

On September 22, *Tribuna*, the Chilean National Party paper, published a curious interview with General Ernesto Baeza Michelsen. He posed for a photo with a postcard identical to the one that Carmen Hertz and Carlos Berger received at their home. "Djakarta is coming," it read. In this case, however, the general claimed that it was actually the left that was sending upstanding conservative officers the threatening message. According to this story—now backed with the full weight of a US-supported military dictatorship—the Marxists had planned to kill all twenty-seven high-ranking officers on September 22, and only the right-wing coup had stopped the murderous left-wing coup from taking place. A few days later, General Jorge Gustavo Leigh, one of the original members of the military junta, told the same story. He said to the newspaper *La Segunda*: "This campaign was destined to totally destroy the Armed Forces . . . a Jakarta that would permit a final collapse. Once this last bastion had fallen, they were going to impose terror on our country."[59]

As this was published on September 22, it was the junta that was terrorizing the nation. Famously, they rounded up thousands of suspected enemies of the regime at the *Estadio Nacional* for questioning, torture, and execution. Less well known is that Brazilian military advisers were there, helping the Chileans to destroy the young men and women they both considered enemies.[60] More than a thousand were immediately executed, their bodies hidden in mass graves.[61] But Carmen Hertz and Carlos Berger weren't among them. They were in the north of the country, where Carlos had been working as a communications officer at the Chuquicamata copper mine, desperately trying to play defense for Allende's nationalization of the copper industry.

Carlos was arrested on September 12 but quickly released; when he was arrested again, on September 14, he stayed in. Carmen, the young lawyer, tried to arrange for his early release. She was sure he would get out; the question was how soon. Since she knew his fate was in the balance, she didn't contact the Communist Party or any other higher-ups in Santiago. She stayed close to him, visiting as much as she could, negotiating with the local officials. His sentence was technically sixty-one days—and Carmen hoped to commute that down to time served.

On October 19, she visited the jail at about five in the afternoon. Carlos was distraught, nervous; something was wrong.

"They took away a group of prisoners. It was some kind of command, a different group. I didn't recognize anyone from the regiment," said Carlos. "They took them away violently, with hoods over their heads."

Later that night, Carmen got an anonymous call. They had taken him away, the voice said. She called the warden. "Yes, they took him, but don't worry, it's just interrogation and they'll be right back." He didn't come back. They executed all of them. Jakarta had arrived.

In their own way, Pinochet's forces eventually confirmed this to her. The next night, they parked a jeep on the road and waited for her to approach. They didn't get out of the car. As she approached, she could see that it was a military priest and someone else, someone in a uniform. That man said, "Carlos Berger and the other prisoners were being driven to the city of Antofagasta, they rebelled on the way, attempted to escape, and were subsequently killed. *Hasta luego.*" The motor was still running; the driver shifted the car into gear and rolled away. Carmen didn't cry. She screamed. "Murderers! Murderers! Sons of bitches, you will see! You will pay for this! Murderers, wretched cowards!"

Officials in Washington watched as developing countries across the world reacted with shock and horror to the rise of Pinochet. An October State Department intelligence report noted that a moderate Cameroonian newspaper called Allende's downfall "a slap in the face of the Third World."[62]

Juraj Domic, the Croatian exile who introduced the "Jakarta" metaphor into Chilean politics, was given a job in Pinochet's foreign ministry.

Before the coup, plotters in Washington were worried the Chileans didn't have what it took to fight socialism. But the Chileans soon surpassed their Brazilian patrons in zeal. The military command was willing to tolerate thousands of deaths, just as Pedro Blaset and the other *constitucionalista* sailors had overheard. In the end, Pinochet and his men killed around three thousand people, mostly in the early days of his dictatorship. They were proud of their efficiency. Manuel Contreras, a close collaborator with the CIA who created Pinochet's deadly DINA secret police, knew that the point of state terror was not just wanton destruction of enemies, but to make resistance impossible and solidify the dominant political and economic structures.

Terrorism had to be unleashed on the population before one man, Augusto Pinochet, agreed to take on the role Washington thought Chile's military was supposed to play. Washington favored Pinochet's government from the very start. Henry Kissinger had a very simple policy regarding South America's new dictator: "Defend, defend, defend."[63]

However, just as with Brazil's military dictatorship, the consequences of Pinochet's violence were far from limited by the borders of his own narrow country. Almost immediately after taking power, he sought to influence events abroad, both by fighting "communism" throughout the hemisphere and by executing civilians around the world.

The international terror began close to home. On September 29, 1974, Pinochet's secret police murdered Carlos Prats, his former boss, and his wife at their home in Buenos Aires, Argentina. Prats had been preparing his memoirs. After murdering him, Pinochet put out a statement saying his death "justifies the security measures the government has adopted."[64]

A few months after Prats was killed, the Brazilian military let slip the existence of its own *Operação Jacarta*.

In August 1975, Luciano Martins Costa was a journalism student in São Paulo. He and other students were able to interview a general named Ednardo D'Avila Mello, who had a reputation for brutality. Military officers had investigated the young journalists before the interview, of course, and they brought in right-wing students to the interview itself, to pack the room as a sort of intimidation tactic. As these things always went, D'Avila Mello delivered pleasant half-truths about the regime while giving it an air of transparency. The problem was, the general became incensed with one of the students' questions. He became enraged at what he saw as her insubordinate attitude. He lost it.

"You're all indoctrinated!" he screamed. "And it's because of this indoctrination that we're going to put into effect Operation Jakarta, and neutralize two thousand communists right here in São Paulo." He began to list the names of targets.

Luciano scribbled down, furiously, *"Neutralizar 2mil comunistas em São Paulo . . ."*

The general had gone off script. This was a dictatorship, however, and he had an easy way to make sure it stayed off the record.

"If you publish a single line of what I just said, it will be 2,001!"

The students kept quiet, for quite some time.[65]

Three months later, Pinochet's regime held a meeting with representatives from Brazil and their like-minded, US-backed anticommunist neighbors. There were a lot of them, now. Representatives from Argentina, Bolivia, Brazil, Paraguay, and Uruguay met with Manuel Contréras, collaborator with the CIA and founder of Chile's secret police, in the grand hall of Chile's War Academy. It was an upbeat meeting. They needed to work together, they had decided. It wasn't enough just to kill communists and subversives in their own countries. They set up a program to collaborate to exterminate their enemies around the world. They established a central data bank in order to trade intelligence. The computers for that system would soon be provided by the United States. The first day ended with a gala dinner, with attractive Chilean women supplied by the secret police.[66]

They named their new alliance after Chile's national bird, the majestic scavenger. In November 1975, they launched Operation Condor.

A Trip to the Movies

Benny arrived in Chile in 1975. He had been transferred from his job in Bangkok, after more than a decade there, to work as a UN economist. Back in Kansas, he had gotten a taste of North America; but this was his first time living in Latin America, and of course, he was excited. He arrived with his wife and children, who did their best to learn the language.

They learned very quickly what life was like under Pinochet. One evening, Benny decided to take a stroll through central Santiago and catch a movie. On the way, a couple *Carabineros*, members of the Chilean police, stopped him on the street. They needed to know who he was and where he was going.

It was suspicious that he was even walking. There was a curfew in Santiago, and it was approaching. But it was also his race that fueled their suspicion. Just as being Chinese had led the US-backed military to harass his community, and Suharto's dictatorship forced him to officially change his name to "Benny Widyono" while working in Bangkok, his face inspired suspicion in Chile, too.

By this point in his life, Benny spoke enough Spanish to understand what the cop said next.

"*Quiere que lo lleve?*" Do you want me to take you away? The subtext was clear as day to Benny. Do you want me to take you in, to be tortured, and maybe never come out? Do you realize you can be disappeared tonight?

Benny tried to be as polite with the cop as possible. It worked—the guy was just trying to intimidate him a bit, which also worked—and Benny was able to walk away. But over his first few weeks in Chile, he realized that not even his plush UN office was a refuge from the chaos of this violent dictatorship. Or rather, the chaos arrived there *because* it was a refuge. As Benny and his colleagues worked, young Chileans would run to the UN compound, fleeing the regime, and jump over the walls. Inside, they couldn't be arrested by the secret police, as the UN facilities, nestled onto the south bank of the Mapocho River, had a little bit of autonomy from the regime. These young men and women were mostly members of the left-wing MIR party, which had heeded the warning of the 1965 massacre in Indonesia and subscribed to the doctrine of armed revolution. Benny watched as the kids kept coming, and coming, and set up a mini encampment inside, sleeping on mattresses on the floor and looking for a way out of the country. They probably didn't know that Operation Condor could hunt them down, anywhere on earth, even if they did get out.

Pinochet hated Benny's office. For him, the whole UN was basically a hive of communists. But even worse, Benny worked at the Economic Commission for Latin America and the Caribbean (CEPAL). This was a bastion of what Pinochet and his global allies considered unacceptably leftist economic thought. CEPAL was the epicenter of development economics and dependency theory; Chile's new dictator, on the other hand, had elevated a group of well-connected Chilean economists who had studied at the University of Chicago, and favored a radical turn toward free-market economics. This group, which came to be known as the "Chicago Boys," were far more zealous than even Benny's old acquaintances in the "Berkeley Mafia" back in Indonesia. Their ascendance was not planned—the Pinochet government's raison d'être was anticommunism, not market fundamentalism—but under these economists, Chile became the world's first test case for "neoliberal" economics, and Benny's CEPAL offered advice that was no longer welcome.[67]

But still, Benny was soon invited to fancy events in *barrio alto*, the eastern neighborhoods up toward the hills, where the elite lived. When you stand in downtown Santiago and look east, it's almost always breathtaking. You can usually see snow capping the peaks of the Andes, towering above you, while down below you stroll through warm air thick with the smell of tropical spices.

It was when Benny went up the hill a bit into the posh neighborhoods that he first saw them: "*Yakarta viene*," "*Djakarta se acerca*," or just "Jakarta."

It was a surprise. He had to ask around to figure out exactly what the graffiti meant, where all the slogans came from. He found out, and that was even more of a shock. The capital of his own country had come to mean not cosmopolitanism, not Third World solidarity and global justice, but rather reactionary violence. "Jakarta" meant brutal elimination of people organizing for a better world. And now he was in another country, also backed by the US, whose governing forces *celebrated* that history rather than condemning it.

The paint was everywhere. But it was slowly fading.

The coup, only two years old now, had been rewritten into a new history by the victors. That was a process he knew very well. There was another similarity with Indonesia that Benny noticed right away. Allende, like Sukarno, was a talker. Pinochet, like Suharto, never really said much. Sometimes, Chilean TV would transmit video of a recent Pinochet speech but dub over his voice to fix what he had actually said. Even the present could be rewritten.[68]

Benny had to get used to seeing "Jakarta" plastered all around, but it never sat well with him. And one day, all these emotions came pouring out. The Indonesian ambassador to Argentina came to give a lecture to Chilean students alongside Benny, who was often the closest thing his country had to an ambassador in Santiago. This meant working with Suharto's government, but like most Indonesians, Benny had resigned himself to that reality.

After the lecture, students pressed the ambassador on how and why the Chilean government looked to Jakarta for an example of glorious, anticommunist terror. What was the meaning of all that graffiti? The ambassador was furious.

"That's simply the name of our capital! How dare you imply it's synonymous with massacre?" Benny was angry too.

But were the students actually wrong? He had to face this. He knew the whole city of Jakarta in its dirty, beautiful complexity. But outside the country—here in Chile—all that arrived was the story of mass murder. A mass murder that absolutely happened, that Pinochet had somehow replicated here. The graffiti wasn't slander. It was reality.

Later, he reflected on this more deeply. He thought back on his own life, to his time in Kansas in the late 1950s and early '60s. He thought of those Indonesian military men coming over to eat Indonesian food at his home and then going out on the town. It was then that those men were being trained, by the United States, in the ways of violent, fanatical anticommunism. It was those men who returned to Jakarta, after nights of strip clubs and heavy drinking with Benny, to help carry out the world's most notorious right-wing extermination program. That's where it all started.

Back in Kansas, he thought. That's why the name of the city I grew up in, where I studied, where I learned about socialism and marched against colonialism and racism, has become a synonym for mass murder.

10

Back Up North

New Theaters

In 1975, the Cold War underwent some geographic shifts. Washington abandoned some of the regions where it had made constant war on communism, while the anticommunist regimes it had helped create continued to scorch the earth all around them.

The United States left South Vietnam. In the Western world, this meant that Saigon "fell." From the perspective of Hanoi, the Vietnamese had only achieved what they should have gotten, through the referendum that Washington had helped cancel, back in 1956. Three million had died, the entire nation was militarized, and huge swathes of the country's lush jungles were rendered poisonous for generations because of US chemical warfare. After the fall of Saigon, there was no communist-led mass murder of civilians in Vietnam.

The massacres came in Cambodia. In 1970, the United States had orchestrated a coup to oust Prince Sihanouk, and installed Lon Nol, a general who was supposed to be Cambodia's Suharto. His forces trained in Bandung, not far from the site of Sukarno's 1955 Afro-Asian Conference.[1] During Lon Nol's rule the United States continued to bomb the country indiscriminately, killing hundreds of thousands of people, mostly peasants, in a futile attempt to stop Vietnamese communists from moving through the countryside. The United States dropped three times the tonnage on Cambodia that fell on

Japan during World War II, atom bombs included. For the people who survived, the effect of the B-52s on those nearby was reminiscent of the *sulfatos* in Guatemala: "The terror was complete. One lost control of bodily functions as the mind screamed incomprehensible orders to get out," one Vietnamese official remembered later.[2]

The disregard for life was staggering, and well understood in Southeast Asia. Traumatized refugees flooded Cambodia's cities. After the US-backed coup that deposed him, the ousted prince, Sihanouk, published a book of memoirs titled *My War with the CIA*. "We refused to become US puppets, or join in the anti-communist crusade," he wrote. "That was our crime."[3] He threw his support behind the small, shadowy, and strange group of Marxists he had repressed while in power. The Khmer Rouge, as he called them in the old colonial language, were the only ones fighting against Lon Nol and the US Army, which was wiping out entire swathes of the population. In 1975, the "Red Khmer" took Phnom Penh back from Lon Nol, without Vietnamese assistance. They closed the borders and set up one of the most horrifying regimes of the twentieth century. It would be years before anyone, even their supposed allies in Hanoi, knew what they were doing.

In 1975, Magdalena and Sakono were still in prison. They were still surviving on starvation rations, and forced to endure backbreaking work in Indonesia's system of concentration camps. For ten years, it had been drilled into them that they were evil, outcast, unwanted. Entirely cut off from family. The tiny bit of rice that prisoners received might have sand or glass in it; they would plant or forage for vegetables to supplement their diets. When working the fields, prisoners were often forbidden from using sickles— because it was one half of the now-banned communist logo.[4]

On Bali, one group of prisoners would carefully collect and utilize their own feces to fertilize tiny bits of soil and grow vegetables. They would pass the time by singing songs, either those from the days of Sukarno or based on their own experiences. The refrain to one of them, sung in Spanish, came from the title of Fidel Castro's 1953 speech—*"La historia me absolverá"*— history will absolve me.[5]

It was also in 1975 that the withdrawal of another colonial power sent ripples throughout the Third World. The dictatorship in Portugal, which had ruled since 1933, had fallen apart. The United States developed a "contingency plan" to invade parts of Portuguese territory if a government it considered communist took over.[6] Lucky for the Portuguese, Washington allowed the elected left-wing (not communist) government to exist. The new Portuguese administration decided on a rapid withdrawal from what was left of its empire.

Suharto looked east, and he pulled out his old bag of tricks. Among Portugal's newly freed colonies was the small nation of East Timor, which shared an island with Indonesian territory. When East Timor gained its independence, Suharto claimed he was threatened by communism on his borders.

Calling this a wild exaggeration would be generous. Neither China, the Soviet Union, nor Vietnam was backing the tiny country. The party that oversaw the Timorese declaration of independence, FRETILIN, did have a left wing, and some of its members used Marxist language, which was hardly surprising for a Portuguese-speaking national liberation movement at the time. But this was enough for Washington, which was convinced that East Timor could become a "Cuba in Asia"—even though Nixon had already re-established relations with the Communist Party in Beijing. He gave Suharto a "big wink," and the Indonesian generals quickly drew up *Operasi Seroja*—Operation Lotus.[7]

Indonesia invaded in December 1975. The people of East Timor did not want the Indonesian military there. FRETILIN radicalized, and launched a "people's war" against the invaders. To put down the freedom fighters, the Indonesian Armed Forces killed up to three hundred thousand people.[8] From 1975 to 1979, while both Gerald Ford and Jimmy Carter sat in the White House, Washington's closest ally in Southeast Asia annihilated up to a third of the population of East Timor, a higher percentage than those who died under Pol Pot in Cambodia.

In former Portuguese colonies in Africa, a different type of bloodshed emerged. In both Mozambique and Angola, full-on Cold War conflicts broke out, with the participation of the world's greater and lesser powers on both sides. Still under Brezhnev, the Soviet Union had begun to intervene more forcefully in the Third World, believing temporarily, and incorrectly, that the United States would grant the Soviets freedom to intervene, just as they had allowed Washington to meddle with Chile in 1973.[9] The United States did not—Washington-backed proxies in both countries, who fought alongside Zaire (as Mobutu's Congo was called at the time), apartheid South Africa, and Rhodesia, all joined together against Moscow's favored movements. Cuba sent twenty-five thousand troops to Angola to assist Moscow's ally. A small number of American and British volunteers, often single, unemployed men responding to magazine classified ads, enlisted to join white suprema-cist forces in Rhodesia and South Africa.[10]

Back in formerly Portuguese South America, there was an internal split within Brazil's dictatorship. Médici was no longer in power, and the new top general, Ernesto Geisel, favored a relaxation of counterinsurgency measures and a so-called *abertura*, or slow "opening," of Brazilian society. The prob-lem was that torture and murder—as they often do—had created powerful elements within the state whose privileges derived from the existence of end-less war. They opposed the *abertura*, and favored expanding the violence to include unsuspecting, law-abiding members of the Communist Party.

It is believed that Brazil's own "Operação Jacarta," or Jakarta Opera-tion, was a plan that aimed to intensify, rather than moderate, repression, and therefore derail *abertura*. It is also believed that a beloved journalist named Vladimir Herzog was one of its few victims. Herzog was a popular middle-class newsman who operated very openly. Though no big fan of the USSR (he had been inspired by Alexander Dubček's "socialism with a hu-man face" in Czechoslovakia), he joined the Brazilian Communist Party in the early 1970s. The PCB was pursuing a moderate path, building a united "democratic front," and was one of the most organized groups opposing the dictatorship, along with parts of the Catholic church. In October 1975, Her-zog became editor in chief of the public station *TV Cultura*. A right-wing journalist called the station "TV Viet-Cultura" because of his communist "infiltration."[11]

On October 25, 1975, Herzog was called for questioning by the Brazilian Army; he went into the military offices voluntarily; he did not come out. No one bought the official version of the story, that he had killed himself—a grisly photo of his body, slung too close to the ground for hanging to be ef-fective, made the dictatorship's claims even more patently offensive—and his death galvanized the nation into protest.

Influential members of the Catholic church hierarchy took up the cause of Herzog's death, and trained increasingly harsh critiques on the military regime.[12] Instead of escalating Brazil's internal war, the "Jakarta Operation" had backfired, and forced the military to back off. Despite the wishes of some hard-line elements, Geisel's *abertura* continued.

Brazil started to slide, little by little, away from its more hard-line anti-communist neighbors. Meanwhile, Chile's Operation Condor continued to expand its activities all around South America, until the continent was a veritable anticommunist killing zone. Thereafter, any real threat to US-aligned authoritarian capitalist development existed mostly in the paranoid minds of the Condor alliance dictators and their US allies. The fanatical anticommunists won the continent.

In 1976, a coup in Argentina brought to power the bloodiest of these regimes. Under General Jorge Rafael Videla, the dictatorship kidnapped, tortured, and disappeared tens of thousands of people. Videla's regime cast a much wider net than Pinochet's men did. This period is often called, somewhat incorrectly, the "Dirty War"—but there was no war. It was a top-down anticommunist extermination campaign with ideological roots in Argentina's homegrown fascist movement.[13] "Subversives" were tortured and killed for their real or perceived communism; for their real or perceived atheism; for their real or perceived Jewishness; or just for union activities. Ford Motor Company and Citibank collaborated with the disappearance of union workers.[14] Even beards were suspect—that's why a Brazilian piano player named Tenorinho was brought in, thrown on a *parrilla*, or grill, for torture in Buenos Aires, and then drowned.[15]

Representatives from Argentina's military had already been at the meeting that launched Operation Condor in 1975, and the murderous "Triple A" alliance—the *Alianza Anticomunista Argentina*—had begun unleashing terror under Isabel Martínez de Perón, who served as president from 1974 to 1976. But the true believers were now in power.

Admiral Emilio Massera declared Argentina was fighting a "Third World War" between "dialectic materialism and idealistic humanism." This meant removing the influence of Marx, as well as Freud and Albert Einstein.[16] General Antonio Domingo explained how this worked: "First we will kill all subversives, then we will kill all of their collaborators, then those who sympathize with subversives, then we will kill those that remain indifferent, and finally we kill the timid."[17]

But the Condor alliance didn't limit their activities to their own continent. They built upon the "stay-behind" armies Frank Wisner had helped to build in Europe to pursue their enemies in Germany, Spain, Italy, and Ireland.[18] The men behind Operation Condor often considered the nonviolent democracy and human rights activists operating abroad to be even more dangerous than armed guerrillas at home.[19] Most infamously, this logic led US citizen, known CIA contact, and Condor operative Michael Townley to murder former Chilean Foreign Minister Orlando Letelier in the heart of

Washington, DC. A car bomb placed on Embassy Row blew Letelier's legs off, killing him instantly; his twenty-five-year-old American assistant, Ronni Moffitt, staggered from the car and slowly drowned in her own blood.[20] Townley is now in FBI witness protection.

In 1978, Ing Giok Tan was admitted to the University of São Paulo (USP). This was a huge accomplishment for an immigrant from a poor Asian country—she would be studying, free, at the best college in Brazil, only fifteen years after she and her family shoved off from Jakarta on that rusty old hospital ship. But for her hardworking family, this seemed natural. She worked like hell at her good—almost entirely white—high school, and her parents put their heads down too, avoiding political conflict like the plague that it had been for their whole lives.

It also felt natural as she drifted toward the left-leaning counterculture at USP. Brazilian universities at the time, especially the elite institutions, were hotbeds of student activism. This wasn't the staid, ultra-disciplined Communist organization of the 1950s and '60s; this was a much more eclectic group of kids. This was the era of *Tropicália*: global rock 'n' roll devoured and reconstituted as a mix of Brazilian high-art concept and savage indigenous pride; cultural liberation; and, more than anything else, opposition to the censorship imposed by the dictatorship. Ing Giok also realized—very quickly—that there were no black students in her class at USP, either.

It was in this milieu that Ing, as everyone called her now, met her Uruguayan friend Hernán Pietro Schmitt, or "Tupa," as they called him. He was always terrified of the police, for reasons she didn't quite understand. He wasn't even a particularly active or left-wing student. But when he told her, it all made sense—as did his nickname. His father had been a *Tupamaro*, a member of the Uruguayan left-wing group that had prompted Brazil to threaten invading the neighboring country in 1971. Under the dictatorship that consolidated power in Uruguay starting in 1973, the new anticommunist regime sent men into Hernán's home and took his father away.

She didn't know it, but this was the fourth time that Washington's violent anticommunist campaign had affected her life personally. First, the US-backed military, the nascent "state within a state," had ignited anti-Chinese riots in her part of Indonesia, forcing her family to flee the country. Second, her family lived through Brazil's US-backed military coup in 1964. Third, the mass murder in Indonesia demolished life for the relatives who had stayed home. And now, one of her college buddies was the victim of an Operation Condor campaign.

That same year, 1978, alarm bells began to ring far north of São Paulo. A new wave of guerrilla movements seemed to threaten the fragile military oligarchies that had been established by Frank Wisner and the CIA back in the 1950s. So with the help of Washington, some of South America's most messianic anticommunists turned their attention north. Essentially, Operation Condor was extended to Central America.[21]

Drain the Sea

The countries of Central America are far more united than the nations of South America. Its peoples know one another well, and they tend to experience the waves of history in a similar fashion. This is especially true of the four most-populous countries in the middle—Guatemala, El Salvador, Nicaragua, and Honduras. (Belize, at the very top, was a British colony; and down at the bottom, Panama took a very different historical path after the US created the nation in order to build a canal.) And world history had crashed over their little subcontinent with punishing violence over the past few centuries. In the late 1970s and '80s, this process rose to astonishing levels of brutality.

Before this new storm of blood and screams even started, brutal oppression was already the rule for the vast majority of the population. The region was ruled by dictators who rarely bothered to hide their cruelty. The practice of "forced labor"—that is, the enslavement of the indigenous peoples that had started centuries prior—was still widespread.[22]

In Guatemala, the terror that started in 1954, and accelerated in 1965 after the arrival of John Gordon Mein and John P. Longan, had never stopped. The year those two men arrived, 1965, El Salvador, Costa Rica, Guatemala, Honduras, Nicaragua, and Panama came together to formalize military links and intelligence sharing within *El Consejo de Defensa Centroamericana* (CONDECA), a kind of proto-alliance to put down the guerrilla threat.[23] That threat was real. Mein himself was killed in 1968 by the FAR, the first rebel group formed in Guatemala in the wake of the 1960 clash over the CIA's use of a Guatemalan base to train Cuban exiles for the Bay of Pigs invasion.[24]

The violence unleashed by the Guatemalan dictatorship during the civil war that followed was indiscriminate. Right-wing terror groups like *La Mano Blanca* ("The White Hand"), the New Anticommunist Organization, and the Anticommunist Council of Guatemala started their own massacres, with the support of US Green Berets, and these death squads were eventually incorporated into the state.[25]

The disappearances that started in 1966 had expanded by the 1970s to transform Guatemala's cities into hunting grounds for any kind of perceived leftist or subversive. The number of people *desaparecido* by the state rose into the tens of thousands. If you were a union member, a student activist, a left-leaning politician, a critical journalist, or even a homeless child, you knew that the regime might come for you. As tension periodically rose around you, friends disappeared forever; you escalated evasive tactics, then settled back into your "normal" life of low-level terror—if you survived this time. Life was a permanent cat-and-mouse game, and Guatemala City became a deadly, sprawling obstacle course, sometimes for the entire life span of its victims.

Miguel Ángel Albizures, the same little schoolboy who never forgot the trauma of the *sulfatos* bombs dropped near his school during the US-backed coup in 1954, grew into a union organizer. The unions were not uniformly left-wing. As a teen, not long after the overthrow of Árbenz, he joined the Catholic Christian Workers' Movement, and by the 1970s he was a bit of a small-time leader. The union movement had moderate communists, and Christian Democrats, as well as some who supported the more radical guerrillas. The government did not care much for these distinctions. In 1977 they busted open the door of a union meeting Miguel was attending, firing their guns. Miguel fled onto to the roof, and jumped from building to building to escape. Another time they shot down several of his colleagues in front of the Coca-Cola factory. He knew he was lucky, in a way, because they apparently didn't want to simply kill him. They easily could have done that in the street, with some men in a car with machine guns. They wanted to capture, torture, and *disappear* him, hopefully getting some information along the way and creating mystery around his death. Since that was a little harder to pull off, he kept bobbing and weaving until he found a way out of the country.[26]

"We could never sleep in the same place for too long. We didn't see our families. It was constant suspicion, unending fear . . . we didn't know what was going on. But we knew that bodies were appearing everywhere around us, so we knew enough."

By 1978, things were changing for Central America. In Nicaragua, a left-wing guerrilla group inspired by the Cuban revolution, the *Sandinistas*, was poised to win power. In El Salvador, the government responded to protests against an obviously rigged election with a massacre. Hundreds were killed. Then a coup there led to a civil-military regime, which also devolved into murderous repression, leading the civilians to quit, and support grew for leftist guerrillas.[27]

All this made Guatemala's government nervous about its own survival. At home, new guerrilla groups were taking over for the older MR-13 and FAR, which had been crushed by the US-backed insurgency campaign. The most prominent new group was the *Ejército Guerrillero de los Pobres* (EGP), or the Guerrilla Army of the Poor. Unlike the FAR, which followed Che Guevara's "*foco*" (focus) strategy of organizing small guerrilla units, the EGP sought to enlist the larger rural population in the guerrilla struggle, emulating the victorious Viet Cong.[28]

The Guatemalan government began to kill indigenous people en masse simply because of their ethnic background. Entire ethnicities, whole tribes, complete villages were marked as either communist or liable to become communist. They were often people who had only a vague idea of what Marxism or the guerrilla groups were. This was new, different from the urban terror tactics, in which government forces kidnapped individual people. For the Mayans and other indigenous groups, the Army would come and simply kill every single one of them.

The close collaboration of US officials with Central American dictatorships as they slaughtered their own populations is well documented, far better than US activities in Indonesia leading up to October 1965.[29] The scale of the violence, however, and the consequences of the actions are often underestimated.

Miguel Ángel Albizures and others who lived through the late 1970s and '80s in Central America always stress that these new Central American guerrilla movements emerged after attempts at peaceful transition to democracy were brutally suppressed or, indeed, exterminated. They say that almost every political ideology in the world—not just the socialism and Marxism dominant in those guerrilla groups—allows for armed resistance against tyrants, and that includes the US revolutionary tradition. Nor is it surprising that the surviving movements were left-wing militants: by the late '70s, most of the moderate dissidents were dead.

In January 1979, the Khmer Rouge fell, and the world found out what had been happening in Cambodia. The government, if it can be called that, fell because the Vietnamese Communists realized what Pol Pot had been doing—and also because he bafflingly attacked his more powerful former allies. Vietnam invaded and easily toppled the secretive, psychotic cabal that had been terrorizing the country since 1975. The Khmer Rouge were driven into the forests and mountains along the Thai border. Vietnam took over most of the country, closed down the killing fields, and allowed Cambodians to return to the cities under a government of their own creation. Around a quarter of Cambodians were dead.[30]

The United States did not celebrate the fall of the murderous Khmer Rouge. China, which had been moving closer to Washington since Nixon's visit in 1973, was allied with Pol Pot. Deng Xiaoping was furious, and unwilling to tolerate what he perceived as Vietnam's aggression against China's ally. He resolved to invade Vietnam, and told the US about the plan.

President Carter said he could not openly condone an attack but assured Deng he understood that "China cannot allow Vietnam to pursue aggression with impunity," and he privately promised to support Beijing if the Soviets threatened to assist the Vietnamese.[31]

The Chinese invasion of Vietnam in 1979 is often forgotten, for two reasons. First, it complicates narratives about the putative international communist conspiracy, or at least the supposedly monolithic Asian communist movement. According to uninformed Western thinking, China and Vietnam were supposed to be on the same side. But more importantly, the episode has been forgotten because the Vietnamese immediately defeated and humiliated the Chinese People's Liberation Army. After decades of battle with France and the US, the Vietnamese were too good for the nation that had once ruled them for more than a thousand years.[32]

Clashes with China in the second half of the 1970s also led to the worst human rights violations under the new communist regime in united Vietnam. Partly as a way to undermine the power of ethnic Chinese in Vietnam—seen as potentially disloyal—Hanoi announced the nationalization of all private businesses. Hundreds of thousands of refugees set off, including the so-called "boat people," penniless and looking for a new life, and tens of thousands died.

At the time, Benny was in Thailand. He had finished his stint in Chile, and returned to Bangkok with the UN. Not long after he arrived, a colleague of his, a young Australian, came back from the Cambodian-Thai border with wild tales. There were Cambodians stumbling out of the jungle, starving and collapsing on Thai soil, he said. After the fall of the Khmer Rouge, they were fleeing to whomever might help them.

Benny went to see for himself. At the border, he broke down in tears. He saw "refugees in rags, fleeing the country by the tens of thousands, often emaciated and barely able to walk, seemingly unable to speak or smile," and immediately sent a cable to New York. "Please, send me to Cambodia."[33] He was sent to New York instead, where he had to witness something just as shocking. The United States chose to recognize the remnants of the Khmer Rouge at the United Nations, keeping its tiny regime alive, and refusing to recognize the Vietnamese-allied government. This would last for years. Partly, it was a way to appease Carter's new ally in Beijing. But Benny knew that it was something else too.

"They hated Vietnam too much," Benny said. "They couldn't forgive them for winning the war."

Much to his chagrin, ASEAN, the organization of Southeast Asian states that Indonesia had helped found in 1967, backed the Khmer Rouge too.[34]

In Central America, however, Jimmy Carter's government tapped the brakes a bit on brutal realpolitik. In this era, after both Watergate and the 1975 Church Committee investigations into the CIA and FBI, the US media were less reflexively uncritical of Washington's covert and overt Cold War schemes abroad. Outlets such as the *New York Times* and *Washington Post* played crucial roles in publicizing the massacre at Panzós, Guatemala, the village where the military was caught gunning down men, women, and children in 1978.[35] Washington banned the sale of weapons to regimes that did not meet basic human rights criteria. Rather than even try, the Guatemalan dictatorship, now run by a man named Fernando Romeo Lucas García, turned to Israel and Taiwan, which stepped in to supply the weapons and assistance instead. US-Guatemala collaboration continued at a number of levels, but Carter's position was enough to enrage some of the most committed anticommunists in the hemisphere.[36] Mario Sandoval Alarcón, one of the founders of *La Mano Blanca* and now vice president, accused the Carter administration's Inter-American Commission on Human Rights of being "a Marxist instrument that has used the cause of human rights as a tool for slander."[37]

In July 1979, the *Sandinistas* took Managua and set up a government in Nicaragua. For leftists across Central America, this was a moment of effervescence, just as 1970 had been for Chilean socialists. The *Sandinistas* had not only won; they had gotten away with it. Even the Clash, the punk band over in England, sang ecstatically about the shocking development:

> *For the very first time ever*
> *When they had a revolution in Nicaragua*
> *There was no interference from America*
> *Human rights in America*
> *The people fought the leader and up he flew*
> *With no Washington bullets what else could he do?*[38]

In its early days, the Communist Party in Nicaragua had opposed the *Sandinistas*' emphasis on armed struggle. Over the years, the *Frente Sandinista de Liberación Nacional* (FSLN) split into three factions. The group that won out, the relatively moderate third faction known as the *terceristas*, favored a broad tactical alliance with the "bourgeoisie."[39] It was this group, led by Daniel and Humberto Ortega, that took power as the dominant part of a coalition government.[40] The *terceristas* would stand in democratic elections.

Like Ho Chi Minh, Mao, Árbenz, Fidel, Sukarno, and Allende before them, the *terceristas* initially hoped to set up a government that Washington could tolerate. Infamously, these hopes would be dashed when Reagan took over and began funding the *Contra* rebels. But the leaders of Operation Condor did not wait for a go-ahead from Reagan to handle the leftist government taking root in Central America.

In 1977, convinced that Carter had abandoned them in their "holy war" on communism, Argentine officials began providing military training to the Somoza regime in Nicaragua. After the 1979 *Sandinista* victory, they set up a base in Honduras to teach Guatemalans and Nicaraguans the arts of counterrevolution and repression.[41] Central American soldiers went to Chile for training in anticommunist counterinsurgency tactics.[42] The 1980 meeting of the Latin American chapter of the World Anti-Communist League, held in Buenos Aires, enabled death squad leaders to form even closer ties with South American governments, as well as US Republican congressmen.[43] The methods that were used in Central America in the following years reflected the defining features of Operation Condor: targeted abductions and murders by multinational "hunter-killer" squadrons, often made up of *Contras* and Honduran commandos in civilian clothes; clandestine transfers of prisoners across borders; methods like disappearance, torture, and assassination of victims, including the use of electric shock, the "*capucha*" (asphyxiation), and the throwing of live people from helicopters; interrogations of prisoners by officers from several countries; and detention centers for foreign disappeared prisoners.[44]

When Reagan took over, Washington returned to more open and aggressive anticommunist tactics than had been seen in two decades. The CIA eagerly joined the Argentines in Honduras and, in the biggest Agency operation since the Bay of Pigs, began training and funding the *Contra* rebels. The *Contras* were not a regular army, and never seriously tried to best the *Sandinistas* in a direct confrontation.[45] They were a well-funded terrorist group, seeking to destabilize the regime however they could.[46] And their worldview and tactics were radically transformed by the fanatical anticommunism of their sponsors.

The former "public relations" chief of the *Contras*, Edgar Chamorro, made clear that the powerful ideological influence of the Argentine officers and CIA operations reshaped their movement. Historian Patrice McSherry writes that "the anti-Sandinistas were originally concerned with retaining their private property and oligarchical power and privilege, or pursuing revenge . . . but the messianic anticommunist ideology of the Argentines and the Americans began to reshape their rationale for the war."

They also learned lessons from abroad. A CIA officer going by John Kirkpatrick, with counterinsurgency experience in the Phoenix Program in Vietnam, compiled a training course that included an assassination manual for the *Contras*. One section was titled "Implicit and Explicit Terror."[47]

According to Argentine journalists Juan Pablo Csipka and Ignácio Gonzalez Janzen, the Argentines and the Central Americans had also discussed employing the Jakarta method. They report that in the early 1970s, before the country had fallen to the brutal Videla dictatorship, the leader of Argentina's far-right Triple A death squad, a politician named José López Rega, was in Franco's Spain. There he met with Máximo Zepeda, the leader of Guatemala's

New Anticommunist Organization death squad. They spoke of the "Plan Yakarta" and what it entailed: a "prophylactic coup" that would allow them to defeat the Marxists by "virtually exterminating" them after conservatives took power. These Argentine authors claim the meeting was arranged by the US ambassador to Spain, Robert Hill, and that frequent CIA collaborator Zepeda not only handed over some "Plan Yakarta" reports he held, but told his anticommunist comrade that Washington could assist him in forming "shock troops" to put the plan into action in Argentina.[48]

"We won't need to kill a million like in Indonesia," López Rega reportedly said, "because we can get it done with ten thousand." He guessed low. Anticommunists killed far more than that in Argentina.

On March 24, 1980, Catholic Archbishop Óscar Romero began to say Mass in San Salvador, the capital of El Salvador. Romero had recently spoken out against the wanton human rights abuses committed by the government. After he finished his sermon that night, a man burst into the church and murdered him.

The assassination was carried out by a death squad led by Major Roberto D'Aubuisson, a fanatical anticommunist who had trained at the School of the Americas in 1972.[49] Whereas Fort Leavenworth is an all-purpose military academy for students from all over the world, the School of the Americas, based in the US-controlled "Panama Canal Zone," was a training ground for Latin American "counterinsurgents." The school became so notorious that Panama expelled it from its territory, and the school changed its name in 2000 to the "Western Hemisphere Institute for Security Cooperation." D'Aubuisson also attended the Political Warfare Cadres Academy in Taiwan, which by then had provided training to officials from almost every Latin American nation.[50]

In 1983, D'Aubuisson summed up the actually existing anticommunist ideology very well. "You can be a Communist," he told reporter Laurie Becklund, "even if you personally don't believe you are a Communist."[51]

When the Salvadoran civil war got underway, the military backed by Ronald Reagan made scorched earth tactics a routine part of its *modus operandi*. On December 11, 1981, reports surfaced of a massacre at El Mozote village. Salvadoran troops executed more than nine hundred men, women, and children with US-made assault rifles. The next day, Reagan appointed a Harvard-trained former liberal named Elliott Abrams to serve as assistant secretary of state for human rights and humanitarian affairs. Put simply, his job was to defend US-allied right-wing regimes to the press, and shield them from criticism coming from appalled human rights groups.

Abrams called the accounts of the slaughter in El Mozote, including those published in the *New York Times*, communist propaganda.[52] This is still the most famous atrocity of the Salvadoran civil war, but it was only a tiny fraction of the violence unleashed on civilians. For years and years, the savagery dragged on and only deepened, because Washington refused to allow the right-wing government to negotiate a political solution with the rebels. Since the rebels had links to "communists" in Nicaragua, no negotiation was possible, according to Reagan's logic.[53]

But it was in Guatemala, Central America's biggest country and the site of the CIA's first major "victory" in the hemisphere, back in 1954, that normal people faced the largest bloodbath unleashed by the Cold War in the Western Hemisphere.

The small community of Ilom is nestled between misty mountains in northwest Guatemala, closer to the Mexican border than to the capital. The people are Mayan, and speak Ixil, not Spanish, and for decades they had been either subsistence farming or working for pennies on a nearby ranch. That ranch was owned by rich white men—and sat on the land taken from the Mayans centuries ago—and over the years, it kept getting bigger and bigger.

Ilom is too far from Guatemala City to have been affected by Jacobo Árbenz's incipient land reform program in 1954. Residents barely heard about the reforms that were snuffed out by the CIA.

In 1981, however, global politics arrived in the village. First, the EGP, the *Ejército Guerrillero de los Pobres*, came to visit. Speaking Spanish, the guerrillas explained that they were on the Mayans' side, that they were building a revolution that would help them get their land back, and they were fighting for them.

Josefa Sanchez Del Barrio, who was sixteen at the time, remembers that most of the villagers were politely receptive to this message, if a bit puzzled about the specifics. Few of them spoke Spanish. It wasn't quite clear what these thirty to forty revolutionaries in green fatigues planned to do, or how the villagers were supposed to help them. But the villagers thanked them, gave them the customary hospitality of thick corn tortillas and some kind words, and waved goodbye.[54]

Not long after, the Army sent in men pretending to be guerrillas. It didn't take long for the villagers to figure out what was going on. The men's costumes were shoddy—one even wore a cheap fake beard. And they were acting all wrong, asking too many questions and treating the villagers aggressively. The guerrillas hadn't acted that way at all when they came. This was not a sophisticated undercover operation. They were clearly just some young military men trying to figure out who was most sympathetic to the rebels.

In January 1982, the military men came back. This time, they were in their Army uniforms, but with black paint on their faces. They burst into Josefa's home. It didn't surprise her that her family was on their list. Her father had been part of a small group that tried, back in the '70s, to ask the local government down in the nearest city to save their land. They dragged away her husband's father. They smashed Josefa in the head with a rock. Then several men shoved a napkin into her mouth and raped her.

All in all, thirty people were taken that day, never to return. A few days later, the soldiers came back and took Josefa's father and brother.

In February, the soldiers came again. Josefa's other brother was working in the field, and they lobbed a grenade at him, and killed him. They took more people away that day, and this time they burned down the empty houses as they left.

Antonio Caba Caba, a young boy, realized something was wrong that day when he came back from working in the fields. As he approached his home, he saw his mother standing in the doorway, wearing the long red skirt worn by Mayan women in the region, staring blankly into the distance. What's wrong, he asked her. She told him about the fires. The soldiers had burned an old woman alive in her home as they left.[55]

Some people began to discuss running—but there was nowhere to go except into the mountains, where they'd soon run out of food. This was the worst violence their community had ever experienced; they came to the conclusion that finally, it must be over.

They were wrong.

On March 23, the soldiers came back at five in the morning and woke up every single person in Ilom. They were wearing black paint again.

"Come on, there is a town meeting, you are going," they told Antonio, and Josefa, and everyone else. They walked the villagers to the tiny town square. They sent the men into the little church behind the plaza and the women into the tiny courthouse next door.

Antonio heard one of them fidgeting on the radio, talking to a superior.

"We're gonna kill the guerrillas," he said.

One by one, then two by two, they brought men out of the church, stood them in front of the schoolhouse, and shot them. Everyone could see each murder. That was clearly the point. After about a hundred were dead, they stopped.

"We're only killing the ones that look guilty. The ones that look afraid," one of the soldiers said.

Other villages weren't so lucky.[56] In many parts of this region, the military simply killed every man, woman, and child. The government had decided that the Ixil were intrinsically communist, or at least very likely to become communist. In Indonesia, it may not have been the case that the mass murder was *genocide*. It was simply anticommunist mass murder. In Guatemala it was anticommunist genocide.

On March 23, 1982, General Efraín Ríos Montt took power in Guatemala in a military coup. He was an Evangelical Christian—which made him a special favorite of Ronald Reagan—and continued the genocide in a slightly different fashion. Some indigenous people from ethnically suspect communities were herded into state-built *aldeas modelos*, "model villages" built to help indigenous people start new lives in suitably noncommunist fashion, which often amounted to little more than deadly concentration camps. For many others, the massacres simply continued apace. As was the case in Indonesia, and Brazil and Argentina, Montt's religious zeal gave the anticommunist violence a theological justification. "They are communists and therefore atheists and therefore they are demons and therefore you can kill them" is how one civil war victim, now the head of one of Guatemala's most prominent research organizations, summarizes the logic.[57] The vast majority of the murdered were practitioners of traditional Mayan religions.

The remaining residents of Ilom were forced into slavery, but this time, they had to work for the military. Antonio was forced to join a militia and grew up "fighting" the guerrillas for the rest of the 1980s. They rebelled quietly, by intentionally missing when shooting at the "enemy." Josefa quickly married—if she had not, she would have been forced to "marry" one of the soldiers watching over the *aldea modelo*, forced into sexual slavery like so many of her friends. Their village was liquidated and burned to the ground.

This was all part of Ríos Montt's new strategy for fighting communism. "The guerrilla is the fish. The people are the sea," he said. "If you cannot catch the fish, you have to drain the sea."[58]

From 1978 to 1983, the Guatemalan military killed more than two hundred thousand people.[59] Around a third of these were taken away and "disappeared," largely in urban areas. Most of the rest were indigenous Mayans massacred in the open air of the fields and mountains where their families had lived for generations. The Salvadoran civil war took seventy-five thousand lives; again, the majority were innocent people killed by the government. Argentina killed twenty thousand to thirty thousand civilians, and other Operation Condor nations killed tens of thousands more. Anticommunist extermination had spread all across Latin America, always with the assistance of the United States. Taken together, the death toll approaches the estimated size of the 1965–66 massacres in Indonesia.

Even the anticommunists' great enemy, the supposed reason for all this terror, did not deploy this kind of violence. Using numbers compiled by the US-funded Freedom House organization, historian John Coatsworth concluded that from 1960 to 1990, the number of victims of US-backed violence in Latin America "vastly exceeded" the number of people killed in the Soviet Union and the Eastern Bloc over the same period of time.[60]

The Fall

The violence in Central America raged on until the fall of the Berlin wall, and then kept going. From 1989 to 1991, the Soviet Union fell apart spectacularly, along with all the states that Moscow directly established in the wake of World War II. The Second World was no more, and its residents experienced this as the literal collapse of their governments. For the rest of the planet, most of which had somehow been affected by the Cold War, some things changed, and some things did not.

In the First World, North Americans and Western Europeans watched triumphantly. Leaders in the West felt vindicated by very persuasive evidence that Soviet Communism was not a sustainable system.

In parts of the Third World, most specifically the regions where the Cold War was still being fought, there was some relief.

Benny was able, finally, to triumph at the UN. He had been lobbying for years to get the US to stop recognizing the Khmer Rouge as Cambodia's official government, and trying to tell the world about the horrors inflicted by

Pol Pot. Benny was influential in getting enough countries on board to end the diplomatic impasse caused by Washington's stubborn opposition to Hanoi. In 1992, he moved to Siam Reap, the most chaotic part of the country, to try to help put together a new UN-coordinated coalition government.[61]

In El Salvador, a truce was finally allowed. In 1992, the FMLN rebels simply became a legal party. Historians suspect that probably could have happened long before, if fanatical anticommunism had not led Washington to block any possibility of negotiations.

In Nicaragua, the *Sandinistas* easily won the 1984 election. Washington told the right-wing opposition not to participate, since the Reagan administration did not want the vote to appear legitimate.[62] The *Contras* never stopped their terrorism. It was clear to everyone, as the country went to the polls again in 1990, that the violence would not stop until the leftists lost power. The Nicaraguan people voted them out, and they left peacefully.

In Afghanistan, where Soviet troops had been trying to prop up a communist ally for nine years, Moscow's forces retreated, the CIA-backed Islamist fundamentalists set up a fanatical theocracy, and the West stopped paying attention.

In Chile, Pinochet had been removed from power by national plebiscite in 1988, but he remained Army commander in chief until 1998, when he became a senator for life.

For the two biggest anticommunist governments ever set up in the former Third World, the end of the Cold War had an indirect effect. Both Indonesia and Brazil transitioned from authoritarian rule to multiparty democracy. They did so at different times—Brazil started the process well before the fall of the Berlin wall, and Suharto left power almost a decade after it fell. Crucially, however, they both did it the same way. In Brazil and Indonesia, the transition from military dictatorship was carried out in a controlled manner. Negotiated transfers of power both maintained the fundamental social structure the dictatorships were set up to protect and provided impunity for the rulers, who remained wealthy and influential. The elites who felt threatened by social movements in the 1950s and '60s remained in charge, and the countries were well integrated into the global capitalist system. This was now the case in almost every country in Latin America, and the vast majority of Southeast Asia. In different ways and to varying degrees, fanatical anticommunism remained a powerful force in both countries and in the surrounding regions. It took different forms, both overt and latent, but it was there, always threatening to reanimate. It certainly did not leave the earth when the putative Soviet threat disappeared.

Nor did Washington change its stance toward Cuba after the fall of the Soviet Union. Instead of moderating pressure on Havana or trying a different tactic, Washington tightened the screws, passing the Helms-Burton Act in 1992 and penalizing all companies doing business with Cuba. But Cuba remained resilient. Castro buckled down, and the island made it through a so-called "Special Period," marked by deprivation worse than it had seen since the 1950s, by reintroducing capitalism and relying on tourism.

It's hard to explain US behavior toward Cuba as a response to the fear of Soviet Communism, or as a defense of freedom. From 1960 to the present, Cuba was very far from the most repressive political system, or the worst violator of human rights, in the hemisphere.

Perhaps Castro had committed the unforgivable sin of very publicly surviving repeated coup and assassination attempts in a way that embarrassed Washington. Or perhaps the real threat Washington perceived was the possibility of a rival model outside the global American-led system, the same thing that we now know bothered US officials about Guatemala in 1954, Bandung in 1955, and Chile in 1973.

There's another thing the US certainly didn't change. Immediately after the end of the Cold War, US officials, especially President George H. W. Bush, had talked about a "Peace Dividend." The idea was that, with Soviet Communism gone, Washington would cut back on military spending and violent foreign engagements. The exact opposite happened. There was a small decrease in spending in the '90s, and then the Pentagon budget exploded again after the turn of the century. Barack Obama ran as an antiwar candidate, yet when he finished his term in 2016, the United States was actively bombing at least seven countries.[63]

The past two decades have led the best historians to take a wider view of US behavior. Before and after the Cold War, the United States was always an expansionist and aggressive power.

"In an historical sense—and especially as seen from the South—the Cold War was a continuation of colonialism through slightly different means," writes Odd Arne Westad. "The new and rampant interventionism we have seen after the Islamist attacks on America in September 2001 is not an aberration but a continuation—in a slightly more extreme form—of US policy during the Cold War."[64]

In Africa, the civil wars ended in different ways, but crony capitalism and resource extraction became the rule almost everywhere.[65] In Eastern Europe, the collapse of communism was not as clean a process as the West often believed.

Nury, the daughter of Sukarno's ambassador to Cuba, had moved to Bulgaria with her Bulgarian husband after she left Fidel's care in Havana. In 1990, Bulgaria held an election. Despite Washington's generous support for the opposition, the Bulgarian Socialist Party—the new name for the Communists—won. But US and European officials made it clear they were unwilling to deal with the Socialists, and after a period of strife and protest, the Socialists handed power to a coalition government. Over the next few years, living standards dropped precipitously. Nury and her husband, who had been used to high employment and decent public services at least, if not democratic freedoms, watched in horror as the economy shrank for nine years in a row and inflation spiraled out of control.[66]

"When I finally got to go back to Indonesia, it was shocking to hear what people think communism is," Nury said. "I lived through it, and they are just wrong. And living in Bulgaria under communism was a hell of a lot better than living in Suharto's Indonesia."

In Guatemala, the civil war ended in 1996. The surviving people of Ilom were finally able to return home and reconstruct their tiny village. The only way to get there now, if you don't have a car, is to climb windy, dangerous roads on a crowded, recycled school bus from the United States. The journey takes two to three days from Guatemala City, about eighty miles away.

The Mayans still wear the red skirts that Antonio's mother was wearing the day she realized her neighbor had been burned alive. Villagers still farm corn, wake up early, and take horses through the trees to work the fields, and come home at sunset to sit and tell stories in Ixil and laugh.

But to participate in the modern economy that has grown up around them, they also need money. For that, they send their teenage sons and daughters to the United States. Josefa's son went in 2016, when he was seventeen. Everyone knows that if you go before you turn eighteen, it's easier to get in the country and stay there. He has a construction job in Florida, where he learned pretty good Spanish. Having paid back his coyote, the man who smuggled him across the border, he can send money home.

Ilom keeps sending more of its youth up north. This is not about love for the United States, or the American dream. They don't want to go. They know who was responsible for the violence they'd suffered.

"A lot of us, just really a lot of us, have gone to the United States," said Antonio Caba Caba as he was showing me around Ilom. We walked by the plaza where he watched almost every man he knew get murdered for being some kind of a suspected communist. He said, "I guess it's funny—well, maybe 'funny' isn't the word—but we know who is responsible for the violence that destroyed this place. We know it was the United States that was behind it. But we keep sending our kids there, because they have nowhere else to go."

11

We Are the Champions

WHAT KIND OF WORLD DID we get after the Cold War? Who won this war? Who lost? And more specifically, how did the anticommunist crusade concretely affect life for billions of people today? These questions were in the back of my head as I traveled the world, reporting this book. I had been raised with a certain set of answers to the questions. To say that what I learned since I started working on this project shook my faith in those answers would be a severe understatement. But rather than just reformulate the answers myself, I wanted to hear from the people who had lived through this, and felt the conflict most intimately.

So I put the questions directly to the survivors I interviewed in Indonesia and around Latin America. For them, the answer was usually quite simple. I asked Winarso, who is the head of *Sekretariat Bersama '65*, or the Unified 1965 Secretariat, a threadbare organization advocating for survivors of the violence in Indonesia.

"The United States won. Here in Indonesia, you got what you wanted, and around the world, you got what you wanted," he said to me in 2018, sitting on the floor of his modest home in Solo, constantly shifting his weight, trying to avoid further inflaming a painful back injury. I had gotten to know him fairly well over years of interviews he helped organize. He continued, "The Cold War was a conflict between socialism and capitalism, and capitalism won. Moreover, we all got the US-centered capitalism that Washington wanted to spread. Just look around you," he said, gesturing to his city, and the entire Indonesian archipelago around him.

How did we win, I asked.

Winarso stopped fidgeting. "You killed us."

Answers like that were very common.

The people I met were not a random selection of the world's population. These were mostly the victims of, and experts on, anticommunist mass murder programs in the twentieth century. There are important other viewpoints out there. But I'm convinced that the perspectives of people like Winarso, and the experiences of people like Francisca and Carmen and Ing Giok and Sakono, are crucial to understanding how our world turned out.

In 1955, Sukarno and much of the rest of the Third World came together with the intention of changing the relationship between the First and Third World. They believed that after centuries of racist colonialism, it was their time to take their place in world affairs as independent nations, to assert their power and intelligence and potential, and to rise as equals.

Back then, they were obviously very far behind, and not just symbolically. A quick look at GDP per capita, the size of a country's yearly economic output divided by the number of inhabitants, in the world's most-populous countries (see Appendix One) confirms that. The numbers for the US, and the economies of the white, former colonial powers were far, far larger than those in the Third World.

Sukarno thought this would change. Richard Wright, the skeptical African American journalist who covered the 1955 Bandung Conference, thought the Third World movement would succeed, too.[1] Colonialism was over. Naturally, these countries would catch up.

But when Winarso waved his hand around him, indicating the current state of the wider world, what was he pointing at? We kept talking about this. One thing is clear as day, even without looking at economic data or quality-of-life tables. The United States is still by far the most powerful nation on earth, and when Americans travel to Indonesia, or Mexico, or Africa, or Paraguay, they are richer than the locals. But citizens of the United States vastly underestimate the size of the gap between them and the rest of the world. The gap between the First World and Third World is enormous. The US economy is not just a little bigger than Indonesia's. It is twenty times larger. Brazil's GDP per capita number is less than one-sixth the US number. With very few exceptions, the countries that were at Bandung have remained in the same structural relationship to the former imperial powers. (See Appendix Two.)

The People's Republic of China has become much more powerful; everyone in Southeast Asia can feel that now. The Chinese economy is now nearly as big as the US economy. But that's because there are four times as many Chinese people as there are Americans. China has gone from being an incredibly poor country to an average country, with GDP per capita around Latin American levels, and the Chinese people remain, on average, incredibly poor by US standards. It is Chinese economic growth over the past few decades that has driven most of the reductions in global inequality that have taken place since 1980. There are heated debates as to whether China has grown because it embraced capitalism or because it had Communist reforms and still remains under the control of a technocratic single party. But what is clear is that China is absolutely not an anticommunist regime created by US intervention in the Cold War. One way of looking at it indicates that global inequality has gone down slightly since 1960, largely because of China (see Appendix Three). Another way of looking at it—that is, by grouping countries into regions—indicates that the Third World has been stuck where it was, while the First World has gotten even better off (see Appendix Four).

There are myriad, complex, and unresolved debates as to why less-rich countries have failed to catch up with rich ones, of course.[2] But it's important to be conscious of the all-too-forgotten size of the gap between nations, and the story of global inequality since World War II, because the events of this book need to fit into that story. One recent study asked US citizens to approximate what the average human earns per year. The number they guessed was ten times too big. They were shocked to find out just how the Third World still lives.[3]

The reality is that the white world, and the countries that conquered the globe before 1945, remain very much on top, while the brown countries that were colonized remain on the bottom. Almost everyone is better off now in a concrete material sense, because of technological advances and global economic growth, but the gap between the First and Third World remains about as cavernous as it was after the Bandung Conference. It would be too much to claim that this is because of the Cold War, or more specifically because of the loose network of anticommunist mass murder programs that the United States organized and assisted. But it's true that the period of the Cold War and its immediate aftermath, the period in which the US made routine violent interventions in global affairs, was not marked by a drop in the power of the white countries.

It is fair to say that the First World won the Cold War, and more generally won twentieth-century history. This is the world that I was born into; I said in the introduction that history is usually written by the victors, and for better or worse, the same is true of this book. I was born and raised in the United States; it is probably no coincidence that it was someone with my background who was able to acquire the contacts and funding to tell this global story, rather than a woman from the Javanese countryside or resident of a Brazilian *favela*.

What about the Second World? Over tea with an aging member of the Vietnamese Communist Party recently, this question came up. He is very open about problems with the socialist system in his country, but said that the government in Vietnam, much like in China and the rest of what's left of the socialist world, watched very carefully what happened to the Soviet Union and its satellites after 1989, and are desperate to avoid repeating those experiences.

Certainly, the leaders of the Communist Parties who ran the Soviet Union and the Warsaw Pact countries lost, and lost big. But what about their citizens, the regular, suffering peoples of the communist world? Did the triumph of global capitalism mean victory for them too? Were they rewarded with prosperity and democracy?

Economist Branko Milanovic, one of the world's foremost experts on global inequality, born and raised in communist Yugoslavia, asked those questions on the twenty-fifth anniversary of the fall of the Berlin wall. We can probably guess that no, they didn't all get that. But it was certainly the *idea* back in 1991, and in many ways it was the promise that was made to the suffering peoples of the communist world, including to Milanovic himself. What happened instead was a devastating Great Depression.[4] Milanovic, in a short essay titled "For Whom the Wall Fell?," looked at postcommunist countries in 2014. Some countries still have smaller economies than they did in 1990. Some have grown slower than their Western European neighbors, meaning they are falling further and further behind even from the low point in 1990, when the collapse of their system cut down the size of their economies. He finds only five real capitalist success cases: Albania, Poland,

Belarus, Armenia, and Estonia, which have been somehow catching up with the First World. Only three are democracies.

Which means, Milanovic calculates, that only 10 percent of the population of the former communist world in Eastern Europe got what they were promised when they tore the wall down. The Second World lost, and lost big. They lost the geopolitical power they had during the Cold War, their citizens often lost material wealth, and many did not even gain democratic freedoms to counterbalance that loss.[5]

And the Third World? Of course, the country I spent the most time on was Indonesia, the world's fourth most-populous country, founder of the Third World movement (and still home to the Non-Aligned Movement, which has its offices in Jakarta).

Often, when I interviewed survivors of the violence in 1965, they assumed I would want to ask them about the torture. What it was like to be beaten, to be starved, to be called a witch or a devil, to lose all contact with your family. To be gang-raped and thrown into the corner of a cell afterward, as if you were nothing. This was not usually what I wanted to talk about. To the extent that journalists or academics have ever spent much time asking survivors to tell their stories, they have already asked them this. Too often exclusively this, with the underlying assumption that it was only the excesses of the repression that were the problem, that if they had just arrested two million people, then proved in a court of law that those people were really communists, and executed half of them, that would have been OK. Personally, I was happy to let the survivors just sketch the worst parts of their stories in quick terms, if it became clear that going through those moments again would retraumatize them.

Unfortunately, though, I did have to ask a question, in two parts, that often proved extremely difficult for them to answer. It took me a long time to perfect the wording of this query in Bahasa Indonesia, so as to make myself very, very clear. At least when talking to those who really had been leftists, I would always say, "Think back to 1963, 1964. In those years, what world did you believe that you were building? What did you believe the world would be like in the twenty-first century?" Then I'd ask, "Is that the world you live in now?"

Often, their eyes would light up when answering the first part. They knew the answer. They were building a strong, independent nation, and they were in the process of standing up as equals with the imperial countries.

Socialism wasn't coming right away, but it was coming, and they would create a world without exploitation or systemic injustice. The answer to the second question was so obvious that it felt cruel even to ask. It might have been one thing if their government had committed horrible atrocities, but recognized the mistake, and built a just, powerful society. This did not happen. They are living out their last years in a messy, poor, crony capitalist country, and they are told almost every single day it was a crime for them to want something different.

If we read Sukarno's opening speech at Bandung; if we look at left-leaning publications across the world from 1955 to 1965; if we read *Afro-Asian Journalist*, the spirit-of-Bandung, pro–Third World magazine that Francisca translated, or democratic socialist publications in Brazil and Chile, we can ask: Were they crazy? Were their expectations wildly unrealistic? Or could things have been different?

As we have seen, in the years 1945–1990, a loose network of US-backed anticommunist extermination programs emerged around the world, and they carried out mass murder in at least twenty-two countries (see Appendix Five). There was no central plan, no master control room where the whole thing was orchestrated, but I think that the extermination programs in Argentina, Bolivia, Brazil, Chile, Colombia, East Timor, El Salvador, Guatemala, Honduras, Indonesia, Iraq, Mexico, Nicaragua, Paraguay, the Philippines, South Korea, Sudan, Taiwan, Thailand, Uruguay, Venezuela, and Vietnam should be seen as interconnected, and a crucial part of the US victory in the Cold War. (I am not including direct military engagements or even innocent people killed by "collateral damage" in war.) The men carrying out purposeful executions of dissidents and unarmed civilians learned from one another. They adopted methods that were developed in other countries. Sometimes, they even named their operations after other programs they sought to emulate. I found evidence indirectly linking the metaphor "Jakarta," taken from the largest and most important of these programs, to at least eleven countries. But even the regimes that were never influenced by that specific language would have been able to see, very clearly, what the Indonesian military had done and the success and prestige it enjoyed in the West afterward. And though some of these programs were wildly misdirected, and also swept up bystanders who posed no threat whatsoever, they did eliminate real opponents of the global project led by the United States. Indonesia is, again, the most important example. Without the mass murder of the PKI, the country would not have moved from Sukarno to Suharto. Even in countries where the fate of the government was not hanging in the balance, mass murders functioned as effective state terror, both within the countries and in the surrounding regions, signaling what could happen to you if you resisted.

I am not saying that the United States won the Cold War because of mass murder. The Cold War ended mostly because of the internal contradictions of Soviet Communism, and the fact that its leaders in Russia accidentally destroyed their own state. I do want to claim that this loose network of extermination programs, organized and justified by anticommunist principles, was such an important part of the US victory that the violence profoundly shaped the world we live in today.

All this depends on what we think the Cold War actually was. The popular understanding in the English-speaking world, I think, is that the Cold War was a conflict between two countries, and although they didn't go to war, they engaged in a number of indirect conflicts. This is not exactly wrong, but it's based on the experiences of a small minority of people on earth, and the Cold War affected almost everyone.

I follow Harvard historian Odd Arne Westad in viewing the Cold War as something different. We can see the Cold War as the global circumstances under which the vast majority of the world's countries moved from direct colonial rule to something else, to a new place in a new global system. If we view it this way, then there is not a simple winner/loser binary between the United States and the Soviet Union. In the Third World, there were many paths each country could take; more importantly, most of them are still on the specific path that was shaped and taken during the Cold War. Something similar is true for the entire structural relationship between the rich and poor countries—the relationship we now have was largely shaped by the way both those two powers behaved in the twentieth century.

None of the systems set up by the Soviet Union are still here. On the other hand, the countries that chose, or were forced onto, paths into the American-led global capitalist system have stayed on them. The countries that did not often fell onto similar paths in the past twenty-five years. Over that same time period, the world has undergone a process often called "globalization." That term certainly caught on for a while. But for those who want to be truly accurate, a better word is "Americanization," Westad says.[6] For better or worse, almost all of us now live in the global economic system that Indonesia and Brazil entered in the mid-1960s, a worldwide capitalist order with the United States as its leading military power and center of cultural production. That may change soon—who knows. But we're still here.

In this book, I spent less time discussing the real atrocities carried out by certain communist regimes in the twentieth century. That's partly because they're so well known already; it's mostly because these crimes truly didn't have much to do with the stories of the men and women whose lives we traced throughout the past one hundred years. But it's also because we do not live in a world directly constructed by Stalin's purges or mass starvation under Pol Pot. Those states are gone. Even Mao's Great Leap Forward was quickly abandoned and rejected by the Chinese Communist Party, though the party is still very much around. We do, however, live in a world built partly by US-backed Cold War violence.

The establishment of Americanization was helped along by the mass murder programs discussed in this book. In a way, they made it possible. They surely weren't the only events that did so—we have not discussed all the nonviolent ways Washington forced regime change in the twentieth century, nor did we analyze the reasons US institutions made the country such a wealthy, dynamic, and powerful nation in the first place—but we can definitely imagine things going a different way without them.

Washington's anticommunist crusade, with Indonesia as the apex of its murderous violence against civilians, deeply shaped the world we live in now, in five ways.

First, most simply, there is the trauma, which is mostly unresolved. Countries like Chile and Argentina did a fairly good job of coming together for national reconciliation. Brazil did a worse job. And Indonesia did absolutely nothing of the kind. But even in the best-case scenario, it's obvious you cannot simply delete the scars of mass terror in a generation or two. The psychological effects of US covert action are felt everywhere, including in North America. More and more citizens there have connections to countries touched by recent US interventions, and even for white Americans, there are psychological effects. When people find out that some things, important things, have been hidden from them, they start to doubt things they shouldn't, and embark on wild conspiracy theorizing.

Second, Washington's violent anticommunist crusade destroyed a number of alternative possibilities for world development. The Third World movement fell apart partly because of its own internal failures. But it was also crushed. These countries were trying to do something very, very diffi-cult. It doesn't help when the most powerful government in history is trying to stop you.

It's hard to say how they might have reshaped the world if they were truly free to experiment and build something different. Maybe, the countries of the developing world would have been able to come together and insist on changing the rules of global capitalism. Perhaps many of these countries would not be capitalist at all. I suppose it's possible—though it seems un-likely to me, considering who the victims were, and considering the strength of the US—that without this violence, authoritarian socialists could have won the twentieth century. It's not clear we even have the ability to imagine what could have been different. When it comes to pure economics, there's in-creasingly robust agreement that the developing nations lost their chances to "catch up" economically with the First World around the early 1980s, when an explosion of debt, a turn to neoliberal structural adjustment, and "global-ization" put them on their current path.[7] Within the current structure, the only real examples of large Third World countries becoming as rich as those in the First World since 1945 are South Korea and Taiwan, and it's very clear that these nations were given special exemptions from the rules of the world order because of their strategic importance in the Cold War.[8]

Third, the operations profoundly affected the nature of the regimes and economic systems set up in their wake. Indonesia and Brazil are two, perhaps the two crucial, examples.

It's now probably broadly accurate to say that all of Latin America, with the exception of Cuba, consists of crony capitalist nations with powerful oli-garchies. In Southeast Asia, the same is true for the majority of countries, and even the communist nations were integrated into ASEAN, which Indonesia and the Philippines set up as anticommunist in 1967. As *The Looting Machine* by Tom Burgis shows, Africa's political economy remains dominated by weak states and violent extraction. If we wanted to try to stretch this analytical focus to its limits, we could even say that when the Second World collapsed, those countries were integrated into a global system that only had two ba-sic structural types—Western advanced capitalist countries and resource-exporting crony capitalist societies shaped by anticommunism—and they slid right into the second category, becoming very much like Brazil.

In the introduction, I said that Brazil and Indonesia were probably the biggest "victories" of the Cold War. In a narrow sense, I figure that is true simply because by population, they are the largest countries that came into play, which seemed like they could go either way but then fell with a thud into the Western camp. In Brazil today, the idea that the João Goulart government was "communist" or that a turn toward the Soviet model was imminent is rightly ridiculed. But the conservatives do have a point. Something else was indeed possible, and the events of 1964 killed that possibility. But another reason that I think Brazil and Indonesia were such important elements of the process of Americanization that ultimately shaped most of the globe is that, after 1964 and 1965, so many of their neighbors landed on paths that were influenced, directly or indirectly, by the anticommunist regimes in the region's largest countries.

As for the victors of the anticommunist crusade, it's clear that as a *nation-state*, the United States has done enormously well since 1945. It is an extremely rich and powerful country. But if we look at individual Americans, or break down the analysis along class and race lines, it's clear that the spoils of that global ascendance were shared extremely unequally. More and more of the flows coming in from other nations have accumulated at the very top, while some US citizens live in poverty comparable to life in the former Third World.

The fourth way that anticommunist extermination programs shaped the world is that they deformed the world socialist movement. Many of the global left-wing groups that did survive the twentieth century decided that they had to employ violence and jealously guard power or face annihilation. When they saw the mass murders taking place in these countries, it changed them. Maybe US citizens weren't paying close attention to what happened in Guatemala, or Indonesia. But other leftists around the world definitely were watching. When the world's largest Communist Party without an army or dictatorial control of a country was massacred, one by one, with no consequences for the murderers, many people around the world drew lessons from this, with serious consequences.

This was another very difficult question I had to ask my interview subjects, especially the leftists from Southeast Asia and Latin America. When we would get to discussing the old debates between peaceful and armed revolution; between hardline Marxism and democratic socialism, I would ask:

"Who was right?"

In Guatemala, was it Árbenz or Che who had the right approach? Or in Indonesia, when Mao warned Aidit that the PKI should arm themselves, and they did not? In Chile, was it the young revolutionaries in the MIR who were right in those college debates, or the more disciplined, moderate Chilean Communist Party?

Most of the people I spoke with who were politically involved back then believed fervently in a nonviolent approach, in gradual, peaceful, democratic change. They often had no love for the systems set up by people like Mao. But they knew that their side had lost the debate, because so many of their friends were dead. They often admitted, without hesitation or pleasure, that the hardliners had been right. Aidit's unarmed party didn't survive. Allende's democratic socialism was not allowed, regardless of the détente between the Soviets and Washington.

Looking at it this way, the major losers of the twentieth century were those who believed too sincerely in the existence of a liberal international order, those who trusted too much in democracy, or too much in what the United States said it supported, rather than what it really supported—what the rich countries said, rather than what they did. That group was annihilated.

Finally, the fifth consequence of the crusade: fanatical anticommunism has never really left us, even in the First World. Not only in Brazil and Indonesia in the past few years, it has become clear that this violent, paranoid style in politics remains a very potent force.

But I think it's clear that the ghosts of this battle most actively haunt the countries of the "developing" world.

12

Where Are They Now? And Where Are We?

Denpasar

Wayan Badra, the Hindu priest, lives on the street where he grew up, in Seminyak, Southwest Bali. But the neighborhood has changed drastically. That same beach that he used to walk on for forty minutes every morning, as he headed to school down in Kuta, is certainly not empty. It's packed wall to wall with luxury resorts and "beach clubs," a very common type of business on the island, where foreigners can sip cocktails all day, and take a dip in a pool, right on the sand.

It's the same sand, of course, where the military brought people from Kerobokan, a few miles east, to kill them at night. Right on the beach, a few feet from Badra's home, is one of the bigger, more upscale beach clubs in Bali. Seminyak has become one of the more expensive places to stay on the island, where the tourism usually revolves around wellness, and spa treatment, or "mindfulness," and meditation and massages, or, of course, sun and surfing.

If aliens from another world landed on Bali, they would immediately conclude that our planet has a racial hierarchy. The white people who come here for vacation are orders of magnitude wealthier than the locals, who serve them. It is just accepted as a natural part of life. Almost everywhere in Southeast Asia, white people have the disposable income to buy lavish

245

hospitality, or sex, from the locals. They were born with this wealth. Compared to the rest of Indonesia, Bali has done OK for itself economically as a result of the tourism, and Balinese people often obediently reproduce the "Bali smile" as they get Australian surfers their eggs or Russian Instagram models their coconuts.

Almost none of the tourists who come, no matter how well meaning and well educated, know what happened here, says Ngurah Termana, the nephew of Agung Alit, the man who spent a darkly absurd afternoon sifting through skulls in search of his father's body. In contrast to Cambodia, where Western backpackers faithfully (or morbidly) visit the Killing Fields Museum outside Phnom Penh, few people who come to Bali are aware that a huge part of the local population was slaughtered right underneath their beach chairs.

"Even when we meet with NGO groups, the most internationally informed type of people, that know about Rwanda, Pol Pot, everything, no one has any idea what happened here," said Ngurah Termana, who is a founding member of Taman 65, or the 1965 Garden, a collective dedicated to promoting memory and reconciliation on the island. The group put out a book on the killings in Bali as well as a CD of songs that prisoners sang in the concentration camps here.[1]

The members of Taman 65 know that there's a reason none of the tourists know about the violence that took the lives of so many of their relatives. The government has buried that history deep, even deeper than it was buried on the island of Java. The tourism boom, which started in the late 1960s, required that. Before Suharto, a huge amount of Bali's land was communal, and often disputed. "They needed to kill the communists so that foreign investors could bring their capital here," said Ngurah Termana.

"Now, all visitors here see is our famous smile," he continued. "They have no idea the darkness and fire that lurks underneath."

The luxury beach club a few steps away from Wayan Badra's home has a name that is almost comically on the nose. It's called Ku De Ta, Bahasa Indonesia for "coup d'état." I asked the staff there if they knew why that might be ironic. They did not.

Over the years, Wayan Badra and his neighbors have found bones and skulls in the sand around Ku De Ta. As the elder priest for this village, he takes it upon himself to give the bodies a proper Hindu funeral. Recently, one of the villagers made a mistake. He kept a skull for himself in his office, and put it next to some flowers on a table. Playing around, he put a hat on the skull.

"Maybe the person who died didn't like being treated like this. The skull started to move" on its own, Wayan Badra said. The man got scared, and quickly brought it to Wayan Badra for a respectful, proper burial.[2]

Stamford

I met Benny Widyono at his home in Connecticut. It took a very long time to find him—at first he was just a rumor: an Indonesian who had lived in Chile under Pinochet. I had to chase leads across a few countries. But he became very real to me, and a valued friend.

After his time trying to help rebuild Cambodia, Benny settled into academic life in the United States, teaching at the University of Connecticut and writing a book about the UN's successes and many failures in Cambodia.

He was wickedly funny in person. When he recounted his stories about trips to strip clubs, back in Kansas in the 1950s, he'd cover his mouth, pretending to hide the story from his smiling wife. After hours of showing me his photos and his materials on Cambodia, he drove me back to the train station, at the spry age of eighty-two. Just a few weeks later, he finally became a US citizen.

We kept in touch for months after that. I'd call to ask follow-up questions, or he'd send me news and links over WhatsApp. One day, he sent me a note; it looked like a mass message, saying that he was going in for heart surgery. I wished him my best; then I sent him a get-well card from Guatemala; then I called his home later to see how he was doing. I had just missed him. His wife told me he had died a week earlier.

I want to dedicate this book to him, and to Francisca Pattipilohy, and to all the innocent victims of state terror in the twentieth century.

São Paulo

Ing Giok Tan met me near Praça da República, just below my apartment in Brazil's largest city. The meeting was convenient for her. It was October 2018, and she was marching in a rally there to stop Jair Bolsonaro from being elected.

Fifty-eight years old, wearing red and absolutely radiant, she was in the square with a few friends, waving flags and passing out pamphlets. This was not one of the huge, all-inclusive anti-Bolsonaro marches that all kinds of people went to. This was a group of dedicated activists, the kind who were out there a few times a week.

And they were going to lose. That was becoming increasingly clear. This very moment, as Bolsonaro breezed to the second round of voting without even showing up to debate his opponent from the left-leaning Workers' Party (PT), was perhaps the lowest point for the Brazilian left since democracy had returned. But Ing Giok was out there with five or six women, unafraid to defend Lula, the popular former president and the country's first left-leaning leader since the fall of the dictatorship. She had been a supporter of the PT, his party, since she voted for him in 1989 (in that election, Brazil's TV Globo manipulated the footage of a key debate between Lula and Fernando Collor, who went on to win and then be impeached for corruption). But she became especially active in 2016, as gathering right-wing forces assembled in the attempt to impeach Dilma Rousseff. She didn't think that would turn out well. She was right.

If you had to sum up Jair Bolsonaro's political career in two words, "violent anticommunism" would be a very good choice. He was an unremarkable soldier and an unremarkable politician, popping between nine parties over two decades in the lower house of the legislature. The only noteworthy thing about him was that he would sometimes scream, into empty congressional chambers or on late-night TV, that everyone was a communist, or that the state should have killed more leftists. He once said, "Voting won't change anything in this country. Nothing! Things will only change, unfortunately, after starting a civil war here, and doing the work the dictatorship didn't do. Killing some thirty thousand people, and starting with FHC [referring to then-President Fernando Henrique Cardoso of the Brazilian Social-Democratic Party]. If some innocents die, that's just fine."[3]

Over the years, his vehement defense of the dictatorship, including its most abhorrent practices, shocked and dismayed even the military high command, who preferred to leave those things in the past, or at least unsaid. Bolsonaro's ideology can be traced directly back to 1975, and to the days of *Operação Jacarta*.

Back then, there was a split within the military. General Geisel wanted a gradual democratic opening, and a radical group within the military, whose power derived from terror, opposed this *abertura*. The leader of this violent, ultra-right faction was Brilhante Ustra, the man Bolsonaro praised during his impeachment vote on the day I met him.

"Bolsonaro represents the faction of the Armed Forces that gained power when torture became an important part of the military regime," wrote Celso Rocha de Barros in *Folha de S. Paulo*. In other words, his presidency is the return of the very impulse that led to anticommunist mass murder in the twentieth century.[4]

Ing Giok is now Brazilian in every way, to the extent that she is now just "Ing," pronounced "Ing-ee" in the local style (words in Brazilian Portuguese can't end on a consonant). I also got to meet much of the Indonesian community in Brazil. They are almost all of Chinese descent. Some were conservative; some were center-left. None of them knew that the original anti-Chinese riots in Indonesia were the result of US policy in the region. Some of them had no idea why they really came to Brazil in the first place. Others, like Hediandi Lesmana and Hendra Winardi, came later, after the chaos of 1965–1966, when anti-Chinese sentiments in Jakarta's student community made life for them very difficult. Hendra went on to start a very successful engineering career in Brazil, literally building some of its most important architectural landmarks. His company helped build five of the World Cup stadiums in preparation for the 2014 event that now feels like it took place in a different, much better world.

Ing Giok and I spoke many times. When I got back to my computer after one of our conversations, I checked Twitter, and something caught my eye. Bolsonaro supporters had already been calling members of the international press "communist" for weeks, because of our critical coverage.

But this time the accusation came with an illustration, clearly old. There was a red, devilish hand holding a long spike, as if to stab the heart of Brazil, and it was being held back by another hand, this one green. It was obvious what it meant—the communists wanted to destroy the country, but the military would save them. But I recognized this one, and checked my history books. It was an illustration created in the 1930s, based on the legend of the communists murdering generals in the middle of the night, the myth surrounding the *Intentona Comunista*.

Bolsonaro was elected on October 28, 2018. I was in Rio, furiously typing up a story as the final results came in. Below me, on the streets of Leme, a few blocks from Copacabana Beach, I heard screaming, and ran to the window to witness a brief, early explosion of political violence. That day, many of the people in the neighborhood had been wearing stickers supporting Haddad, the left-leaning candidate.

"*Comunistas! Comunistas!*" a group of bulky men started screaming at them "*Fascistas!*" a few women screamed back. But they were scared. These guys were a lot bigger than them, and they shuffled off quickly, removing their stickers.

After the results, I spoke to Ivo Herzog, the son of Vladimir Herzog, the journalist killed in the putative *Operação Jacarta*. "I think we may be taking a huge step backwards. I'm very afraid," he said. "The political situation puts me under intense stress. I can't sleep without medication. But I've decided now is not the time to back down from the fight."

Paris

I was sitting and waiting in Djakarta Bali, an Indonesian restaurant a few blocks from the Louvre, when an elderly woman came zooming toward the front door. I couldn't see her feet, so I was confused how she was going this fast.

But then she hopped off a Razor scooter and walked in. It was Nury Hanafi, the daughter of Sukarno's ambassador to Cuba. This restaurant is her family's, opened in Paris after they came here from Cuba. On the walls, there are photos of her father with Che, and with Fidel, back in the days when they thought they were building a tricontinental movement. We had the excellent *daging sapi rendang*, one of my favorite dishes from Indonesia. She told me the scooter was her "Harley Davidson."

It might have looked strange, a white American man and an old Asian woman speaking Spanish in Paris.

After years in Bulgaria, she came back here, and was reunited with her family. But even in Paris, they couldn't escape the stigma of communism. The Indonesian embassy in Paris refused to recognize the restaurant ever existed. She doesn't know what country she belongs to; she feels she lost Indonesia back in 1965.

"When I talk to younger people from Indonesia now, I realize we don't have the same history," she said. "I don't mean that we have different personal stories. I mean they don't even know the truth of what our country used to be—our struggle for independence, and the values we held."

Life for the exiles in Europe and Asia remains hard. But, she admits quickly, things for victims back home have been much worse.

Solo

Magdalena has been beautiful her entire life. All throughout the time she was in prison, guards tried to marry her. She resisted, even though she knew this would improve her situation, maybe even get her out early. She didn't want a relationship like that.

When she did get out of prison, more men tried to marry her. She resisted. She didn't feel safe with any man who had not been imprisoned himself.

She knew that she was marked for life as a communist, as a witch. Any regular man was likely to view her as a reject, she worried, and treat her like garbage if and when he felt like it.

"How could I trust a regular man to be my husband?" she asked me. "What if he got angry? He could just beat me, call me a communist, and no one would help me."

Much worse things happened than this to the families of communists and accused communists. In Indonesia, being communist marks you for life as evil, and in many cases, this is seen as something that passes down to your offspring, as if it were a genetic deformity. Children of accused communists were tortured or killed.[5] Some women were prosecuted simply for setting up an orphanage for the children of communist victims.[6] One Indonesian businessman close to Washington warned US officials, years after the killings, that a strong military was needed because the offspring of the communists were growing up.[7]

Magdalena is serene and radiant at seventy-one, but also shy and guarded. She lives alone, in a tiny one-bedroom shack, down an alleyway in the city of Solo, in Central Java.

She lives on two hundred thousand rupiah a month, or about fourteen US dollars. She gets a tiny bit of help from her local church, which supplies her with a monthly stipend of five kilos of rice. But she has no family, and she has none of the traditional ties to her community that sustain most women her age. Those were cut when she was accused of being a communist. When I first pushed my motorcycle down the little road to her home, and walked into her living room, I couldn't believe my eyes. This is not how elderly Indonesians live. They live in houses with big families—and if they don't have that, the neighborhood takes care of them. As I walked into her house, no one on her street greeted us. She was not wrong when she figured that she would be marked for life.

This kind of situation is extremely common for survivors of the 1965 violence and repression. There are an estimated tens of millions of victims or relatives of victims still alive in Indonesia, and almost all live in worse situations than they deserve. This ranges from abject poverty and social isolation to simply being denied the admission that a parent or grandparent was killed unjustly—that their family was not guilty of anything at all.

The small organization that advocates for survivors in this region, *Sekretariat Bersama '65*, has fought for decades for recognition of the crimes committed against people like Magdalena. The survivors thought there could be some kind of a truth commission or national reconciliation process; they thought there should be reparations paid to the victims; they thought, at least, there should be a public apology for what happened to them, an affirmation that they are not less than human. None of that has taken place.

Back in 2017, when I first arranged to meet survivors, Baskara Wardaya, a Jesuit Catholic priest and historian who specializes in 1965, warned me, "Many survivors are tired of talking, tired of fighting. It's been so long, and they've gotten absolutely nowhere."

The mayor of Solo in 1965 was a member of the Communist Party named Utomo Ramelan. Over the years, as I visited Solo and met survivors, I met quite a few people who had worked in his administration, young Indonesians just excited to get an official job at City Hall. After Suharto took over the country, he was arrested and sentenced to death.

In 2005, a former businessman in the furniture industry, Joko "Jokowi" Widodo, was elected mayor of Solo. In 2014, he was elected president. His candidacy was supported by a range of human rights groups, many of which thought that as the first leader of Indonesia who did not come from Suharto's military-oligarchical nexus, he would recognize and apologize for the crimes of 1965, or start some inquiry on the fiftieth anniversary of the killings.

They were wrong. Not long after starting, he smiled and told reporters he had "no thoughts about apologizing."[8] In 2017, the year my roommate was terrorized in Jakarta for attending a conference on 1965, Jokowi, who had been accused of being a communist himself, took a stronger position. "If the PKI comes back, just beat them up," he said.[9] In 2019, Jokowi was re-elected for another five-year term.

I had a very hard time in Solo. These interviews are very hard to do, and I had to go slow, so the weeks were long and languorous. At first I thought

I could speak to Indonesians with the help of an interpreter, but it quickly became clear that many people are still far too traumatized, and too afraid of the stigma still attached to them in their old age, to speak freely in front of an Indonesian they don't know or trust. Even for those who would speak to me through an interpreter, the questioning was far too delicate to pass the responsibility for wording on to someone else. So I improved my skills in that language enough to do one-on-one interviews, and slowly earn their trust. I talked to many, many people whose stories I could not include; some, it became clear, did not really feel comfortable telling their full stories, and many others did bravely, helping to shape my understanding of the events as I selected the few stories I could pick for a book like this. I feel guilty even admitting the process was very psychologically difficult for me, since my tiny ordeal pales in comparison to theirs—and because I could go back and live a comfortable life in the United States whenever I wanted.

In Solo, I had to spend a lot of time in the town's new megamall, where all the important businesses are. In some ways the megamall now functions as the cultural center of Indonesian cities, with children's concerts in the lobby. People can wander aimlessly, buying iced coffee and doughnuts. Often, the escalators leave you quite literally trapped on its upper floors, so you wander more and buy something else. And like every other mall in Indonesia, the music on the speakers is American-produced pop almost all the time. You do not hear Indonesian music. You do not hear Japanese music, even K-pop, or anything from Asia. No European or Latin American music. It will all have been packaged and sold in the USA.[10]

Sakono also lives near Solo. He's still very feisty, and still applying sharp political analysis to the world around him. Unlike Magdalena, he can talk about the old days without going quiet, without staring off into the distance, or breaking into tears. Like Magdalena, he converted to Christianity in prison. This is also very common among survivors, especially among 1965 victims who were raised to observe the Javanese form of Islam. After being accused of atheism, communists were rejected by the large Muslim institutions in Java, which often collaborated in the killings, but they still believed in God and sought spiritual comfort from the material horrors of their lives.

The only thing Sakono likes to talk about more than Marxism is grace and forgiveness. He is adamant that he holds nothing against his captors or the men who killed his friends. He wants no vengeance and is at peace with his past. But he's equally adamant that the country is not at peace with this history.

"The solution is for this nation to recognize its sins and to repent. I value even the most difficult experiences I went through, because they taught me to show love to everyone," he said. "If we can recognize what our nation has done, and ask for forgiveness, we can move forward."

New York City

Thirty Rockefeller Plaza is a big building in Midtown Manhattan. I had never been there before, though I had heard of it—I think I caught a couple episodes of *30 Rock*, with Tina Fey and Tracy Morgan, whose title made the address even more famous.

It's clearly a place tourists visit. On the ground floor, the walls display pictures of *Seinfeld* and *Friends* and all the other shows that NBC has produced. On the twenty-third floor is Squire Patton Boggs, a "white-shoe" law firm.

Frank Wisner Jr. has an office there. He served in the State Department for decades, including as Reagan's ambassador to Egypt and the Philippines, and as Bill Clinton's ambassador to India. But I mostly asked him about his father, things he remembered him saying about Indonesia or the fight against communism. It would be unfair to make him answer for the deeds of his father, but there was one thing he could tell me, one myth he wanted to dispel.

He told me that whether or not the CIA overestimated the strength of the Soviet Union, and despite what the outcome might have been, his father truly thought that he was fighting communism. He didn't think he was doing it to help his business buddies back in New York; he thought it was about the cause. For what it is worth, I believe that he believed that.

After going very carefully over the 1950s and 1960s, we talked about life in Indonesia now. Packing my bag, I remarked that for many countries, that history is hugely important to this day. While Americans may have forgotten about these events and those countries, the residents don't have the option to forget. Wisner agreed with me quickly and enthusiastically.

That's true, he said, as I stood up to leave. In many ways, we are "the land of the great amnesiac," he said.

"We have a psychological habit of looking ahead and not behind," he said. Musing freely, as friendly men in their eighties often do, he said the US government would not have gotten itself into its current situation in the Middle East if we had paid attention to history. Speaking with dark sarcasm, he finished: "There's a long and honorable record of American indifference to the world around us."

Santiago

Carmen Hertz is a busy woman. She's a congresswoman now, elected in 2017. She's still in the Communist Party, which has eight members in the *Cámara de Diputados*, led by a young former student leader, Camila Vallejo.

When I tell Indonesian victims of 1965–66 that it's sort of OK to be a communist now in parts of Latin America, or even that former guerrillas, once imprisoned, became presidents, they can't believe it. But reconciliation did happen, of some kind, in much of South America.

Chile as a center-right capitalist country is far from perfect. It's certainly not what Carmen thought the world would be like back in 1970, when she and her friends believed they were on their way to building a world without poverty or exploitation.

Santiago has a powerful monument to the victims of the Pinochet regime, called the *Museo de la Memoria y los Derechos Humanos*. As you walk in, there's a single candle lit for every single person killed by the dictatorship. The guides on the walls do not shy from the fact that many of the victims were indeed leftists, even communists or supporters of Marxist armed struggle. One wall has a small display of every single truth and reconciliation process that has ever taken place: in South Africa, in Argentina, in more than thirty countries. There's the beginning of a small plaque for Indonesia. Then it ends abruptly: "Indonesia abolished the law that would establish their truth commission."

Jakarta

In the center of Indonesia's capital, there is a structure called the *Monumen Pancasila Sakti*, or Sacred Pancasila Monument. My ride there, just like any ride between two points in Jakarta, was through gridlock traffic, slowly making my way through crowded, polluted streets.

For reasons that are hard to describe, in many parts of Indonesia, if you're a white foreigner, people will ask you for a selfie. It is deeply strange, disturbing even, but I usually comply. I do not at the Sacred Pancasila Monument—because I think I have technically snuck onto the grounds. Recently, Indonesia's military has banned foreigners from entering this complex of memorials and museums—it appears authorities don't want international researchers to examine the site.[11] After visiting, I understand why.

The Sacred Pancasila Monument is a large white marble wall with life-size figures representing the victims of the September 30th Movement standing in front of it. It's just a few steps from *Lubang Buaya*, the well where the generals' bodies were found.

But as for everyone else who was killed, there's no memorial. There is an entire museum—the *Museum Pengkhianatan PKI (Komunis)*, or the Museum of Communist Betrayal—that exists to reinforce the narrative that the communists were a treacherous party that deserved to be eliminated. As you walk down a bizarre series of darkened halls, a series of diorama installations take you through the history of the party, demonstrating each and every time they betrayed the nation, or attacked the military, or plotted to destroy Indonesia, down to reproducing Suharto's propaganda narrative about the events of October 1965. There is no reference to the up to one million civilians killed as a result.

At the exit, kids pose for photos in front of a big sign that says, "Thank you for observing some of our dioramas about the savagery carried out by the Indonesian Communist Party. Don't let anything like this ever happen again."

Guatemala City

I rode back from Ilom to the capital in one of those old, cramped American school buses that serve as the only "public" transportation in this part of rural Guatemala. I've traveled a lot, rarely having the money to do so luxuriously, and often in places where luxurious travel doesn't even exist. But being on these buses meant being in constant pain, for almost two days straight.

But I was grateful for the ride. The bus belonged to Domingo, the brother of Antonio Caba Caba. They had both watched that morning in 1982 as the US-backed military executed most of the people in their village. Domingo had worked in the United States for years so he could save up and make this investment, and generate some income for the family. It is painted beautifully and he is proud of it. On the front, he had written, "God is love."

In Guatemala City, if you ask people when democracy ended in the country, many will give a quick answer: 1954. Árbenz was the last chance for social justice, they say. Most above a certain age will know someone who was killed in the decades of violence that followed. Stop and ask someone on the street, and they'll often have a horror story, and be able to tell you about the importance of 1954, of America's power here.

When I spoke with experts like Clara Arenas, head of the *Asociación para el Avance de las Ciencias Sociales en Guatemala*, we used slightly different terminology.

"Was the relationship that the United States had to Guatemala in 1954 imperialist?" I asked.

An easy one: "Yes."

Is the relationship between Washington—the government now—and Guatemala still imperialist? Still easy. Still yes.

On the bus from the town of Ilom to Nebaj, people had a slightly different understanding of twentieth-century politics. There was a different way of speaking employed by the Ixil people, most of whom still speak broken or accented Spanish. I asked them what they thought communism was. Domingo, the owner of the bus, had this answer: "Well, they said they were communists and that communists are dangerous. But actually, the government are the ones who did all the killing. So if anyone was dangerous, if anyone was 'communist,' it must be them."

Amsterdam

Like many other Indonesian exiles, Francisca Pattipilohy lives in Amsterdam. She's just a few miles outside the city center, in a tasteful little apartment packed with books. She reads slower than she used to, but she gets excited when each new title comes out—on Indonesia 1965, on Dutch colonialism, on art theory and capitalism, on US foreign policy—and makes her way through each.[12] I love visiting. She'll prepare snacks and talk for hours—maybe repeating herself sometimes, but spilling out more information than I'll ever have in my head.

Lots of older Indonesians live in the Netherlands too. Gde Arka and Yarna Mansur, the student couple trapped in the Soviet Union in 1965, finally made their way here. Sarmadji, who was stuck in China on October 1, 1965, lives here, and has other exiles round his small apartment for Indonesian food.

They were all born in Dutch territory, and now they are back. Over their entire lives, the dream of an independent Indonesia they could call their home only lasted a short fifteen years.

It was often hard to schedule interviews with Francisca. I'd have to make arrangements far in advance, because at ninety-four years old, she's extremely busy. She was deeply involved in the formation of the International People's Tribunal on the crimes of 1965–66. And now she's active in a new group lodging protests with the Dutch government. The group is opposing the direction of some new Dutch research into the period just before Indonesian independence, arguing it pays insufficient attention to colonial brutality. She's still fighting to tell the world what really happened in Indonesia.

She does take some breaks. She went on a family trip to Bali; then she had a stroke. But that didn't stop her, either. After a few months of rest, she started fighting again.

Appendixes

Appendix 1

The World in 1960: The 25 Most Populous Countries

Country	Population Rank	GDP / Capita (nominal)	Structural Position in 1945
China	1	$90	Third World
India	2	$82	Third World
Soviet Union	3	$991*	Second World
USA	4	$3,007	First World
Japan	5	$479	First World
Indonesia	6	$65**	Third World
Germany	7	$1,127***	First World
Brazil	8	$210	Third World
United Kingdon	9	$1,381	First World
Italy	10	$804	First World
Bangladesh	11	$89	Third World
France	12	$1,344	First World
Nigeria	13	$93	Third World
Pakistan	14	$82	Third World
Mexico	15	$345	Third World
Vietnam	16	$70 (N); $110 (S)****	Third World
Spain	17	$396	First World
Poland	18	$573*****	Second World
Turkey	19	$509	Third World
Thailand	20	$101	Third World
Egypt	21	$191**	Third World
Philippines	22	$245	Third World
South Korea	23	$158	Third World
Ethiopia	24	$61**	Third World
Iran	25	$192	Third World

All data (including population ranking) from the World Bank Data Bank (databank .worldbank.org) unless otherwise stated.

* This is derived from the US government estimate of the size of the Soviet economy as 38.1% of that of the United States (See "A Comparison of Soviet and US Gross National Products, 1960–1983," accessible via the CIA FOIA Reading Room, www.cia.gov/library /readingroom/docs/DOC_0000498181.pdf) and Soviet census data from 1959 (208,800,000, see www.foreignaffairs.com/articles/russian-federation/1959-07-01 /soviet-population-today) as well as US GDP data from the World Bank.

** Penn World Tables 9.1 (PWT91) (www.rug.nl/ggdc/productivity/pwt/)—output side, Year 1961

*** PWT91, 1960

**** These Vietnamese figures are drawn from contemporary CIA analysis: Economic Intelligence Report, A Comparison of the Economies of North and South Vietnam, December 1961, accessible via the CIA FOIA Reading Room, www.cia.gov/library /readingroom/docs/CIA-RDP79R01141A002200070001-8.pdf.

***** Data provided by Branko Milanovic, who relied on World Bank World Development Indicators, and adjusted using PWT91 Price Index.

Appendix 2

The World Today: The 25 Most Populous Countries (plus South Korea) in 2018

Country	Population Rank	GDP / Capita (nominal)	Structural Position in 1945
China	1	$9,771	Third World
India	2	$2,016	Third World
United States	3	$62,641	First World
Indonesia	4	$3,894	Third World
Pakistan	5	$1,473	Third World
Brazil	6	$8,921	Third World
Nigeria	7	$2,028	Third World
Bangladesh	8	$1,698	Third World
Russia	9	$11,289	Second World
Japan	10	$39,287	First World
Mexico	11	$9,698	Third World
Ethiopia	12	$772	Third World
Philippines	13	$3,103	Third World
Egypt	14	$2,549	Third World
Vietnam	15	$2,564	Third World
DR Congo	16	$562	Third World
Germany	17	$48,196	First World
Turkey	18	$9,311	Third World
Iran	19	$5,628*	Third World
Thailand	20	$7,274	Third World
France	21	$41,464	First World
United Kingdom	22	$42,491	First World
Italy	23	$34,318	First World
South Africa	24	$6,374	Third World
Tanzania	25	$1,051	Third World
South Korea	27	$31,363	Third World

All data (including population ranking) is from the World Bank Data Bank, databank.worldbank.org.

South Korea is included because it is the rare exception of a large country moving from the Third World to First-World levels of wealth. See Robert Wade, "Escaping the periphery: the East Asian 'mystery' solved," United Nations University World Institute for Development Economics Research, September 2018, for discussion of the exceptional treatment South Korea and Taiwan were given by Washington due to their strategic importance in the Cold War.

* 2017

Appendix 3

Global Inequality Between Countries, 1960–2017

The measure of inequality used here is the GINI coefficient. Purely for reference, inequality *within* the United States is around 41.5 (World Bank estimate). Some of the most equal societies on Earth, often in Northern Europe, hit lows of around 25, and South Africa, one of the world's most unequal nations, has a GINI index of 65.

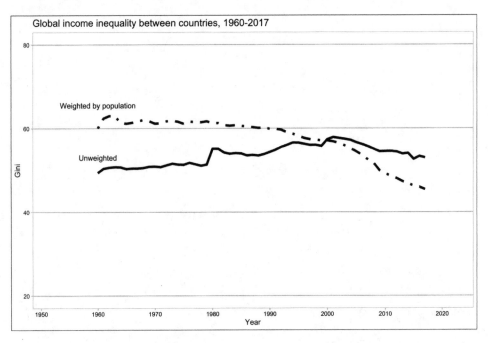

Data for the graph was provided by economist Branko Milanovic. The dotted line (weighted by country population) more clearly shows the effects of Chinese growth. For more on his methods, see Branko Milanovic, *Global Inequality*.

Appendix 4

Global Inequality, 1960-2017

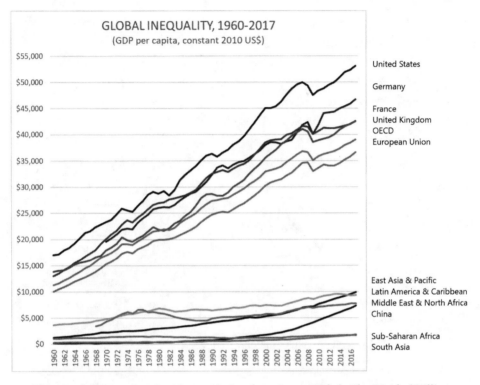

This graph is reproduced with permission from Jason Hickel, *The Divide* (William Heinemann, 2017).

Appendix 5

Anticommunist Extermination Programs, 1945–2000

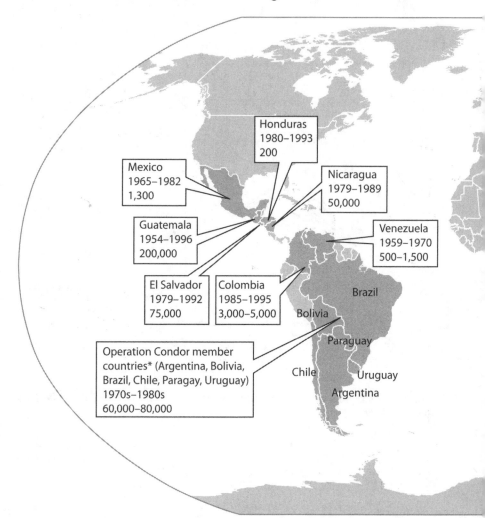

The map above illustrates intentional mass murder carried out to eliminate leftists or accused leftists, and does not include deaths from regular war, collateral damage from military engagements, or unintentional deaths (starvation, disease) caused by anticommunist governments.

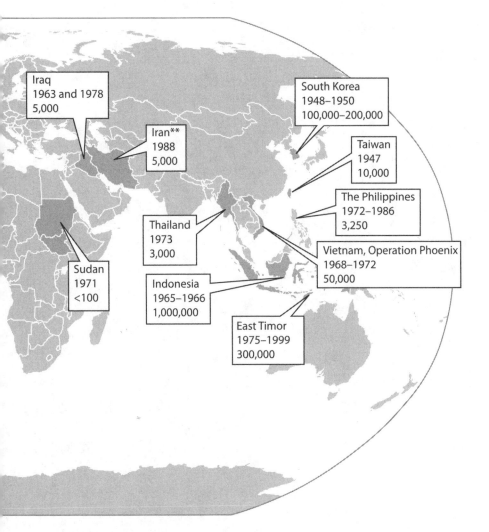

Iraq
1963 and 1978
5,000

South Korea
1948–1950
100,000–200,000

Iran**
1988
5,000

Taiwan
1947
10,000

The Philippines
1972–1986
3,250

Thailand
1973
3,000

Vietnam, Operation Phoenix
1968–1972
50,000

Sudan
1971
<100

Indonesia
1965–1966
1,000,000

East Timor
1975–1999
300,000

* Operation Condor itself was concerned with cross-border operations, which killed 400–500. This graphic includes all violence employed domestically by states that were part of the anticommunist alliance undergirding Condor.

** Please note that in this one case, the violence was carried out by a geopolitical rival of the United States.

Notes for the figures begin on page 305.

Acknowledgments

I'm fairly certain that even a talented expert could not write a book like this alone, and I am not a talented expert. So lots of thanks are in order.

First, I owe a debt of gratitude to my mother, and father, and brothers and sister, for always being there to support me, and to Sung, for being my smartest critic.

I have already thanked Baskara Wardaya, whose expertise and kindness made this book possible; and Bradley Simpson, whose diligent work and expansive generosity were crucial; and Febriana Firdaus, whose introductions and early encouragement were vital; but I want to thank them again here for allowing this project to exist in the first place. I'm also deeply grateful to John Roosa, Patrick Iber, Matias Spektor, Tanya Harmer, and Kirsten Weld for patiently explaining how I could write a book like this, or reading an early manuscript to (even more patiently) explain how it could be better, or doing both.

More than deserving thanks, there are a few people who should be recognized as coauthors of this book. I worked with a number of brilliant researchers who did some part-time work for me around the world. In the world of journalism, there is a spot after an article where you can write "additional reporting by"—that doesn't exist on book covers, but I want to note that the following people contributed crucial investigation: Willian de Almeida Silva at USP in São Paulo; Tyson Tirta and Stanley Widianto in Jakarta; Benjamin Concha at the Universidad Católica de Chile in Santiago; Yen Duong in Hanoi; Andrea Ixchíu in Guatemala City; Molly Avery at LSE in London; and João Vítor Rego-Costa at Cornell.

Of course, I am deeply grateful to everyone at *Sekretariat Bersama '65* in Solo, especially Winarso, Didik Dyah Suci Rahayu, and Nicholas Gebyar Krishna Shakti. They were my hosts for weeks and weeks, and held my hand through a long, difficult process. They're still holding my hand.

I'm truly unsure how I can ever pay back the survivors and witnesses who sat with me and told me their stories. Obviously, that goes for Francisca, and Benny, and Ing, and Sakono, Carmen Hertz, and Magdalena Kastinah, and Nury, Sumiyati and Agung Alit and Ngurah Termana and Wayan Badra, and Gde Arka, Yarna Mansur, and Sarmadji, Pedro Blaset and Guillermo Castillo, Clara Arenas, Antonio Caba Caba, Miguel Ángel Albizures, and Josefa Sanchez Del Barrio.

But it also goes for the many people who are not in the final version of the book. So I also want to offer my deepest thanks to Sunaryo, Vanius Silva Oliveira, Adriano Diogo, Sri Tunruang, Bedjo Untung, Rangga Purbaya, Maridi Marno, Sanusi, Nin Hanafi, Soe Tjen Marching, Djumadi, Franchesca Casauay, Zevonia Vieira, Coen Husain Pontoh, Made Mawut, Suratman, Sutarmi, Darsini, Soegianto and Maria Sri Sumarni, Rusman Prasetyo, Pramono Sidi, Supriyadi, Hariyono Sugiyono Raharjo, Hadi Pidekso, Liem Gie Liong and The Siok Swan, Hendra Winardi and Hediandi Lesmana, Ivo Herzog, Francina Loen, Tjin Giok Oey, Manuel Cabieses, Roberto Thieme, Orlando Saenz, Eduardo Labarca, Patricio "Pato" Madera, Pedro del Barrio Caba, Magdalena Caba Ramirez, Inenga Wardita, everyone at Taman 65 in Bali, Martin Aleida, Dilma Rousseff, and Zuhair Al-Jezairy.

The experts, scholars, and authorities who took the time to explain things to me, trade ideas, or point me in the right direction were more valuable than any amount of time I could have spent in the library. I want to offer my sincere gratitude, and apologizes for when I—perhaps behaving too much like a journalist—went to smarter people to ask for help, rather than trying to find the answer myself. So thank you, so much, to Ratna Saptari, Elio Gaspari, Mario Magalhães, Olímpio Cruz Neto, Marcos Napolitano, Petrik Matanasi, Ivan Aulia Ahsan, Hizkia Yosie Polimpung, Windu Jusuf, Andreas Harsono, Yerry Wirawan, Greg Grandin, Robert Wade, Lê Đăng Doanh, Jess Melvin, Taomo Zhou, Saskia Wieringa, Frank G. Wisner Jr., Peter Kornbluh, Greg Poulgrain, Joma Sison, Pedro Dallari, Rodrigo Patto Sá Motta, Luciano Martins Costa, Mariana Joffily, João Roberto Martins Filho, Fathi Alfadl, Ascanio Cavallo, Hector Reyes, Mario Castañeda, Noam

Chomsky, Ben Kiernan, Alfred McCoy, Vijay Prashad, Patrice McSherry, Federico Finchelstein, Jason Hickel, Branko Milanovic, Frederick Cooper, Ben Fogel, Adam Shatz, Kate Doyle, Tim Weiner, Sean Jacobs, Alexander Aviña, E. Ahmet Tonak, Ghassane Koumiya, Raimundos Oki, and Carlos H. Conde.

Thank you very much to Athena Bryan, and Clive Priddle, and Anupama Roy-Chaudhury at PublicAffairs. To Clive for giving the project the green light and guiding it to the end, to Athena for spotting the biggest errors in the first draft and pushing me in the right direction, and to Anu for helping me in every way imaginable. I'm grateful to Pete Garceau for the cover design and for being open to my input, to Brynn Warriner and Mark Sorkin for the copyediting, to Brooke Parsons and Miguel Cervantes for their book world expertise, and of course to Rob McQuilkin for finding a place for my idea in the first place.

My cousin Paige Evans, and my good friends Juliana Cunha and Niken Anjar Wulan (who is also in the book), provided much-needed advice and encouragement on the project as a whole, and I owe all three of them big time.

And though it might seem silly, I'd like to thank everyone that (still, for some reason) follows me on social media. For better or worse, they are likely part of the reason I was allowed to write a book. So if I get too annoying on there, please mute, don't unfollow. I'm also grateful to the many people I have learned from online, especially dedicated young people around the world.

I would have been lost without the support of the institutions, public or private, that allowed me to further my research: Perpustakaan Nasional Republik Indonesia, Arquivo Nacional do Brasil, the National Security Archive, Biblioteca Nacional de Chile, the British Library, the New York Public Library, the University of Malaya Library, Cornell University Library (especially Ekarina Winarto and Astara Light), the National Archives in Washington, DC, the Fundação Getúlio Vargas and its CPDOC Center, the Hoover Institution, SOAS University of London, University of São Paulo, Los Archivos Del Terror in Paraguay (with special thanks to Rosa Palau), the Museum Konferensi Asia Afrika in Bandung, and the National Library of Vietnam.

My deepest thanks to everyone above, and my apologies—and even deeper thanks—to anyone I have forgotten.

Notes

Introduction

1. *Bradley Simpson, Economists with Guns: Authoritarian Development and U.S.-Indonesian Relations, 1960–1968* (Palo Alto, CA: Stanford University Press, 2008), 5. Simpson notes here that "until the mid-1960s most officials still considered Indonesia of far greater importance than Vietnam or Laos." As we will see later, newspaper reports in 1965 confirm this balance of priorities.

2. Vincent Bevins, "The Politicians Voting to Impeach Brazil's President Are Accused of More Corruption Than She Is," *Los Angeles Times*, March 28, 2016.

3. Jonathan Watts, "Dilma Rousseff Taunt Opens Old Wounds of Dictatorship Era's Torture in Brazil," *The Guardian*, April 19, 2016.

4. Vincent Bevins, "Brazil Is in Turmoil, an Impeachment Trial Looms, and Still, Dilma Rousseff Laughs," *Los Angeles Times*, July 5, 2016.

5. The memorable phrase I'm referencing here is from Hegel: "Death that achieves nothing. . . . It is thus the most cold-blooded and meaningless death of all, with no more significance than cleaving a head of cabbage or swallowing a draught of water." In *Phenomenology of Spirit*, "Absolute Freedom and Terror," Section 590.

6. I am in great debt to Odd Arne Westad's *The Global Cold War: Third World Interventions and the Making of Our Times* (Cambridge: Cambridge University Press, 2005) for his meticulously researched affirmation that the Cold War was as much about shaping life in the Third World as it was a conflict between superpowers. I wish I already knew his arguments well before I started this project, but I confess I only read his work after I wrote my proposal, which relied upon a similar thesis. Perhaps my decade working in the "developing world" led me to the same conclusions as his scholarly research.

Chapter 1. A New American Age

1. For the Puritans in New England, their ideological commitment to the colonies, extremism in relation to England, and their conclusion that God "providentially cleared the land of its inhabitants to accommodate His people," see Virginia DeJohn Anderson, "New England in the Seventeenth Century," in *The Oxford History of the British Empire, Vol. 1: The Origins of Empire* (Oxford: Oxford University Press, 1998), 193–96.

2. Alexander Koch et al., "Earth System Impacts of the European Arrival and Great Dying in the Americas after 1492," *Quarternary Science Reviews* 207 (March 2019), www.sciencedirect.com/science/article/pii/S0277379118307261#!.

3. Adam Serwer, "White Nationalism's Deep American Roots," *The Atlantic*, April 2019. The affirmation that the systematic segregation amounted to "apartheid" in the contemporary usage of that term is mine, not Serwer's. On the fact that soldiers were segregated in World War II and the consequences of racialized justice in the military at the time, see, for example, Francis X. Clines, "When Black Soldiers Were Hanged: A War's Footnote," *New York Times*, February 7, 1993.

4. Alden Whitman, "'The Lightning' Strikes in War," *New York Times*, December 27, 1972, www.nytimes.com/1972/12/27/archives/harry-s-truman-decisive-president-the-lightning-strikes-in-war.html.

5. The official estimate is 27 million. Some claim the number is significantly higher. See Leonid Bershidsky, "A Message to Putin from 42 Million Dead," *Bloomberg*, May 10, 2017.

6. See Ronald Grigor Suny, *The Soviet Experiment: Russia, the USSR, and the Successor States* (Oxford: Oxford University Press, 2011), Chap. 3, "Socialism and Civil War," and Part III: Stalinism.

7. Westad, *The Global Cold War*, 10, 30.

8. Elizabeth Brainerd, "Uncounted Costs of World War II: The Effects of Changing Sex Ratios on Marriage and Fertility of Russian Women," 1–3. National Council for Eurasian and East European Research, www.ucis.pitt.edu/nceeer/2007_820-4g_Brainerd1.pdf.

9. The Louisiana Purchase (1803); the territories ceded by Mexico (1848) and the annexation of Texas (1845); as well as the acquisition of Florida (1819) all resulted from war or the threat of war. In *The Global Cold War*, Westad calls Manifest Destiny a "rather concrete imperialist program." See the first pages of Chapter 1 for this discussion.

10. Westad, *The Global Cold War*, 15.

11. The original coinage is from Alfred Sauvy, "Trois Mondes, Une Planété," *L'Observateur* no. 118, August 14, 1952. Cited and discussed in Vijay Prashad, *The Darker Nations: A People's History of the Third World* (New York: New Press, 2007), 6–11.

12. The figure is 68 percent for "developing countries." See "Urbanization: Facts and Figures," United Nations Centre for Human Settlements, 2001.

13. Westad, *The Global Cold War*, 83. For the discussion of whether or not Wilson's performance at Versailles directly caused Ho Chi Minh to take this position, see Brett Reilly, "The Myth of the Wilsonian Moment," Woodrow Wilson Center, www.wilsoncenter.org/blog-post/the-myth-the-wilsonian-moment. Whatever his motivations, it was right after the conference ended that he began lecturing on "Bolshevism in Asia" and urging French Socialists to join the Third International.

14. "Declaration of Independence," *Socialist Republic of Vietnam Government Portal*, www.chinhphu.vn/portal/page/portal/English/TheSocialistRepublicOfVietnam/AboutVietnam/.

15. Eric Hobsbawm, *The Age of Extremes* (London: Penguin, 1994), 235. Hobsbawm says "Americanism" can be "virtually defined as the polar opposite of communism."

16. Westad, *The Global Cold War*, 20–21.

17. In the 1945 French legislative election, the PCF (French Communist Party) came in first place, and in the 1946 Italian general election, combined votes for the Communists (PCI) and Socialists outnumbered those for the Christian Democratic Party. Under leader Pietro Nenni, the Italian Socialist Party was in close coalition with the PCI. See Alessando Brogi, *Confronting America: The Cold War between the United States and the Communists in France and Italy* (Chapel Hill, NC: University of North Carolina Press, 2011), 95–102.

18. Odd Arne Westad, *The Cold War: A World History* (New York: Basic Books, 2017), 92–95.

19. Ellen Schrecker, *The Age of McCarthyism: A Brief History with Documents* (Boston: Bedford/St Martin's, 2002), 27.

20. Stalin called the Greek rebellion "foolishness" because the British and Americans would never tolerate a "red" Greece. Vladislav Zubok and Constantine Pleshakov, *Inside the Kremlin's Cold War: From Stalin to Khruschev* (Cambridge: Harvard University Press, 1996), 56–57.

21. Tito wrote to Stalin: "Stalin. Stop sending assassins to murder me. We have already caught five, one with a bomb, another with a rifle . . ." Zhores A. Medvedev and Roy A. Medvedev, *The Unknown Stalin* (London: Tauris, 2003), 62.

22. On Stalin's goals and attitudes at the time, see Zubok and Pleshakov, *Inside the Kremlin's Cold War*, 28–50; on his "surprise and alarm" at Western confrontation, see ibid., 75, as well as Bert Cochran, *The War System* (New York: Macmillan, 1965), 42–43.

23. Brogi, *Confronting America*, 112–13. On both the left and the right in France and Italy, there was opposition to the American "productivist," mass-consumption model of capitalism that Washington was pushing.

24. A. James McAdams, *Vanguard of the Revolution: The Global Idea of the Communist Party* (Princeton, NJ: Princeton University Press, 2017), Chaps. 1–6.

25. On the uneasy alliance, see Patricia Stranahan, *Underground: The Shanghai Communist Party and the Politics of Survival 1927–1937* (Lanham, Maryland: Rowman & Littlefield, 1998), 7–11; for the broader overview, see also Rebecca E. Karl, *Mao Zedong and China in the Twentieth Century World* (Durham, NC: Duke University Press, 2010), 24–25.

26. Ruth McVey, *The Rise of Indonesian Communism* (Ithaca: Cornell Press, 1965; reprinted in Jakarta by Equinox, 2006), 76–81.

27. Karl, *Mao Zedong and China*, 25–33.

28. Ibid., 71.

29. On the US in relation to the expulsions in Italy and France, see Brogi, *Confronting America*, 82–87.

30. Ibid., 96; William Blum, *Killing Hope: U.S. Military and CIA Interventions since World War II* (Monroe, ME: Common Courage Press, 2004), chap. 2.

31. For a summary of Togliatti's 1947 remarks, see Brogi, *Confronting America*, 1. For the "Sinews of Peace" speech, which popularized a term that already existed, see Winston Churchill, "The Sinews of Peace ('Iron Curtain Speech')," March 5, 1946, International Churchill Society, at winstonchurchill.org/resources /speeches/1946-1963-elder-statesman/the-sinews-of-peace/.

32. Zubok and Pleshakov, *Inside the Kremlin's Cold War*, 53.

33. Karl, *Mao Zedong and China*, 77.

34. See Schrecker and Deery, *The Age of McCarthyism*.

35. Schrecker, *The Age of McCarthyism*, 28.

36. J. Edgar Hoover, Testimony before HUAC, March 26, 1947, printed in Schrecker, *The Age of McCarthyism*, 127–33.

37. Westad, *The Cold War*, 120; Schrecker, *The Age of McCarthyism*, 101; Owen Lattimore, "Far East Scholar Accused by McCarthy, Dies at 88," *New York Times*, June 1, 1989.

38. Rodrigo Patto Sá Motta, *Em Guarda Contra o Perigo Vermelho: O anticomunismo no Brasil 1917–1964* (São Paulo: Editora Perspectiva, 2002), 2.

39. For an overview of the Madiun Affair, especially in relation to the Soviet Union and events in Yugoslavia, see Ruth McVey, *The Soviet View of the Indonesian Revolution: A Study in the Russian Attitude towards Asian Nationalism* (Singapore: Equinox, 1959), 63–87.

40. Westad, *The Global Cold War*, 119.

41. Robert Dallek, *An Unfinished Life: John F. Kennedy 1917–1963* (New York: Little Brown, 2003), 175.

42. Ibid., 130.

43. Ibid., 132.

44. David M. Oshinsky, *A Conspiracy So Immense* (Oxford: Oxford University Press, 2005), 33, 490.

45. Dallek, *An Unfinished Life*, 165.

46. Papers of John F. Kennedy: Pre-Presidential Papers, House of Representative Files, Speeches, 1947–1952, Boston Office Speech Files, 1946–1952, Trip to Middle and Far East, November 14, 1951, JFKREP-0095-037, John F. Kennedy Presidential Library and Museum; Dallek, *An Unfinished Life*, 165–66. Kennedy's impression of Jakarta from this trip are recorded in a separate folder relating to this trip. See Papers of John F. Kennedy: Personal Papers, Boston Office, 1940–1956: Political Miscellany, 1945–1956, Asian trip, 1951.

47. Ibid.

48. Shashi Tharoor, "In Winston Churchill, Hollywood Rewards a Mass Murderer," *Washington Post*, March 10, 2018, www.washingtonpost.com/news/global-opinions /wp/2018/03/10/in-winston-churchill-hollywood-rewards-a-mass-murderer/?utm _term=.a162f746f9ab. See also Shashi Tharoor, "The Ugly Briton," *Time*, November 29, 2010, http://content.time.com/time/magazine/article/0,9171,2031992,00.html.

49. This episode is recounted in Arthur M. Schlesinger, Jr., *Robert Kennedy and His Times* (London: Andre Deutsch, 1978), 91.

50. Family testimony is drawn from author interviews with Frank Wisner Jr. in 2018 and 2019. For Wisner in Romania, see Tim Weiner, *Legacy of Ashes: The History of the CIA* (New York: Doubleday, 2007), 11–12; Evan Thomas, *The Very Best Men: Four Who Dared: The Early Years of the CIA* (New York: Simon & Schuster, 2006), 19–22; George Cristian Maior, *America's First Spy: The Tragic Heroism of Frank Wisner* (London, Washington DC: Academia Press, 2018), chaps. 1–12.

51. Author interview, Frank Wisner Jr., 2018.

52. Maior, *America's First Spy*, 190–91.

53. For details on Wisner's early life, see the first chapter of Thomas, *The Very Best Men*, and Maior, *America's First Spy*, chaps. 1–8.

54. Beverly Bowie, who was stationed in Romania at the same time, later wrote Wisner into the novel *Operation Bughouse* as a manic operative who sets up in a large madam's house and immediately tries to declare war on the Soviet Union. See *Operation Bughouse* (New York: Dodd, Mead, 1947).

55. Weiner, *Legacy of Ashes*, 18.

56. Author interview with Frank Wisner Jr. in 2018.

57. The anecdote regarding the German soldiers is in a biographical sketch found in Howard Palfrey Jones Papers, Box 51, Biographical Materials, Hoover Institution Library and Archives.

58. "'Soft-Sell' Envoy; U.S. Accused of Meddling," *New York Times*, April 5, 1962; Howard Palfrey Jones Papers, Biographic Sketch of Ambassador Howard Palfrey Jones, Box 51, Biographical Materials, Hoover Institution Library and Archives, Stanford University.

59. For early childhood recollections, see Howard Palfrey Jones Papers, Box 51, Biographical Materials, Hoover Institution Library and Archives.

60. Howard Palfrey Jones, "The Life of an American Diplomat," in Marcy Babbit, *Living Christian Science: Fourteen Lives* (Prentice Hall, 1975), 34–35.

61. For Wisner's stance on the currency, see Maior, *America's First Spy*, 179; for Stalin's understanding of events in Berlin 1947–1949, see Zubok and Pleshakov, *The Kremlin's Cold War*, 50–53. For the importance of the new currency in the partition of Germany, see Westad, *The Cold War*, 111–16.

62. Kyle Burke, *Revolutionaries for the Right*, 14.

63. Burton Hersh, *The Old Boys*, 159. Cited in Thomas, *The Very Best Men*, 23.

64. Author interview, Frank Wisner Jr., 2018.

65. Thomas, *The Very Best Men*, 207.

66. Ibid., 91.

67. Weiner, *Legacy of Ashes*, 33.

68. Thomas, *The Very Best Men*, 25–36.

69. Ibid., 111.

Chapter 2. Independent Indonesia

1. Francisca's story is based on the author's interviews between 2018 and 2020, in Amsterdam and over the phone.

2. Anthony Reid, *A History of Southeast Asia* (Oxford: Wiley Blackwell, 2015), 70–73.

3. For the relationship between the nationalist movement and Japanese occupation, see J. D. Legge, *Sukarno: A Political Biography* (New York: Praeger Publishers, 1972), chap. 7.

4. For this reason it is incorrect to call Indonesian just "Bahasa." There are also "Bahasa Jawa" (Javanese), "Bahasa Inggris" (English), etc. Correct usages are "Bahasa Indonesia" in Indonesian, or just "Indonesian."

5. In the 1930 census, only 2 percent of Dutch East Indies residents spoke Malay as a first language. By 1980, Indonesian was used at home by 12 percent of the population, but by 36 percent of city dwellers and a large proportion of age groups. Now in

Indonesia, almost everyone in Indonesia can speak Bahasa Indonesia to some degree, though they may speak other languages at home or in their regions. See Reid, *History of Southeast Asia*, 397.

6. A note on names in this part of the world: Some Indonesians have two names, and some only have one, but often, the second name isn't a patronymic "last name," passed down from the father. "Sukarno" is the full, correct way to refer to him, and virtually the only thing he is ever called within Indonesia. Francisca, being from the Maluku Islands (which have different naming conventions), does indeed have a surname, but because this is not universal in Indonesia, calling someone simply by their first name is very common, and in no way diminutive. I will very often refer to Indonesians only by a single name, whereas I might refer to Westerners by their surname only, for these reasons.

7. Tim Hannigan, *A Brief History of Indonesia* (Tokyo: Tuttle, 2015), chap. 8.

8. David Van Reybrouck, *Congo: The Epic History of a People* (London: Fourth Estate, 2014), 168–70.

9. Saskia Wieringa, *Propaganda and Genocide in Indonesia: Imagined Evil* (London and New York: Routledge, 2018), 61–65. First, in 1914 Henk Sneevliet helped found the Indies Social Democratic Association (ISDV), whose name was changed to Communist Association (PKH) in 1920. Finally, they settled on Partai Komunis Indonesia (PKI) in 1924.

10. We've been unable to confirm that *the* Patrice Lumumba was in Hungary at the time, so it's possible this memory is apocryphal, or that there was simply someone else with a similar name she met from the Congo that year. In any case, when she began reading about events in that country later in her life, she immediately connected them to her experience with this man in Hungary.

11. Washington P. Napitupulu, "Illiteracy Eradication Programme in Indonesia," presented at the workshop on Planning and Administration of National Literacy Programs, Arusha, Tanzania, November 27–December 2, 1980.

12. *Harian Rakjat* archives, University of Malaya, Kuala Lumpur.

13. Westad, *The Cold War*, 161; Michael J. Seth, *A Concise History of Modern Korea* (Lanham, Maryland: Rowan & Littlefield, 2010), 88.

14. Bruce Cumings, *The Korean War: A History* (New York: Modern Library, 2010), subsections on "The Cheju Insurgency" and "The Yosu Rebellion," chap. 5.

15. Ibid.

16. Weiner, *Legacy of Ashes*, 54.

17. On the famine, see Weiner, *Legacy of Ashes*, 81; and for the James A. Bill quote, see Stephen Kinzer, *Overthrow: America's Century of Regime Change from Hawaii to Iraq* (New York: Times Books, 2006), 122.

18. For an overview of CIA activity in Iran, see Weiner, *Legacy of Ashes*, chap. 9; For Roosevelt's threat against Iranian agents, see Kinzer, *Overthrow*, 127.

19. Lansdale cited in Westad, *The Global Cold War*, 115; for Lansdale as the model for Burdick and Lederer's *The Ugly American*, see Thomas, *The Very Best Men*, 57.

20. Westad, *The Global Cold War*, 117.

21. Thomas, *The Very Best Men*, 57.

22. For Iran, see *Harian Rakjat*, August 18, 21, 22, and 24, 1953. The front page on June 26, 1954, reports on use of napalm in the Philippines. University of Malaya archives, Kuala Lumpur.

23. For Wisner's successful efforts to control the press in the United States, see Maior, *America's First Spy*, 197–98.

24. Author interview with former *Harian Rakjat* employee Martin Aleida, Jakarta, 2019.

25. For background on the Guatemalan revolution and presidency of Juan José Arévalo, see Ralph Lee Woodward Jr., *A Short History of Guatemala* (La Antigua, Guatemala: Editorial Laura Lee, 2008), chap. 7; and Stephen Schlesinger and Stephen Kinzer, *Bitter Fruit: The Story of the American Coup in Guatemala* (Cambridge, MA: Harvard University Press, 2005), chaps. 2–3.

26. Walter LaFeber, *Inevitable Revolutions: The United States in Central America* (New York: Norton, 1993), 120–21; Schlesinger and Kinzer, *Bitter Fruit*, 51–53, 58.

27. United Fruit's lobbying operation in Washington is detailed in Schlesinger and Kinzer, *Bitter Fruit*, 88–97. United Fruit also held extensive direct ties to key individuals in the Eisenhower White House: both John Foster Dulles and Allen Dulles had carried out legal work for United Fruit through its subsidiary, International Railways of Central America (IRCA). The family of John Moors Cabot, assistant secretary of state for inter-American affairs, owned stock in United Fruit, and his brother Thomas served as president of the corporation in 1948. US Ambassador to the United Nations Henry Cabot Lodge was also a stockholder, and Eisenhower's personal secretary, Anne Whitman, was the wife of United Fruit's director of public relations. Undersecretary of State Walter Bedell Smith was seeking an executive job with United Fruit *at the same time* as he was helping to plan the coup against Árbenz. Schlesinger and Kinzer, *Bitter Fruit*, 106–07.

28. Ibid., 101.

29. The first coup attempt, Operation Fortune, in 1952, was aborted after Dean Acheson convinced Truman to withdraw his support; the second, which involved using United Fruit money to support disgruntled right-wing officers in the Guatemalan army in staging an uprising in Salamá, failed. Schlesinger and Kinzer, *Bitter Fruit*, 102–03.

30. Ibid., 132.

31. Ibid., 183–90.

32. Author interview with Miguel Ángel Albizures, Guatemala City, November 2018.

33. Schlesinger and Kinzer, *Bitter Fruit*, 195–98.

34. Ibid., 205–08.

35. Greg Grandin, *The Last Colonial Massacre: Latin America in the Cold War* (Chicago: University of Chicago Press, 2004), 66–67. For details on Peurifoy's insistence that this be done as well as Anticommunism Day, see Schlesinger and Kinzer, *Bitter Fruit*, 207–16.

36. Thomas, *The Very Best Men*, 124.

37. *Harian Rakjat*, June 21, 1953; June 23, 1953; and June 25, 1953. *Harian Rakjat* archives, University of Malaya, Kuala Lumpur.

38. These assertions were repeated throughout *New York Times* coverage. See, in particular, editions from June 20, June 29, and July 1, 1954. I compared this coverage extensively to *Harian Rakjat* issues viewed in Malaysia and made my own judgment based on my knowledge of current historical consensus.

39. Thomas, *The Very Best Men*, 117. See also Schlesinger and Kinzer, *Bitter Fruit*, 154–55, and Maior, *America's First Spy*, 198.

40. *Harian Rakjat*, June 26, 1954.

41. "Memorandum by Louis J. Halle, Jr. of the Policy Planning Staff to the Director of the Policy Planning Staff (Bowie)," Washington, May 28, 1954, *Foreign Relations of the United States (FRUS) 1952–1954, Vol. 4, The American Republics* (Washington, DC: Government Printing Office, 1983).

42. Piero Gleijeses, *Shattered Hope: The Guatemalan Revolution and the United States, 1944–54* (Princeton, NJ: Princeton University Press, 1991), 366.

43. Author interview with Frank Wisner Jr., July 2018.

44. Ernesto "Che" Guevara, *Back on the Road: A Journey to Central America* (London: Vintage, 2002), 67.

45. Howard P. Jones, *Indonesia: The Possible Dream* (Stanford, CA: Hoover Institution, 1971; fourth printing, Singapore: Toppan Printing, 1980), 38–40.

46. This quote is drawn from a draft chapter of Jones's autobiography. Draft book manuscript, Box 51, Folder 1, Howard Palfrey Jones Papers, Hoover Institution Archives and Library (herein HI). Interestingly, the first draft was savaged by an unidentified critic who wrote in the margins that it "shouldn't be published."

47. Ibid.

48. Jones, *Indonesia: The Possible Dream*, 47–49.

49. Arnold M. Ludwig, *King of the Mountain: The Nature of Political Leadership* (Lexington, KY: University Press of Kentucky, 2004), 150.

50. Jones, *Indonesia: The Possible Dream*, 49.

51. On Sukarno's early life, see Legge, *Sukarno*, chap. 1.

52. For identification of socialism and independence, see McVey, *Rise of Indonesian Communism*, 20; for Muslim communist thinking, see 171–76.

53. Ibid., 73.

54. Legge, *Sukarno*, 97–98.

55. The PKI signed off on Pancasila in 1954. Rex Mortimer, *Indonesian Communism under Sukarno: Ideology and Politics 1959–1965* (Ithaca, NY: Cornell University Press, 1974), 66–67. For D. N. Aidit's tortured theoretical justifications, see also 92.

56. When I first started covering Southeast Asia, I was shocked to find that in Malaysia, Malays speak Malay, ethnic Chinese speak a Chinese dialect, and "Indians" speak Tamil. There is no language that everyone speaks fluently, at least not compared to Indonesia. Similarly, I was taken aback to learn that Duterte does not even speak Tagalog fluently—he gives his national addresses in English, which not every Filipino speaks.

57. Jones, *Indonesia: The Possible Dream*, 42–44.

58. Legge, *Sukarno*, 260–61.

59. Jones, *Indonesia: The Possible Dream*, 80.

60. Christopher J. Lee, "Between a Moment and an Era: The Origins and Afterlives of Bandung," in *Making a World after Empire: The Bandung Moment and its Political Afterlives*, Christopher J. Lee, ed. (Athens, OH: Ohio University Press, 2010), loc. 217 of 4658, Kindle.

61. I'm using the official transcript, which can be found in many places online, such as www.cvce.eu/content/publication/2001/9/5/88d3f71c-c9f9-415a-b397-b27b8581a4f5/publishable_en.pdf. However, in the video of the original speech (easily found online as well), he stops himself at this point and says, ". . . so-called colored peoples."

62. Lee, "Between a Moment and an Era," loc. 195 of 4656, Kindle.

63. Dipesh Chakrabarty, "The Legacies of Bandung: Decolonization and the Politics of Culture," in *Making a World After Empire*, loc. 641 of 4658, Kindle; Richard Wright, *The Color Curtain: A Report on the Bandung Conference* (Jackson, MI: Banner Books, 1956), 158–65.

64. Prashad, *Darker Nations*, 12, 33, and 68 for discussion of Bandung nationalism, Sukarno's plan, and terms of trade goals, respectively.

65. *Harian Rakjat*, April 18, 1955, and April 19, 1955. *Harian Rakjat* archives, University of Malaya, Kuala Lumpur. Coincidentally, the paper did promote cure-all tablets and medicines in the back section. No matter how communist they were, it seems they could use the advertising revenue.

66. Wright, *The Color Curtain*, 12.

67. Ibid.,16, 35–60.

68. Ibid., 78, 103.

69. Ibid., 180–81. Wright says the book was *Bahasa Indonesia*, compiled by S. van der Molen (and adapted to English by Harry F. Cemach).

70. See James R. Brennan, "Radio Cairo and the Decolonization of East Africa, 1953–1964," in *Making a World After Empire*.

71. Van Reybrouck, *Congo*, 233.

72. Laura Bier, "Feminism, Solidarity, and Identity in the Age of Bandung," in *Making a World After Empire*, loc. 1789 of 4685, Kindle.

73. Ibid., loc. 1695 of 4685, Kindle.

74. Thomas, *The Very Best Men*, 157.

75. John F. Kennedy, Remarks to the US Senate, July 2, 1952, www.jfklibrary.org /archives/other-resources/john-f-kennedy-speeches/united-states-senate-imperialism -19570702.

76. Thomas, *The Very Best Men*, 157–58; Jess Melvin, *The Army and the Indonesian Genocide: Mechanics of Mass Murder* (New York: Routledge, 2018), 7.

Chapter 3. Feet to the Fire, Pope in the Sky

1. Nikita Khrushchev, "On the Cult of Personality and Its Consequences," February 25, 1956, https://digitalarchive.wilsoncenter.org/document/115995.

2. Suny, *The Soviet Experiment*, 413.

3. For the importance of the "secret speech" in laying the foundations for the Sino-Soviet split, see Lorenz M. Luthi, *The Sino-Soviet Split: Cold War in the Communist World* (Princeton, NJ: Princeton University Press, 2008), chap. 2.

4. Mortimer, *Indonesian Communism Under Sukarno*, 26, 36, 44–45, 57–65, 171.

5. Thomas, *The Very Best Men*, 145–47.

6. Westad, *The Global Cold War*, 125–28. According to Westad, Eisenhower opposed intervention in Egypt (in contrast to his very enthusiastic support elsewhere) for two reasons: One, he wanted to contrast US behavior with the Soviet crackdown in Hungary; and two, it seemed that Nasser wasn't going anywhere, whether the Europeans got the canal back or not.

7. Stanley Karnow, *Vietnam: A History*, 2nd ed. (New York: Penguin, 1991), 238–39.

8. Both this quote and the claim that he was overworked and emotional are from my interviews with Frank Wisner Jr.

9. Joseph Burkholder Smith, *Portrait of a Cold Warrior* (New York: G. P. Putnam, 1976), 205.

10. Geoffrey B. Robinson, *The Killing Season: A History of the Indonesian Massacres, 1965–66* (Princeton, NJ: Princeton University Press, 2018), 43–44. On December 19, 1960, the National Security Council recognized that the PKI stood in marked contrast to the "venality and incompetence" of the non-Communist organizations. National Security Council Report, NSC 6023, Draft Statement of US Policy on Indonesia, December 19, 1960, Document 293, *FRUS, 1958–1960*, Indonesia, Volume XVII, at https://history.state.gov/historicaldocuments/frus1958-60v17/d293.

11. Editorial Note, NSC Meeting on April 5, 1956, *FRUS, 1955–1957*, Vol. XXII, 254. Cited in Simpson, *Economists with Guns*, 32.

12. Jones, *Indonesia: The Possible Dream*, 45.

13. Spoiler alert: stop here if you don't want to know how things go for Sakono. All information pertaining to his life comes from author interviews with him in Solo, 2018–19.

14. Mortimer, *Indonesian Communism under Sukarno*, 64–65.

15. In Indonesian, BTI is Barisan Tani Indonesia, LEKRA is Lembaga Kebudayaan Rakyat, and SOBSI is Sentral Organisasi Buruh Seluruh Indonesia. In English, these are sometimes translated as the Peasants Front of Indonesia, the Institute for the People's Culture, and the All-Indonesian Federation of Workers' Organizations, respectively.

16. Wieringa, *Propaganda and Genocide*, 106. For more on *Gerwani*, see also Saskia Wieringa, *Sexual Politics in Indonesia* (The Hague: Palgrave, 2002).

17. Author interviews with Sumiyati, 2018, in Solo, Indonesia.

18. *Harian Rakjat*, May 19, 1958.

19. Jones, *Indonesia: The Possible Dream*, 115–18.

20. Ibid., 119–20.

21. "Aid to Indonesian Rebels," *New York Times*, May 9, 1958.

22. For an account of Pope's attacks on Ambon, told from the perspective of the pilots, see Kenneth Conboy and James Morrisson, *Feet to the Fire: CIA Covert Operations in Indonesia, 1957–1958* (Naval Institute Press, 1999), 115–140. For the bombing of the market, killing people on the way to church, see Jones, *Indonesia: The Possible Dream*, 129. Evans says that the bomb actually hit the church itself: *The Very Best Men*, 158.

23. Conboy and Morrisson, *Feet to the Fire*, 166.

24. "Indonesian Operation—Original Concept of Operation," CIA Library, approved for release in 2002, www.cia.gov/library/readingroom/docs/CIA-RDP89B00552R000100040006-9.pdf.

25. Thomas, *The Very Best Men*, 158.

26. Jones, *Indonesia: The Possible Dream*, 130.

27. Ibid., 135. Other accounts have put the rice figure at 37,000 tons. See, for example, Thomas, *The Very Best Men*, 159; and Maior, *America's First Spy*, 251.

28. For the similarities in the CIA's perception and planning in Guatemala and Indonesia, see Maior, *America's First Spy*, 250.

29. Jones, *Indonesia: The Possible Dream*, 342.

30. Ibid., 121.

31. Ibid., 122.

32. Thomas, *The Very Best Men*, 160; Maior, *America's First Spy*, 251–52.

33. Simpson, *Economists with Guns*, 29–30.

34. "Summary of Facts, Investigating CIA Involvement in Plans to Assassinate Foreign Leaders," Executive Director of the CIA Commission, May 30, 1975, 4, www.archives.gov/files/research/jfk/releases/docid-32112745.pdf.

35. Thomas, *The Very Best Men*, 158.

36. Smith, *Portrait of a Cold Warrior*, 238–40; and Robert Maheu and Richard Hack, *Next to Hughes: Behind the Power and Tragic Downfall of Howard Hughes by His Closest Advisor* (New York, NY: HarperCollins, 1992), 71–115.

37. Jones, *Indonesia: The Possible Dream*, chap. 9.

38. Ibid., chap. 10.

39. Jones, *Indonesia: The Possible Dream*, 181.

Chapter 4. An Alliance for Progress

1. On Chinese immigration to Southeast Asia, see Reid, *History of Southeast Asia*, in particular 81–85, 191–95. All information on Benny Widyono's life is from author interviews.

2. Legge, *Sukarno*, 282–83.

3. Jones, *Indonesia: The Possible Dream*, 242; Mortimer, *Indonesian Communism under Sukarno*, 120–22.

4. Telegram 272 from Singapore to the Foreign Office, April 25, 1958, Records of the Prime Minister's Office (PREM) 11-2370, UK National Archives, cited in Simpson, *Economists with Guns*, 35.

5. Jones, *Indonesia: The Possible Dream*, 160.

6. Legge, *Sukarno*, 297.

7. Bryan Evans III, "The Influence of the United States Army on the Development of the Indonesian Army (1954–1964)," *Indonesia* 47 (April 1989): 27, 44.

8. In his masterful intellectual history of Modernization Theory, Nils Gilman explains that it was a response to the seemingly attractive model for Third World development offered by the Soviet Union, and in many ways transformed anticommunism "from the hysterical red-baiting populism of McCarthy into a social-scientifically respectable political position." Nils Gilman, *Mandarins of the Future: Modernization Theory in Cold War America* (Baltimore, MD: Johns Hopkins Press, 2003), loc. 221 of 4567, Kindle.

9. Simpson, *Economists with Guns*, 36.

10. Ibid., 19.

11. Dallek, *An Unfinished Life*, 294.

12. Telegram 2154 from Jakarta to State, January 25, 1961, RG 59, Central Files, 611.98/1-2561, NA. Cited in Simpson, *Economists with Guns*, 39.

13. John F. Kennedy Presidential Papers, President's Office Files, Speech Files, Inaugural Address, January 20, 1961, at www.jfklibrary.org/asset-viewer/archives/JFKPOF/034/JFKPOF-034-002.

14. Van Reybrouck, *Congo*, 259.

15. Ibid., 299.

16. Ibid., 296–98.

17. Quoted in "Alleged Assassination Plots Involving Foreign Leaders, an Interim Report of the Select Committee to Study Governmental Operations with Respect to

Intelligence Activities," US Senate, November 20, 1975 (US Government Printing Office, Washington, DC: 1975), 53, at www.intelligence.senate.gov/sites/default/files/94465.pdf.

18. Thomas, *The Very Best Men*, 221. See also Senate Report, "Alleged Assassination Plots Involving Foreign Leaders," 57.

19. On August 26 Dulles signed a cable emphasizing the priority of the "removal" of Lumumba; this was taken by CIA operatives in the Congo as a "circumlocutious means of indicating that the President wanted Lumumba killed." See Senate Report, "Alleged Assassination Plots Involving Foreign Leaders," 15–16.

20. For discussion of Project MK-Ultra, see Thomas, *The Very Best Men*, 211–12. There is now extensive declassified information on the illegal program.

21. Van Reybrouck, *Congo*, 304.

22. Thomas, *The Very Best Men*, 222–24.

23. Van Reybrouck, *Congo*, 306–08.

24. Ibid., 336–39.

25. Dallek, *An Unfinished Life*, 357.

26. Ibid., 367.

27. Zubok and Pleshakov, *Inside the Kremlin's Cold War*, 245–53.

28. Simpson, *Economists with Guns*, 51.

29. Jones, *Indonesia: The Possible Dream*, 197.

30. Ibid., 144.

31. Philip Short, *Pol Pot: Anatomy of a Nightmare* (New York: Henry Holt, 2004), 124–28.

32. Prince Norodom Sihanouk, *My War With the CIA: The Memoirs of Prince Norodom Sihanouk, as related to Wilfred Burchett* (London: Penguin, 1974), 110.

33. Short, *Pol Pot*, 128.

34. Thomas, *The Very Best Men*, 286–91.

35. Ibid., 207, 225–29.

36. Ibid., 294–95.

37. Ibid., 287–89.

38. Dallek, *An Unfinished Life*, 400. They did not do this. Bowles considered the idea "half-cocked."

39. Simpson, *Economists with Guns*, 73–75.

40. National Security Council, "Urgent Planning Problems," June 9, 1961, NSF, Komer Series, Box 438, JFK Library, cited in Simpson, *Economists with Guns*, 53.

41. CIA paper for the Special Group, December 11, 1961, and December 14, 1961, mentioned in *FRUS 1964-1968, Vol. XXVI*, 234–35. Cited in Simpson, *Economists with Guns*, 75.

42. Thomas, *The Very Best Men*, 36–37.

43. Roger Morris, "A Tyrant 40 Years in the Making," *New York Times*, March 14, 2003.

44. Author interview with Zuhair Al-Jezairy, September 2019.

Chapter 5. To Brazil and Back

1. Peter Dale Scott, "The United States and the Overthrow of Sukarno, 1965–1967," *Pacific Affairs* 58, no. 2 (Summer 1985): 249.

2. Legend has it in the Indonesian Brazilian community, mostly in São Paulo, that the immigration started around 1960, when an Indonesian pilot first visited the country and started spreading the word to his friends and relatives.

3. All information about Ing Giok and the Tan family based on author interviews in São Paulo, 2017–2019.

4. A number of postcolonial countries owed their names to a commodity exported in the early days of European contact. For example: Argentina (silver), Gold Coast (now Ghana), Ivory Coast, etc.

5. The original text is Hans Staden's *True Story and Description of a Country of Wild, Naked, Grim, Man-eating People in the New World, America* (Andreas Kolbe Publishing, 1557, with woodcuts). For more discussion of the text, see also Vincent Bevins, "The Correct Way to Be a Cannibal," *The Outline*, September 20, 2017.

6. Lilia M. Schwarcz and Heloisa M. Starling, *Brazil: A Biography* (London: Allen Lane, 2018), 86.

7. Thomas E. Skidmore, *Brazil: Five Centuries of Change*, 2nd ed. (Oxford: Oxford University Press), 83.

8. Jeffrey Lesser, "Negócios com a 'raça brasileira,'" *Folha de S.Paulo*, June 6, 1999.

9. W. Michael Weis, *Cold Warriors and Coups d'Etat: Brazilian-American Relations, 1945–1954* (Albuquerque, NM: University of New Mexico Press, 1993), 11, 21–22.

10. Schwarcz and Starling, *Brazil*, 450. It's also worth noting that in many ways, Brazil was an earlier and more enthusiastic anticommunist nation in the Cold War than the United States. See also Patto Sá Motta, *Em Guarda Contra O Perigo Vermelho*, 3.

11. Weis, *Cold Warriors*, 24–30; the use of the word "gringo" is my own—in Brazilian Portuguese, the word has no negative connotations.

12. In his annual address to the Brazilian National Congress in March 1953, Vargas elaborated on Brazil's support for colonial freedom struggles in the UN General Assembly the previous October. See Getulio Vargas, Mensagem ao Congresso Nacional, Rio de Janeiro, March 15, 1953, 17–19, accessed online September 17, 2019, at www.biblioteca .presidencia.gov.br/publicacoes-oficiais/mensagem-ao-congresso-.

13. Weis, *Cold Warriors*, 71–75.

14. "Brazil Oil Monopoly Created by New Law," *New York Times*, October 5, 1953.

15. Weis, *Cold Warriors*, 77.

16. Ibid., 85. Weis's footnote for this is as follows: "Regarding the goals and activities of USIS/Brazil, see Trimble to Kemper, Sept. 28, 1954, file 320, Rio Post file, State Department archives. USIS received 490,000 dollars for 1955, compared to 360,000 dollars for 1954."

17. Ibid., 128.

18. Telegram from the Ambassador to Brazil (Gordon) to the Department of State, Rio de Janeiro, March 28, 1964, *FRUS, 1964–1968*, Vol. XXXI, 187, at https://history .state.gov/historicaldocuments/frus1964-68v31/d187.

19. Bruce L. R. Smith, *Lincoln Gordon: Architect of Cold War Foreign Policy* (Lexington, KY: Kentucky University Press, 2015), chaps. 8–10, chaps. 12–13.

20. Ibid., 150–55, 202, 224. There are other mentions of their interaction throughout the book, but since meeting in World War II and consulting him about entering Harvard Business School, he was certainly an "old friend" by the early 1960s.

21. Ibid., 237.

22. Weis, *Cold Warriors*, 143.

23. John Gerassi, *The Great Fear in Latin America* (New York: Collier Books, 1971), 83.

24. Marcos Napolitano, *1964: História do Regime Militar Brasileiro* (São Paulo: Contexto, 2014), 32–33.

25. Ibid., 33–38.

26. "Meeting on Brazil on July 30, 1962," Presidential Records, Digital Edition. Recording of the conversation hosted by the University of Virginia at https://prde.upress .virginia.edu/vl/documents?uri=8010002.xml.

27. Thomas, *The Very Best Men*, 323. I am assuming this is based on an interview Thomas conducted with either Hogan or Fitzgerald, because the source he cites—John Ranelagh, *The Agency* (London: Weidenfeld and Nicolson, 1986)—for the relevant passage contains no mention.

28. For characterization as "counterinsurgency assessment," see Weis, *Cold Warriors*, 156. For the conclusions, see "Report From the Inter-Departmental Survey Team on Brazil to President Kennedy," *FRUS, 1961–1963, Vol. XII*, 228.

29. Weis, *Cold Warriors*, 131.

30. Elio Gaspari, *A Ditadura Envergonhada (Coleção Ditatdura Livro 1)*, chap. 1, "O Exército dormiu Janguista," loc. 1088 of 13184, Kindle. Gaspari demonstrates that Walters did not want to come; it was certainly not a promotion, which lends more weight to the supposition (widely held in Brazil) that he was sent to "fix" things. I return to Walters and his memoirs in the last subsection of this chapter.

31. Vernon A. Walters, *Silent Missions* (New York: Doubleday, 1978).

32. Dallek, *An Unfinished Life*, 522.

33. Schwarcz and Starling, *Brazil*, 501–07.

34. Weis, *Cold Warriors*, 161. The organization was Instituto Brasileiro de Ação Democrática. When Pernambucan Governor Miguel Arraes credibly alleged that AID was being used for elections, the US withdrew assistance in his region, and tensions worsened between the governments.

35. Weis, *Cold Warriors*, 231. The footnotes section makes reference to an author interview with Miguel Osorio de Almeida, who was sent to the Soviet Union in 1963 to appeal for increased trade. He was told that Brazil was in the US orbit and they "did not want to be mixed up with communism in Brazil."

36. Schwarcz and Starling, *Brazil*, 377.

37. Marly de Almeida Gomes Vianna, *Revolucionários de 35* (São Paulo: Camponahia das Letras, 1992) 40–43. Even when the Comintern took its most radical turn in 1928, the organization never believed in immediate revolution in colonial and semicolonial countries, and the line for parties in those nations was to avoid open conflict with other nationalist forces, including the local capitalist "bourgeoisie," at all costs.

38. Prestes, from Southern Brazil, led a march across the country demanding secret ballots, public schools for all, and, technically, the overthrow of President Arthur Bernardes—though the protesters intentionally avoided confrontation with government troops and sought more to rally soldiers and citizens to their cause. Prestes then went into exile for five years, and became more radical, attempting to join the Communist Party. At first, the PCB—and Moscow—weren't so sure about him. They called him a "petty bourgeois" *caudilho* and, because Communists had been burned by making

alliances with Nationalists in China, worried about accepting a kind of a Brazilian Chiang Kai-shek. He was only finally admitted in 1934, as the government of Getúlio Vargas was taking its hard turn toward fascism (Vianna, *Revolucionários*, 50–51).

39. Ibid., 117.

40. This account of the rebellion draws on Vianna, *Revolucionários*, 230–48.

41. *O Globo*, June 26, 1935, 1st ed. Cited in Vianna, *Revolucionários*, 132–33.

42. Rodrigo Patto Sá Motta, *Em Guarda Contra O Perigo Vermelho*, 223.

43. Patto Sá Motta, *Em Guarda Contra O Perigo Vermelho*, 60, 66–67.

44. Schwarcz and Starling, *Brazil*, 419–22.

45. Patto Sá Motta, *Em Guarda Contra O Perigo Vermelho*, 116.

46. Federico Finchelstein, *The Ideological Origins of the Dirty War: Fascism, Populism, and Dictatorship in Twentieth Century Argentina* (Oxford: Oxford University Press, 2014), 47–48.

47. Patto Sá Motta, *Em Guarda Contra O Perigo Vermelho*, 49–52.

48. Ibid.,169.

49. Weis, *Cold Warriors*, 20.

50. Patto Sá Motta, *Em Guarda Contra O Perigo Vermelho*, 156.

51. Fundação Getúlio Vargas, CPDOC, "Verbete: Movimento Anti-Comunista (MAC)," summary at www.fgv.br/cpdoc/acervo/dicionarios/verbete-tematico/movimento-anticomunista-mac.

52. Patto Sá Motta, *Em Guarda Contra O Perigo Vermelho*, 149–52.

53. Napolitano, *1964*, 38–39.

54. *O Globo*, January 25, 1964, reprinted in Patto Sá Motta, *Em Guarda Contra O Perigo Vermelho*, 93.

55. Kinzer, *Overthrow*, 169.

56. Dallek, *An Unfinished Life*, 697–98.

57. Weiner, *Legacy of Ashes*, 225–26.

58. For Johnson's career before the presidency, see Doris Kearns Goodwin, *Lyndon Johnson and the American Dream* (New York: Integrated Media, 2015), chaps. 1–6.

59. Ibid., 175–77.

60. *Jornal do Brasil*, September 13, 1963, 6. Cited in Napolitano, *1964*, 46.

61. Ordem do Dia do Exercito, General Jair Dantas Ribeiro, November 1963, printed in General Fernando de Carvalho, *Lembrai-Vos de 35!* (Rio de Janeiro: Biblioteca do Exército Editora, 1981), 375–77. *Lembrai-Vos* is an edited volume of all *Intentona* memorial speeches from 1936 to 1980. My translation maintains some of the stilted, overwrought language of the original. As cops often do in the US, Brazilian police and military officers tend to try too hard, using arcane grammatical structures and obscure vocabulary when attempting to speak formally.

62. Napolitano, *1964*, 50, 61.

63. Telegram from the Ambassador to Brazil (Gordon) to the Department of State, Rio de Janeiro, March 28, 1964, *FRUS, Vol. XXXI*, South and Central America; Mexico, 187, https://history.state.gov/historicaldocuments/frus1964-68v31/d187.

64. Walters, *Silent Missions*, 77, 123.

65. Brazil's EBC has the full transcript (in Portuguese) and some photos, "Discurso de Jango na Central do Brasil em 1964," at www.ebc.com.br/cidadania/2014/03/discurso-de-jango-na-central-do-brasil-em-1964.

66. Benjamin Cowan, *Securing Sex: Morality and Repression in the Making of Cold War Brazil* (Chapel Hill, NC: University of North Carolina Press, 2016), 75–77.

67. Napolitano, *1964*, 56–57.

68. Patto Sá Motta, *Em Guarda Contra O Perigo Vermelho*, 74. It is notable that in his memoirs, Vernon Walters makes it clear he shares the vast majority of the anticommunist assumptions I just outlined here. First, he believes that because of the "sinister precedent" of the *Intentona Comunista*, and the murder of the generals in their sleep, they had special reason to be worried about Jango's appeals to rank-and-file soldiers. Second, he waves away abuses ("excessive zeal," he says) committed by Brazil's dictatorship by saying, with apparent sincerity, that we can be sure things would have been much worse "if Brazil had gone Communist." Third, he puts forward the belief (also enunciated by Nixon) that "authoritarian rightist regimes always disappear eventually. Communist regimes, once they seize power, never let go." Walters, *Silent Missions*, 371–89.

69. Here and below I have expanded the language and approach I used in my October 12, 2018, piece for *The New York Review of Books*. See Vincent Bevins, "Jair Bolsonaro, Brazil's Would-be Dictator," *NYR Daily*, October 12, 2018.

70. *FRUS*, 1964–1968, Volume XXXI, South and Central America; Mexico, 198. Telegram from the Department of State to the Embassy in Brazil, March 31, 1964.

71. Bevins, "Jair Bolsonaro, Brazil's Would-be Dictator."

72. Ruth Leacock, *Requiem for Revolution: The United States and Brazil, 1961–1969* (Kent, Ohio: Kent State University Press, 1990), chap. 11.

73. General-de-Exercito Pery Constant Bevilaqua, Alocucao Do Representante Das Forcas Armadas, December 1, 1964, printed in *Lembrai-Vos De 35!*, 381.

74. Leacock, *Requiem for Revolution*, 197.

75. Napolitano, *1964*, 62. For analysis of Soviet responses to the coup, see Gianfrano Caterina, "Um grande oceano: Brasil e União Soviética atravessando a Guerra Fria (1947–1985)" (PhD diss., Fundação Getúlio Vargas, 2019), 267–75. Moscow only registered mild criticisms of the new government's anticommunist posture, and expressed a desire to continue developing bilateral relations between the countries.

Chapter 6. The September 30th Movement

1. *The Afro-Asian Journalist*, Djakarta 1964, 1-1964, no.1, viewed at SOAS University London.

2. Declassified documents from Eastern Europe point to Zain as a member of the Central Committee of the Communist Party, and Martin Aleida confirmed this. Francisca, however, said they never really talked about his specific party activities at this time, though the team he was on was obvious, so I just call him an "influential figure on the left" here. Later in the text I discuss his party role. "Memorandum about talks with the Deputy Head of the Department for International Relations of the Central Committee of the PKI, Comrade Zain Nasution, on 30 June 1965," Stiftung Archiv Parteien und Messenorganisationen der DDR im Bundesarchiv (SAP-MO-BArch) DY 30 / IV A2 / 20, 66. Cited in Wardaya, *1965: Indonesia and the World* (Jakarta, 2013); Author interview with Martin Aleida.

3. Mortimer, *Indonesian Communism under Sukarno*, 125–26.

4. Jones, *Indonesia: The Possible Dream*, 260.

5. For background on *The Afro-Asian Journalist*, see Taomo Zhou, "The Archipelago Reporting Global: The Afro-Asian Journalist Association, the Indonesian Left, and the Print Culture of the Third World, 1963–65" *Medium*, medium.com/afro-asian-visions/the-afro-asian-journalist-association-the-indonesian-left-and-the-print-culture-of-the-third-7f6463b185b0.

6. Karl, *Mao Zedong and China in the Twentieth-Century World*, 109–13.

7. Sugiono, a teacher at the PKI's own theoretical school, submitted a thesis on the party's populist approach, which consisted of positing the "dual aspect of the state,"—one being "pro-people," and the other "anti-people." He was indeed disappointed when ideologues in North Korea rejected it as "un-Marxist," but the Indonesians certainly weren't going to abandon their philosophy as a result. Recounted in John Roosa, *Pretext for Mass Murder: The September 30th Movement and Suharto's Coup d'Etat in Indonesia* (Madison, WI: University of Wisconsin Press, 2006), chap. 5.

8. These numbers, three million for full members and twenty million for affiliates, respectively, come from the PKI and have been widely reproduced by historians as well as US officials. See, for example, Wieringa, *Propaganda*, 5, and Robinson, *The Killing Season*, 8. In 1964, Guy J. Pauker arrived at the estimate of between 25 percent and a third of registered voters in a paper for the Rand Corporation titled "Communist Prospects in Indonesia," and this was only working with the affiliate figure of sixteen million rather than twenty million. It is difficult to know how much, if any, double counting occurred in these estimations.

9. On the PKI's agitation for parliamentary elections under Guided Democracy, see Mortimer, *Indonesian Communism under Sukarno*, 120–22. More broadly, Chapter 2 of this volume includes an explanation of the party's decision to stay very close to Sukarno in this period.

10. Jones, *Indonesia: The Possible Dream*, 265.

11. Simpson, *Economists with Guns*, 117.

12. "Crossroads for Sukarno," *New York Times*, May 30, 1963.

13. Simpson, *Economists with Guns*, 88–89.

14. Ibid., 121.

15. Jim Baker, *Crossroads: A Popular History of Malaysia and Singapore* (Singapore: Marshall Cavendish, 2010), loc. 4000–4088 of 8869, Kindle.

16. Simpson, *Economists with Guns*, 34.

17. Magdalena's account is based on author interviews with Magdalena Kastinah, in Solo, Indonesia, 2018–2019.

18. Simpson, *Economists with Guns*, 125.

19. Jones, *Indonesia: The Possible Dream*, 297

20. Ibid., 299–300.

21. Simpson, *Economists with Guns*, 133.

22. Greg Poulgrain, *The Incubus of Intervention: Conflicting Indonesia Strategies of John F. Kennedy and Allen Dulles* (Petaling Jaya: Strategic Information and Research Development Centre, 2015), 247.

23. Jones, *Indonesia: The Possible Dream*, 321. See also Simpson, *Economists with Guns*, 131–34.

24. Jones, *Indonesia: The Possible Dream*, 325–26.

25. Weiner, *Legacy of Ashes*, 241.

26. Simpson, *Economists with Guns*, 134; author interviews.

27. Jones, *Indonesia: The Possible Dream*, 343–44, 359–60.

28. Copy of Resignation Letter, Howard P. Jones to President Johnson, November 1, 1964, Box 10, Howard Palfrey Jones Papers, Hoover Institution.

29. Dinner Invitation for May 18, Folder: Subandrio, Box 18, Howard Palfrey Jones Papers, Hoover Institution.

30. Warren Unna, "Jones Was Sukarno's Pal," *Washington Post*, January 17, 1965.

31. Warren Unna, "Our Man in Indonesia: Patsy for Sukarno or Unique Envoy?" *Los Angeles Times*, January 17, 1965.

32. For a summary of the limited glimpses that we have, see Robinson, *Killing Season*, 105–115, and Simpson, *Economists with Guns*, 139–58. The quote "Premature PKI coup" is from Edward Peck, assistant secretary of state in the Foreign Office, in conversation with the New Zealand high commissioner in London (cited in Simpson, 144). "Director of political warfare" is from Simpson, 158. "Virtual certainty" is a quotation from Robinson's measured analysis of probable activities, 110.

33. Howard Jones, presentation at 1965 Chief of Mission conference, "American-Indonesian Relations," Howard P. Jones Papers, Hoover Institution, Box 22, HI. Cited in Simpson, *Economists with Guns*, 157.

34. Roro Sawita, "Tanah, *Landreform* dan Kemelut 1965," in *Melawan Lupa: Narasi-Narasi Komunitas Taman 65 Bali* (Denpasar, 2012), 3–13; Wieringa, *Propaganda*, 89–90.

35. Taomo Zhou, "China and the Thirtieth of September Movement," *Indonesia* 98 (October 2014): 35.

36. Simpson, *Economists with Guns*, 165–66.

37. Zhou, "China and the Thirtieth of September Movement," 48–49.

38. Ibid., 49–51. Zhou here interprets this passage as a kind of advance outline of the approach that developed into the September 30th Movement, but it appears in the context of a discussion regarding what the PKI might do if Sukarno dies or is removed from the scene. Upon reading the same conversation I concluded (similarly to Geoffrey Robinson) that Aidit could have been speaking about a contingency plan for a future without Sukarno, or really just speaking extemporaneously as to how they might take more power without provoking the right. What I find most interesting about the China-Indonesia exchange in 1965 is that the Chinese Communists seem to stress the need to prepare for the possibility of violent struggle and suspect the US-backed right may attempt to seize power. Zhou herself concludes unequivocally that Mao was not the architect of the September 30th Movement.

39. Robinson, *The Killing Season*, 112.

40. Simpson, *Economists with Guns*, 156.

41. Ibid., 154.

42. Memorandum Prepared for the 303 Committee, *FRUS 1964–1968*, Vol. XXVI, 110, https://history.state.gov/historicaldocuments/frus1964-68v26/d110.

43. George Ball Telephone Conversation (Telcon) with McGeorge Bundy, August 16, 1965, George W. Ball Papers, Mudd Library, Princeton, NJ. Cited in Robinson, *The Killing Season*, 103.

44. Cited in Robinson, *The Killing Season*, 110. His footnote for the document is as follows: "Neville Maxwell, a British scholar, discovered the document in the Pakistan

Foreign Ministry archive. His unpublished letter of June 5, 1978, to *The New York Review of Books* describing the document's contents was later printed as Neville Maxell, 'CIA Involvement in the 1965 Military Coup: New Evidence from Neville Maxwell,' *Journal of Contemporary Asia* 9, no. 2 (1979): 251–52."

45. Roosa, *Pretext for Mass Murder*, chap. 1. For the narrative of October 1, I largely follow the narrative flow provided by Roosa's account, though I do not include any elements that are unique to him and controversial.

46. Roosa, *Pretext for Mass Murder*. The entire volume is dedicated to making this case, using extensive analysis of documents in several languages.

47. Robinson discusses a range of theories in *Killing Season*, 65–80. I have very briefly summarized these and added some other questions, mostly those asked by Saskia Wieringa, survivors (in author interviews), and Subandrio (in his volume, cited below).

48. Benedict Anderson and Ruth McVey, "A Preliminary Analysis of the October 1, 1965, Coup in Indonesia," Cornell Modern Indonesia Project, 1971.

49. This anecdote was passed on to me secondhand by Andreas Harsono, head of Human Rights Watch in Indonesia, in 2018.

50. Soebandrio, *Kesaksianku tentang G30S*. The entire volume lays out the explanation for this theory, but the most relevant sections are chaps. 2 and 3.

51. Abdul Latief, *Pledoi Kol. A. Latief: Soeharto Terlibat G 30 S* (Jakarta, ISAI: 2000).

52. I asked the Agency directly in 2019 what their role was. Their response was that, unfortunately, nothing new had been declassified.

53. CIA Intelligence Info Cable TDCS-315-00846-64, "US-Indonesian Relations," September 19, 1964, *DDC*, 1981. Cited in Robinson, *Killing Season*, 103.

54. Scott, "The United States and the Overthrow of Sukarno, 1965–1967," 245–49.

55. Soebandrio, *Kesaksianku tentang G30S*, 5.

56. Roosa, *Pretext for Mass Murder*, 114.

57. *Harian Rakjat*, October 2, 1965. The headline reads, "Lieutenant Colonel Untung and the Tjakrabirawa Batallion [Presidential Guard] save President and the Republic from a Council of Generals Coup," with the subtitle "The September 30th Movement is an internal Army movement." Copy supplied by Cornell University Library.

58. Author interviews with Aleida, 2018 and 2019.

59. Simpson, *Economists with Guns*, 181.

60. Scott, "The United States and the Overthrow of Sukarno, 1965–1967," 260.

61. *Angkatan Bersendjata*, October 5, 1965. Copy supplied by Cornell University Library.

62. Memorandum of Telephone Conversation Between Acting Secretary of State Ball and Secretary of Defense McNamara, October 1, 1965, *FRUS, 1964–1968*, Vol. XXVI, Indonesia; Malaysia-Singapore; Philippines, 143, https://history.state.gov/historicaldocuments/frus1964-68v26/d143.

63. Telegram from the Embassy in Indonesia to the Department of State, October 14, 1965, *FRUS, 1964–1968*, Vol. XXVI, 155, https://history.state.gov/historicaldocuments/frus1964-68v26/d155.

64. Melvin, *The Army and the Indonesian Genocide*, 9–10, 25; author interviews with survivors in Central Java also confirm they heard this propaganda line on foreign outlets.

65. Wieringa, *Propaganda and the Genocide in Indonesia*, 102. See chap. 6 for the context of this particular aspect of military propaganda concerning the events of October 1.

66. See Benedict Anderson, "How Did the Generals Die?" *Indonesia* 43 (April, 1987): 109–34.

67. Simpson, *Economists with Guns*, 181.

68. Kyle Burke, *Revolutionaries for the Right* (Chapel Hill, NC: University of North Carolina Press, 2018), 20–25.

Chapter 7. Extermination

1. Melvin, *The Army and the Indonesian Genocide*, 127.

2. Telegram from the Embassy in Indonesia to the Department of State, October 5, 1965, *FRUS, 1964–1968*, Vol. XXVI, Indonesia; Malaysia-Singapore; Philippines, 147, at https://history.state.gov/historicaldocuments/frus1964-68v26/d147.

3. Melvin, *The Army and the Indonesian Genocide*, 82.

4. Ibid., 89.

5. Ibid., 78.

6. Ibid., 143.

7. Ibid., 3, 72.

8. Ibid., 125.

9. *Angkatan Bersendjata*, October 8, 1965. Copy provided by Cornell Library. This illustration is discussed in Melvin, *The Army and Indonesian Genocide*, 41.

10. Ibid., 1.

11. Telegram from the Embassy in Indonesia to the Department of State, Djakarta, October 20, 1965, 0330Z, *FRUS, 1964–1968*, Vol. XXVI, 158, at https://history.state.gov/historicaldocuments/frus1964-68v26/d158.

12. Telegram, Djakara to SecState, "1. PII Moslem Youth Leader," October 21, 1965, RG 59, Central Files 1964–1966, Pol 23-9 Indon, National Archives and Records Administration (NARA).

13. Memorandum from the President's Special Assistant for National Security Affairs (Bundy) to President Johnson, October 22, 1965, *FRUS, 1964–1968*, Vol. XXVI, Indonesia; Malaysia-Singapore; Philippines, 160.

14. Telegram, Djakarta to Sec State, October 22, 1965, "PAGE TWO RUMJBT." Copy from original document held in the Lyndon Baines Johnson Presidential Library provided by Bradley Simpson.

15. Ibid.,186–87.

16. Kathy Kadane, "US Officials' Lists Aided Indonesian Bloodbath in '60s," *Washington Post*, May 21, 1990, www.washingtonpost.com/archive/politics/1990/05/21/us-officials-lists-aided-indonesian-bloodbath-in-60s/ff6d37c3-8eed-486f-908c-3eeaf c19aab2/?utm_term=.d9f3a266673c.

17. Some authors have suggested that Wisner's death was somehow caused by the consequences of the actions he took in Indonesia and elsewhere years ago. His son Frank Wisner Jr. rejects this theory, and also says he was unlikely to be reading the news or following global affairs in his final days. Author interviews, 2018 and 2019.

18. Wieringa, *Propaganda*, 15, 87. The "largest Muslim organization" is Nahdlatul Ulama.

19. Melvin, *The Army and the Indonesian Genocide*, 168, 211. For interviews with witnesses to the violence, see also Baskara Wardaya, "Truth Will Out" (Victoria: Monash University Publishing, 2013).

20. Telegram, Djakarta to SecState, Joint Sitrep No. 47, "Page 5 RumJBT 272A S E C R E T," November 6, 1965, RG 59, Central Files 1964–1966, Pol 23-9 Indon, NARA.

21. Airgram A-545, Djakarta to State, "Subject: Alleged Aidit Confession Reported in Asahi Shimbum is Apparently False," March 4, 1966, RG 59, Central Files 1964–1966, Pol 23-9 Indon, NARA.

22. The event was the *Konferensi Internasional Anti Pangkalan Militer Asing*, or KIAPMA for short. Author interviews with Martin Aleida, 2019.

23. Simpson, *Economists with Guns*, 196–97.

24. Telegram 741 from State to Jakarta, December 8, 1965; and Telegram 1605 from Jakarta to State, December 1, 1965, both in RG 59, Central Files, 1964–1966, POL 23-9, Indonesia, NA. Cited in Simpson, *Economists with Guns*, 197.

25. Simpson, *Economists with Guns*, 198–99.

26. Ibid., 199.

27. Geoffrey Robinson, *The Dark Side of Paradise: Political Violence in Bali* (Ithaca, NY: Cornell University Press, 1995), 293.

28. Ibid., 251–54, 300.

29. Ibid., 273

30. Ibid., 184.

31. Ibid., 301.

32. Airgram A-453, Djakarta to State, "Subject: U.S. Policy Assessment," January 14, 1966, RG 59, Central Files 1964–1966, Pol 2-3 Indon, NARA.

33. Roosa, *Pretext for Mass Murder*, 200.

34. Soebandrio, *Kesaksianku tentang G30S*, 41.

35. Wieringa, Propaganda, 35.

36. Legge, Sukarno, 402.

37. Simpson, *Economists with Guns*, 231–32.

38. Telegram, Singapore to SecState, "1. Several American Correspondents," March 17, 1965, RG 59, Central Files 1964–1966, Pol 15-1 Indon, NARA.

39. "Amok" is from Malay, which is simple enough to say, but I didn't want to confuse readers who are likely to think "Malaysia" when they hear Malay.

40. C. L. Sulzberger, "Foreign Affairs: When a Nation Runs Amok," *New York Times*, April 13, 1966.

41. Robinson, *Killing Season*, 138.

42. For a discussion of *amok* in the US press, see Roosa, *Pretext for Mass Murder*, 26–27. The well-documented episodes of mass murder in Indonesia up to this point all involve foreign actors to some extent, and took place during the colonial period, attempts to reconquer the archipelago after World War II, and the Japanese occupation (1942–45).

43. One survivor and party member, Sunaryo, recalled that he and a few friends did consider trying to mount some resistance. But they were held back by PKI leadership in Solo. Author interviews in Solo, 2018.

44. For Sarwo Edhie's claims, see Robinson, *Killing Fields*, 339 (footnote 3); for a concise discussion of the various estimates, see Ibid., 119.

45. Wieringa, *Propaganda*, 132.

46. Ibid., 105, and author interview with Sumiyati and other victims.

47. For the best defense of the use of the term to describe the events of 1965–66, see Melvin, *The Army and the Indonesian Genocide*, chap. 1. See also Helen Jarvis and Saskia

E. Wieringa, "The Indonesian Massacres as Genocide," in *The International People's Tribunal for 1965 and the Indonesian Genocide* (Routledge, 2019).

48. Ragna Boden, "The 'Gestapu' Events of 1965 in Indonesia: New Evidence from Russian and German Archives," *Bijdragen tot de Taal-, Land- en Volkenkunde* 163, no. 4 (2007): 515–17; "Memorandum about talks with the Deputy Head of the Department for International Relations of the Central Committee of the PKI, Comrade Zain Nasution, on 30 June 1965," Stiftung Archiv Parteien und Messenorganisationen der DDR im Bundesarchiv (SAP-MO-BArch) DY 30 / IV A2 / 20, 66. Cited in Wardaya, *1965: Indonesia and the World* (Jakarta 2013).

49. *Final Report of the IPT 1965: Findings and Documents of the International People's Tribunal on Crimes against Humanity Indonesia 1965* (The Hague, Jakarta, 2016).

50. Christian Gerlach, *Extremely Violent Societies* (Cambridge: Cambridge University Press, 2010), 82.

51. Roosa, *Pretext for Mass Murder*, 13.

52. "A Gleam of Light in Asia," *New York Times*, June 18, 1966.

53. Maior, *America's First Spy*, 192–94.

54. Kathy Kadane, "US Officials' Lists Aided Indonesian Bloodbath in '60s."

Chapter 8. Around the World

1. Robert McNamara, *In Retrospect: The Tragedy and Loss of Vietnam* (New York: Times Books, 1995), 215.

2. Ibid., 219.

3. Ibid., 270.

4. *Nhân Dân*, October 7–18, 1965. Accessed at National Library of Vietnam in Hanoi.

5. These are official statistics from Hanoi cited approvingly by Christopher Goscha in *Vietnam: A New History* (New York: Basic Books, 2016), 329. As Goscha argues elsewhere in the book, the Vietnamese government tended to underplay, not overexaggerate, the sacrifices required by the war in the subsequent years. See also Philip Shenon, "20 Years After Victory, Vietnamese Communists Ponder How to Celebrate," *New York Times*, April 23 1995.

6. For a discussion of why the war went on as long as it did, see Goscha, *Vietnam*, 333–40.

7. Ibid., 329–36.

8. Burke, *Revolutionaries for the Right*, 148.

9. Boden, "The 'Gestapu' Events," 515.

10. Ibid.

11. For a discussion of international reactions elsewhere, especially Europe, see Gerlach, *Extremely Violent Societies*, 80–85.

12. For official comments and GDR commentary, see Boden, "'Gestapu' Events," 515–19.

13. Author interviews, 2018 and 2019, Amsterdam.

14. Ratna Saptari, "Persecution through Denial of Citizenship: Indonesians in Forced Exile Post 1965," in Saskia E. Wieringa, Jess Melvin, and Annie Pohlman, eds., *The International People's Tribunal for 1965 and the Indonesian Genocide* (New York: Routledge, 2019).

15. Thomas, *The Very Best Men*, 186.

16. LaFeber, *Inevitable Revolutions*, 166.

17. For a very general overview of this period, see Ralph Lee Woodward Jr., *A Short History of Guatemala* (Guatemala: Laura Lee, 2008), 140–50. For a more extensive treatment in Spanish, see Ricardo Sáenz de Tejada, "Modernización y conflictos, 1944–2000," in Babara Arroyo et al., *Los Caminos de Nuestra Historia: estructuras, procesos y actores, Volumen II* (Guatemala: Editorial Cara Parens, 2015), 150–52.

18. Greg Grandin and Elizabeth Oglesby, "Washington Trained Guatemala's Mass Murderers—and the Border Patrol Played a Role," *The Nation*, January 3, 2019; Greg Grandin, "The Border Patrol Has Been a Cult of Brutality since 1924," *The Intercept*, January 12, 2019.

19. Grandin, *The Last Colonial Massacre*, 73.

20. It was John Roosa who suggested I look into this connection, and who originally asserted to me that disappearances were put to use for the first time in Asia in 1965. For someone without special expertise on this specific issue, it's hard to check or prove that there was not the use of disappearances before 1965 in Indonesia. So I put the question, "Do you know of the use of mass disappearance as a form of state terror in Asia prior to Indonesia 1965" to the following experts: Noam Chomsky, Ben Kiernan, Alfred McCoy, Bradley Simpson, and Baskara Wardaya. None could recall an incident that would refute Roosa's thesis.

21. On Longan's arrival and Operation Limpieza, see Greg Grandin, *The Last Colonial Massacre: Latin America in the Cold War* (Chicago: University of Chicago Press, 2004), 11–12, 73–75. For discussions of disappearance within the history of Latin American violence in the twentieth century, see Greg Grandin's introductory essay, "Living in a Revolutionary Time: Coming to Terms with the Violence of Latin America's Long Cold War," in Greg Grandin and Gilbert M. Joseph, eds., *A Century of Revolution: Insurgent and Counterinsurgent Violence During Latin America's Long Cold War* (Durham, NC, and London: Duke University Press, 2010).

22. Martin Aleida, *Tanah Air Yang Hilang* (Jakarta, 2017), chap. 1.

23. Taomo Zhou, *Migration in the Time of Revolution* (Ithaca, NY: Cornell University Press, 2019), chap. 8, 163.

24. Ibid., 4.

25. Ibid., 167–68.

26. Ibid., 174.

27. Author interview with Sarmadji, Amsterdam, 2018. He described years of living in Beijing while the Cultural Revolution blew up around him, but never exactly engulfing Indonesian students like him; Zhou, *Migration*, 176–78.

28. Zhou, *Migration*, 188–89.

29. Zhou notes in Chapter 9 that Zhou Enlai also endorsed the idea of a "Fifth Force" in Indonesia. The description of the influence on the Cultural Revolution is also in this chapter. I want to re-emphasize the point I made earlier, that despite reviewing both of Taomo Zhou's presentations of Aidit's final in-person conversation with Mao, I follow Robinson in disagreeing with her interpretation that the exchange proves that Aidit had already formulated broad plans for the September 30th Movement, and shared this plan with Mao. Like Robinson, I don't think the evidence Zhou presents supports this theory.

30. Schlesinger Jr., *Robert Kennedy and His Times*, 733.

31. Memorandum of Conversation, Visit to Department of Time-Life Inc. Officials, January 5, 1967, RG 59, Central Files 1967–1969, FN 9 Indonesia, NARA.

32. Robinson, *The Killing Season*, 209–25; author interviews.

33. Proceedings of the Indonesian Investment Conference, "To Aid in Rebuilding a Nation," November 2–4, 1967, RG 59, Central Files 1967–1969, FN 9 Indonesia, NARA.

34. Short, *Pol Pot*, 135–45.

35. In a "historical lessons" document composed in early 1977, Pol Pot looked back on the 1966 period as follows: "If our analysis had failed, we would have been in greater danger than [were the communists] in Indonesia. But our analysis was victorious, because our analysis was agreed upon, because most of our cadres were in life-and-death contradiction with the enemy; the enemy sought to exterminate them constantly." Ben Kiernan, *Pol Pot Plans the Future: Confidential Leadership Documents from Democratic Kampuchea*, (New Haven, CT: Yale University Press, 1988), 213–226. The quotation appears on page 218, and Kiernan explained it to me as follows: "By that statement, Pol Pot conveyed that the Communist Party of Kampuchea, as he had renamed it in 1966 after visiting China, had decided on armed struggle against Sihanouk's Cambodian government, rather than peaceful competition or cooperation (i.e. to 'live together with Sihanouk inside the country') as was the policy of the Indonesian Communists towards Sukarno's government."

36. John Henrik Clarke, "Kwame Nkrumah: His Years in America," *The Black Scholar* 6, no. 2 (October 1974): 9–16.

37. The notion of "black" Africa, of course, is incoherent and itself a product of external, colonial imposition, but it certainly existed as a geopolitical category for Western observers in the twentieth century.

38. Kwame Nkrumah, *Neo-Colonialism: The Last Stage of Imperialism* (Melbourne: Thomas Nelson and Sons, 1965), x–xi.

39. Kwame Nkrumah, *Handbook of Revolutionary Warfare* (New York: International Publishers, 1968), 42. Cited in Prashad, *Darker Nations*, 111.

40. Prashad, *Darker Nations*, 163–64.

41. Gerlach, *Extremely Violent Societies*, 86.

42. Weiner, *Legacy of Ashes*, 307.

43. "Covert Action in Chile 1963–1973," Staff Report of the Select Committee to Study Governmental Operations, US Senate, December 18, 1975, 15, at www.intelligence.senate.gov/sites/default/files/94chile.pdf.

44. Paul E. Sigmund, *The Overthrow of Allende and the Politics of Chile, 1964–1976* (Pittsburgh, PA: University of Pittsburgh Press, 1977), 297.

45. "Covert Action in Chile," 7.

46. Author interviews with Carmen Hertz, in person (Santiago) and by phone, 2018 and 2019.

47. Orlando Millas, *Memorias 1957–1991: Una digresión* (Santiago: ChileAmerica, 1996), 162–63.

48. *Punto Final*, Año 1, 2 quincena de octubre de 1966, no. 14, 25.

49. *Punto Final*, Año 1, 1 quincena de marzo de 1967, no. 24, 21.

50. Tanya Harmer, *Allende's Chile and the Inter-American Cold War* (Chapel Hill, NC: University of North Carolina Press, 2011), 34–36.

51. Thomas, *The Very Best Men*, 36.

52. Bernard Eccleston, Michael Dawson, and Deborah J. McNamara, eds., *The Asia-Pacific Profile* (London and New York: Routledge, 1998), 311–12.

53. Tyrell Haberkorn, "Getting Away with Murder in Thailand: State Violence and Impunity in Phatthalung," in Ganesan and Chull Kim, eds., *State Violence in East Asia* (Lexington, KY: University of Kentucky Press, 2013), 185–87.

54. Author interviews with Endang Tedja Nurdjaya "Nury" Hanafi, in Paris (2018) and by phone (2019).

55. Harmer, *Allende's Chile*, 34–36.

56. Zhou, *Migration*, 173–74.

57. Scott Anderson and Jon Lee Anderson, *Inside the League: The Shocking Exposé of How Terrorists, Nazis, and Latin American Death Squads have Infiltrated the World Anti-Communist League* (New York: Dodd, Mead, 1986).

58. Burke, *Revolutionaries for the Right*, 55.

59. Anderson and Anderson, *Inside the League*, chaps. 1 and 2.

60. Barack Obama, *Dreams from My Father* (New York: Crown, 1995), 40.

Chapter 9. Jakarta Is Coming

1. Simpson, *Economists with Guns*, 20.

2. Obama, *Dreams from My Father*, 45–46.

3. This is the 1967 parliamentary elections. At the time the "Socialists" were called the Federation of the Democratic and Socialist Left *(Fédération de la gauche démocrate et socialiste or FGDS)*.

4. Charlotte Denny, "Suharto, Marcos and Mobutu Head Corruption Table with $50bn Scams," *Guardian*, March 26, 2004.

5. Robinson, *Killing Season*, 209.

6. Napolitano, *1964*, 70–85.

7. Napolitano, *1964*, 86–90.

8. *El Pais*, "Atentados de direita fomentaram AI-5," October 2, 2018.

9. It was President Artur da Costa e Silva who put AI-5 into effect, and Médici used it to unleash terror when he took over. See Napolitano, *1964*, 71–72, 91–95.

10. João Roberto Martins Filho, "Military Ties between France and Brazil during the Cold War, 1959–1975," *Latin American Perspectives* 198, Vol. 41, no. 5 (September 2014): 167–183.

11. Sandra Kiefer, "Dilma Rousseff Revela Detalhes do Sofrimento Vivido Nos Porões da Ditadura," *Correio Braziliense*, June 17, 2012.

12. Napolitano, *1964*, 126.

13. Paulo Coelho, "I Was Tortured by Brazil's Dictatorship. Is That What Bolsonaro Wants to Celebrate?" *Washington Post*, March 29, 2019.

14. Tanya Harmer, "Brazil's Cold War in the Southern Cone, 1970–1975," *Cold War History* 12, no. 4 (November 2012): 659–681.

15. Memorandum for the Record, Washington, June 27, 1970, *FRUS, 1969–1976*, Vol. XXI, Chile, 1969–1973, https://history.state.gov/historicaldocuments/frus1969-76v21/d41.

16. Weiner, *Legacy of Ashes*, 308–10.

17. *El Mercurio*, September 7, 1970. Cited in Harmer, *Allende's Chile*, 664.

18. Harmer, *Allende's Chile*, 3.

19. Peter Kornbluh, *The Pinochet File: A Declassified Dossier on Atrocity and Accountability* (New York: New Press, 2003), 36.

20. Weiner, *Legacy of Ashes*, 310.

21. It's not clear it was actually meant to resemble a spider, but it became common to refer to it as that "araña" logo. See José Díaz Nieva, *Pátria y Libertad: El Nacionalismo Frente a la Unidad Popular* (Santiago: Centro de Estudios Bicentenario, 2015), 80–82, on the symbol's origin.

22. John Dinges, *The Condor Years: How Pinochet and His Allies Brought Terrorism to Three Continents* (New York: New Press, 2004) 18–20; Weiner, *Legacy of Ashes*, 310–13.

23. Author interviews with Chileans who were both left-wing journalists and low-level military officers at the time, 2018.

24. Kristian C. Gustafson, "Re-examining the Record: CIA Machinations in Chile 1970," CIA Library, www.cia.gov/library/center-for-the-study-of-intelligence/kent-csi /vol47no3/html/v47i3a03p.htm#_ftn76.

25. Carmen Hertz, *La Historia Fue Otra* (Santiago: Debate, 2017), 45.

26. Harmer, *Allende's Chile*, 81–83.

27. Ibid., 78–79.

28. Ibid., 24.

29. Ariel Dorfman, "Salvador Allende Offers a Way Out for Venezuela's Maduro," *The Nation*, February 11, 2019.

30. Kornbluh, *The Pinochet File*, 119–20.

31. Harmer, "Brazil's Cold War," 660.

32. Ibid., 669–70.

33. Gabriel Warburg, *Islam, Nationalism, and Communism in Traditional Society* (London: Frank Cass, 1978), 130–35. The SCP had paid close attention to what happened in Indonesia in 1965, and for this reason had been trying to avoid direct confrontation, according to Alain Gresh, "The Free Officers and the Comrades: The Sudanese Communist Party and Nimeiri Face-to-Face, 1969–1971," *Journal of Middle East Studies* 21. no. 3 (August 1989): 13. According to the SCP itself, thirty-seven members were executed by hanging. Author interview with Fathi Alfadl, 2019, by email.

34. On Operação Jacarta as part of Operation Radar, starting in 1973, see Graziane Ortiz Righi, "Angelo Cardoso da Silva: Herzog gaúcho," Comissão Nacional da Verdade (CNV) Processo no 00092.000932/2013-01, Sistema de Informações do Arquivo Nacional (SIAN) do Brasil. The same assertion, as well as the claim that Operação Jacarta took the life of Vladimir Herzog, is made in "Comissão Estadual da Verdade Rubens Paiva," (Assembleía Legislativa do Estado de São Paulo), CNV-SIAN. For more on Operation Radar itself, see "Depoimento de Marival Chaves Dias," divided among BR RJANRIO CNV.0.DPO.00092000585201317, BR RJANRIO CNV.0.RCE.00092000122201317, v.107/1, and BR RJANRIO CNV.0.RCE.00092000122201317, v.106/2, at CNV-SIAN. For several references to Operação Jacarta, see "Relatório sobre a morte de João Goulart," *Comissão de Cidadania e Direitos Humanos da Assembléia Legislativa do Estado do Rio Grande do Sul—Subcomissão para Investigar as Circunstâncias da Morte do ex-Presidente João Goulart*, CNV-SIAN. For the declaration that former president Goulart was monitored in Uruguay as part of Operação Jacarta since 1973, before the creation of Operation Condor, see "Termo de declarações, que presta o senhor Mario Ronald Neyra Barreiro,"

00092.000311/2013-10, CNV-SIAN. For "Operação Jacarta" in reference to a threat made against a leftist named Jesse Jane, see "Relatório de Pesquisa para a Comissão Estadual da Verdade do Rio de Janeiro," CEV-RIO. I should note again here that no smoking gun exists proving that Brazil's military officially used the phrase "Operation Jakarta" internally. To prove or disprove that would require more access to military materials. What we have is widespread reports that the term was used (including many not cited here), and a firsthand account of the first-known use of the term in public, later in this chapter.

35. Díaz Nieva, *Pátria y Libertad*, 176–79. His Croatian background made me wonder if he might have links to the far right in that country, which was active early in the Anti-Bolshevik Bloc of Nations and the World Anti-Communist League, but I could find no evidence either way. Díaz Nieva writes that Domic was "almost obligatory reading" for right-wing Chileans at the time. For an early example of Domic's output on Indonesia, see Juraj Domic, *Fundamentos de la Praxis Marxista-Leninista en Chile* (Santiago: Vaitea, 1977), 33, on a 1969 article blaming the PKI for their own destruction. According to Manuel Fuentes Wendling, who was chief of propaganda for Pátria y Libertad, Domic and Wendling spoke as early as 1970 about painting five hundred thousand slogans on the walls of Chile, at this point with the goal of supporting presidential candidate Jorge Alessandri. This is recounted in Manuel Fuentes Wendling, *Memorias secretas de Patria y Libertad y algunas confesiones sobre la Guerra Fría en Chile* (Santiago de Chile: Grupo Grijalbo-Mondadori, 1999), 61–76 and 320–25. I corresponded with Pátria y Libertad leader Roberto Thieme by email in 2018. When I asked about "Yakarta" he only responded that "no Chilean, on the left or right, cares about or knows the history of Jakarta." During a 2018 interview in Santiago, Orlando Saenz Fuentes, who was active on the right in the early 1970s, said it was very credible that Pátria y Libertad would have been responsible for the graffiti.

36. *El Rebelde*, January 25–31, 1972, no. 14. Accessed at Biblioteca Nacional de Chile, Sección Periódicos.

37. Carlos Berger, "La conspiración derechista está tomando vuelo," *Revista Ramona*, February 22, 1972. Accessed at Biblioteca Nacional de Chile. Berger asserts that Plan Djakarta was given to the Chilean right wing by "el gerente yanqui de Purina," or "the Yankee boss at Purina." At the time, Ralston Purina was a pet food company owned in Chile by Rockefeller and Edwards.

38. Author interview with Patricio "Pato" Madera, Santiago 2018; "Patricio Madera: un muralista patrimonial de la histórica Brigada Ramona Parra," *Radio Universidad de Chile*, at https://radio.uchile.cl/2018/07/17/patricio-madera-un-muralista-patrimonial-de-la-historica-brigada-ramona-parra/.

39. Hertz, *La Historia Fue Otra*, 65–73.

40. Harmer, *Allende's Chile*, 182–83.

41. Weiner, *Legacy of Ashes*, 315.

42. Harmer, *Allende's Chile*, 237.

43. Luis H. Francia, *A History of the Philippines: From Indios Bravos to Filipinos* (New York: Overlook Press, 2010), 223.

44. Author interview with Joma Sison. I reported on the CPP for the *Washington Post* in 2018, so I had the contact of its "Information Bureau." The bureau advised me to email Sison my questions, and this is his full response relating to 1965 and its bearing on this thinking:

I observed and learned the lessons that the PKI members and most active mass activists were easily massacred to the extent of 3 million (according to the strategic command in charge of the slaughter) without any effective resistance because the PKI had no people's army and was thoroughly exposed to its enemies by its NASAKOM and electoral activities.

Of course, the lesson from Indonesian massacre in 1965–66 had a bearing on my thinking in the years afterwards. Since then, I have thought that it is ultimately fatal for a communist party to expose itself mainly or completely before it can seize political power. Thus, the CPP has been clandestine since its founding in 1968 and has preserved itself and grown in strength for more than 50 years despite all the strategic plans to destroy it and the full restoration of capitalism in China, the collapse of the Soviet Union and other factors that have made US imperialism and the world capitalist system look like eternal, as if the epochal struggle between the bourgeoisie and proletariat has come to an end forever.

45. Stanley Karnow, *In Our Image: America's Empire in the Philippines* (New York: Random House, 1989), 380.

46. Alfred McCoy, "Dark Legacy: Human Rights under the Marcos Regime," paper delivered at Ateneo de Manila University, September 20, 1999, at www.hartford-hwp .com/archives/54a/062.html; Karnow, *In Our Image*, 356–60.

47. Author interviews with Pedro Blaset and Guillermo Castillo, Santiago 2018. As I noted previously, Jakarta was not the site of the most intense and visible violence. If any Chilean sailors did see scenes of bodies lying everywhere, it might have been somewhere else, or they might have just been passing on horror stories secondhand. There were, for example, reports of "heads on stakes along the road" in Aceh. See Prashad, *Darker Nations*, 154.

48. Harmer, "Brazil's Cold War," 673.

49. *Puro Chile*, July 12, 1973; See also *El Siglo*, July 8 and 9, 1973, for reports of Godoy Matte's declaration. On August 1, 1973, Orlando Millas, official in the PCCh, wrote of his own experiences in Indonesia and used the nationalist politician's words to claim that the Chilean right wanted to reproduce the CIA-backed 1965–66 massacre. Both newspapers at Biblioteca Nacional de Chile, Seccíon Periodicos.

50. *Las Noticias de Última Hora*, August 3, 1973, at Biblioteca Nacional de Chile, Sección Periodicos.

51. See especially *El Mercurio*, July 14, 1973. Though the article is unsigned, the language used here is very similar to that used by Juraj Domic in an earlier article, "Modelo Indonesio de Golpe de Estado Comunista," published in *Revista PEC* (January/February 1973), which was later published as a small book titled *Modelo Indonesia de Golpe de Estado* (Santiago de Chile: Vaitea, 1975). Also notable is that on September 7, radio host Sergio Onofre Jarpa compared the situation to Jakarta in 1965. Reprinted on September 10, 1973, one day before the coup. Biblioteca Nacional de Chile, Sección Periodicos.

52. Harmer, *Allende's Chile*, 133.

53. Mary Helen Spooner, *Soldiers in a Narrow Land: The Pinochet Regime in Chile* (Berkeley, CA: University of California Press, 1999), 31–35.

54. Ibid., 35–36.

55. Patricia Politzer, *Altamirano* (Santiago, 1990), 132.

56. For a long time, the theory that Allende did not actually pull the trigger was widely circulated, and many people, especially outside Chile, still automatically assume this is the case. These rumors persisted for good reason, but we can also put them to rest for good reason. Allende's suicide was witnessed by a member of his medical team, Patricio Guijón, who had returned to the room in which they had been sheltering to take a gas mask as a souvenir for his son. The rifle itself bore Allende's fingerprints. Nevertheless, the theory that Allende was murdered by the military was fueled by Allende's widow, Hortensia Bussi de Allende. While Bussi de Allende originally accepted Guijón's testimony from her new position in exile in Mexico City, three days later she retracted that statement and insisted that her husband once told her that the only way he would leave La Moneda would be "dead, but fighting." This revised version of Allende's death offered more comfort to his supporters, especially outside Chile, and was amplified by the likes of Pablo Neruda, the Nobel Prize–winning Chilean poet who succumbed to cancer just twelve days after the coup. Guijón's testimony is now widely accepted as the true course of events that day. This episode is recounted in Mary Helen Spooner, *Soldiers in a Narrow Land: The Pinochet Regime in Chile* (Berkeley and Los Angeles, CA: University of California Press, 1994), 40–44, 50–54.

57. I listened to this speech at the Museo de la Memoria y los Derechos Humanos in Santiago, Chile, but it is also available online at www.bbc.com/mundo/noticias-america-latina-45458820.

58. Harmer, "Brazil's Cold War," 680.

59. *La Segunda*, September 21, 1973.

60. Ibid., 660.

61. Dinges, *The Condor Years*, 3.

62. Intelligence Note, State Department Bureau of Intelligence and Research, "Coup in Chile Reveals African Mistrust of US," October 10, 1973, Box 2198, RG 59, NARA.

63. Dinges, *The Condor Years*, 158.

64. Spooner, *Soldiers in a Narrow Land*, 45–47.

65. Author interview with Luciano Martins Costa, São Paulo (2018) and by phone (2019).

66. Dinges, *The Condor Years*, 110–25.

67. For discussion of the strange rise of the "Chicago Boys" in Chile, see Spooner, *Soldiers in a Narrow Land*, 108–10.

68. Ibid., 12.

Chapter 10. Back Up North

1. Benny Widyono, *Dancing in Shadows: Sihanouk, the Khmer Rouge, and the United Nations in Cambodia* (Lanham: Rowman & Littlefield, 2007), 25.

2. Short, *Pol Pot*, 216.

3. Sihanouk, *My War with the CIA*, 130.

4. Wieringa, *Propaganda*, 140.

5. From the film *Sekeping Kenangan* (*Fragment of Memory*), by Hadhi Kusuma, produced by Komunitas Taman 65 (Indonesia, 2018).

6. On US contingency planning in Portugal, including links to now-declassified government documents, see "Document Friday: The US Military Had 'a

Contingency Plan to Take Over' Portuguese Islands!?," *Unredacted: The National Security Archive Blog*, November 19, 2010, accessed October 2019, https://unredacted.com/2010/11/19/document-friday-the-us-military-had-a-contingincy-plan-to-take-over-portugal/.

7. Irena Cristalis, *East Timor: A Nation's Bitter Dawn* (London: Zed Books, 2009), loc. 1582 of 8861, Kindle.

8. Cristalis, *East Timor*, loc. 1523–3162 of 8861, Kindle.

9. Westad, *The Global Cold War*, 283–84.

10. Burke, *Revolutionaries for the Right*, 107–15.

11. Mário Sérgio de Morães, *O Ocaso da Ditadura* (São Paulo: Barcarolla, 2006), 74.

12. "Dom Paulo Evaristo Arns: O Cardeal do Povo," *Historia Imediata*, 1979. The report explains Operation Jakarta in the context of the military repression the cardinal fought.

13. Finchelstein, *The Ideological Origins of the Dirty War*, 3 and chaps. 1, 2, and 6.

14. Ibid., 115 (on anti-Semitism), 124 (on Citibank and Ford), and 127 (on atheism).

15. J. Patrice McSherry, *Predatory States: Operation Condor and Covert War in Latin America* (Lanham: Rowman & Littlefield, 2005), 188.

16. Greg Grandin, "Living in Revolutionary Time: Coming to Terms with the Violence of Latin America's Long Cold War," in Greg Grandin and Joseph M. Gilbert, eds., *A Century of Revolution: Insurgent and Counterinsurgent Violence During Latin America's Long Cold War* (Durham, NC: Duke University Press, 2010), 22.

17. Finchelstein, *The Ideological Origins of the Dirty War*, 127.

18. McSherry, *Predatory States*, chap. 2 (on the connection to "stay-behind" armies); Dinges, *The Condor Years*, 129, 220.

19. Dinges, *The Condor Years*, 11.

20. Ibid., chap. 7.

21. McSherry, *Predatory States*, 207–08. "Messianic," used on page 213, describes both Argentine and US officials.

22. For a firsthand account of conditions for indigenous people forced to work on Guatemala's *fincas* in the 1970s, see Rigoberta Menchú's famous testimony. Rigoberta Menchú and Elizabeth Burgos, *Me Llamo Rigoberta Menchú y Así Me Nació La Conciencia* (Siglo XXI Editores: Mexico, 2013).

23. McSherry, *Predatory States*, 210.

24. Henry Giniger, "Guatemala Reds Say They Slew Envoy," *New York Times*, August 30, 1968.

25. Grandin, *The Last Colonial Massacre*; Michael McClintock, *The American Connection, Vol. 2: State Terror and Popular Resistance in Guatemala* (London: Zed Books, 1985), 60; LaFeber, *Inevitable Revolutions*, 171–72.

26. Author interview with Miguel Ángel Albizures, Guatemala City, November 2018.

27. James Dunkerley, *Power in the Isthmus: A Political History of Modern Central America* (London: Verso, 1988), 375. On the rise of the *Sandinistas* in Nicaragua, see chap. 6, "The Nicaraguan Revolution: Origins," in the same volume.

28. Carlota McAllister, "A Headlong Rush into the Future: Violence and Revolution in a Guatemalan Indigenous Village," in Grandin and Joseph, *A Century of Revolution*, 276–80.

29. For example, see the two volumes by Michael McClintock on this subject. Michael McClintock, *The American Connection, Volume I: State Terror and Popular Resistance in El Salvador* (London: Zed Books, 1985) and *The American Connection, Volume II: State Terror and Popular Resistance in Guatemala* (London: Zed Books, 1985).

30. Ben Kiernan, "The Demography of Genocide in Southeast Asia: The Death Tolls in Cambodia, 1975–79, and East Timor, 1975–80," *Critical Asian Studies* 35, no. 4 (2003): 585–597.

31. Westad, *The Cold War*, 490–92.

32. Goscha, *Vietnam*, 395–96.

33. Widyono, *Dancing in Shadows*, 5; Author interview.

34. Ibid., 28.

35. Marlise Simons, "Army Killings in Indian Village Shock Guatemala," *Washington Post*, June 24, 1978.

36. On Taiwanese and Israeli support for Guatemala's military in this period, see Anderson and Anderson, *Inside the League*, 136–37; and Milton Jamail and Margo Gutierrez, "Guatemala: The Paragon," in *NACLA Report on the Americas* 21, no. 2 (1987): 31–39.

37. Anderson and Anderson, *Inside the League*, 110.

38. "Washington Bullets," from *Sandinista!*, the Clash, 1980.

39. Eline van Ommen, "Sandinistas Go Global: Nicaragua and Western Europe, 1977–1990" (PhD diss., London School of Economics and Political Science, 2019), 37–38.

40. Westad, *The Global Cold War*, 339–43.

41. McSherry, *Predatory States*, 207–11.

42. As the perceived revolutionary threat in Central America grew from 1978 onward, the Pinochet dictatorship increased the number of scholarships offered to members of the Salvadoran and Guatemalan armed forces, with a particular focus on counterinsurgent police training provided by Chile's *carabineros* (armed police). The Chilean and Argentine dictatorships' involvement in the armed conflicts in Guatemala and El Salvador is the subject of ongoing PhD research by Molly Avery in the Department of International History at the London School of Economics.

43. Anderson and Anderson, *Inside the League*, 146–47, 206–07.

44. McSherry, *Predatory States*, 207–11.

45. By 1983, the CIA had concluded the *Contras* could never actually win a military victory. See LaFeber, *Inevitable Revolutions*, 301.

46. LaFeber, *Inevitable Revolutions*, 305–07.

47. McSherry, *Predatory States*, 218.

48. Ignácio Gonzalez Janzen, *La Triple A* (Buenos Aires: Contrapunto, 1986), 95–100. These passages are also cited by Juan Pablo Csipka in *Los 49 Dias de Campora* (Buenos Aires: Sudamericana, 2013), 115–16.

49. Biographic Sketch, Roberto D'Aubuisson, November 1980, Folder El Salvador (01201981-05301981) [5], Box 30, Exec Sec, NSC Country File, Ronald Reagan Presidential Library.

50. Anderson and Anderson, *Inside the League*, 135–37.

51. Ibid., 194.

52. Raymond Bonner, "What Did Elliott Abrams Have to Do With the El Mozote Massacre?" *The Atlantic*, February 15, 2019.

53. LaFeber, *Inevitable Revolutions*.

54. Author interview with Josefa Sanchez Del Barrio, Ilom, November 2018.

55. Author interviews with Antonio Caba Caba, Guatemala City and Ilom, November 2018.

56. For a complete summary of the genocide committed by the Guatemalan military against the Ixil, see the testimonies recorded during Efraín Ríos Montt's trial in 2013. Sentencia por Genocidio y Delitos Contra los Deberes de Humanidad Contra el Pueblo Maya Ixil, dictada por el Tribunal Primero de Sentencia Penal, Narcoactividad y Delitos contra el Ambiente "A," Guatemala, May 10, 2013.

57. Author interview with Clara Arenas, from AVANCSO, Guatemala City, 2018.

58. John Otis, "Efraín Ríos Montt, Former Guatemalan Military Dictator Charged with Genocide, Dies at 91," *Washington Post*, April 1, 2018.

59. *Guatemala: Memory of Silence—Report of the Commission for the Historical Clarification, Conclusions and Recommendations*. La Comisión para el Esclarecimiento Histórico (CEH) found that "over 200,000" people were killed, with 93 percent victims of military violence; AVANCSO, La Asociación para el Avance de Las Ciencias Sociales en Guatemala, estimates the total number of victims at 250,000, with the majority indigenous people killed en masse, in the countryside, and 45,000 of the total number of "disappearances," which more often took the lives of targeted individuals in the cities.

60. John H. Coatsworth, "The Cold War in Central America," in *The Cambridge History of the Cold War, Vol. 3*, eds. Melvyn P. Leffler and Odd Arne Westad (Cambridge: Cambridge University Press, 2010), 221.

61. Widyono, *Dancing in Shadows*, Part I.

62. LaFeber, *Inevitable Revolutions*, 309.

63. Micah Zenko and Jennifer Wilson, "How Many Bombs Did the United States Drop in 2016?" Council on Foreign Relations blog post, January 5, 2017.

64. Westad, *The Global Cold War*, 396, 405.

65. Tom Burgis, *The Looting Machine* (New York: PublicAffairs, 2016).

66. Report for Selected Countries and Subjects, International Monetary Fund.

Chapter 11. We Are the Champions

1. Wright, *Color Curtain*, 206.

2. I wrote a dissertation on the effects of Federal Reserve interest rate policy in the early 1980s on debt burden and development programs. I know how complicated this is, and we're not going to resolve it now.

3. Gautam Nair, "Most Americans Vastly Underestimate How Rich They Are Compared with the Rest of the World. Does It Matter?" *Washington Post*, August 23, 2018.

4. Branko Milanovic, "Income, Inequality, and Poverty during the Transition from Planned to Market Economy," *World Bank Regional and Sectoral Studies*, chap. 3, www

.gc.cuny.edu/CUNY_GC/media/CUNY-Graduate-Center/PDF/Centers/LIS/Milanovic/papers/Income_ineq_poverty_book.pdf.

5. Branko Milanovic, "For Whom the Wall Fell?" *The Globalist*, November 7, 2014.

6. Westad, *The Global Cold War*, 387.

7. On the "strong and widespread global trend toward neoliberalism since the 1980s," see Jonathan D. Ostry, Prakash Loungani, and Davide Furceri, "Neoliberalism: Oversold?" an IMF paper questioning the effectiveness of that policy trend, at www.imf.org/external/pubs/ft/fandd/2016/06/ostry.htm.

8. Robert Wade, "Escaping the Periphery: The East Asian 'Mystery' Solved," United Nations University World Institute for Development Economics Research, September 2018.

Chapter 12. Where Are They Now? And Where Are We?

1. *Prison Songs Nyannyian Yang Dibunkam* (Bali: Taman 65, 2015).

2. This story was first told in Steph Vaessen's excellent short documentary *Indonesia's Killing Fields* for Al-Jazeera.

3. I cited this quote in this format in "Jair Bolsonaro, Brazil's Would-be Dictator," *The New York Review of Books*, October 12, 2018. The original 1999 interview was with TV Bandeirantes and is widely available on YouTube.

4. Celso Rocha de Barros, "Bolsonaro representa facção das Forças Armadas que ganhou poder com a tortura," *Folha de S.Paulo*, October 22, 2018.

5. Gerlach, *Extremely Violent Societies*, 28.

6. Ibid., 74

7. Ibid., 41.

8. Melvin, *The Army and the Indonesian Genocide*, 6.

9. Wieringa, *Propaganda*, 2.

10. Part of this is adapted from my article "Stuck in the Shopping," *Popula*, December 18, 2018.

11. "Foreign Researchers' Access to TNI Museums Restricted," *Jakarta Post*, February 9, 2018.

12. Recently she was raving to me about Mark Fisher's *Capitalist Realism*.

Map Citations

Argentina, Bolivia, Brazil, Chile, Paraguay, Uruguay: Estimates vary, with a low number of at least 50,000 offered in 1992 by Archivos del Terror. See *National Geographic Resource Library*, "Archives of Terror Discovered;" A higher number of 90,000 is offered by La Federación Latinoamericana de Asociaciones de Familiares de Detenidos-Desaparecidos (FEDEFAM), but that includes other countries, such as Colombia, not a party to Condor. I have gone with the estimate offered by Víctor Flores Olea, "Operation Cóndor," *El Universal*, April 10, 2006. Argentina was the most violent offender, with an estimated 30,000 dead.

Colombia: The violence was carried out against the Patriotic Union (UP), the leftist political party founded as part of 1985 peace negotiations with guerrillas. See *Deutsche Welle*, "In Colombia, It's Dangerous to Be Left Wing," www.dw.com/en/in-colombia-its-dangerous-to-be-left-wing/a-44131086—DW reports at least 3,000 dead, whereas groups and analysts closer to the UP, the victims of the violence, estimate 5,000 dead;

For fuller treatment see Centro Nacional de Memoria Histórica, "Todo pasó frente a nuestros ojos. Genocidio de la Unión Patriótica 1984–2002."

East Timor: See page 213 of this volume.

El Salvador: The truth commission gives a total number of 85,000, with 85% of the cases consisting of extrajudicial executions and enforced disappearances. "Those giving testimony attributed almost 85 per cent of cases to agents of the State, paramilitary groups allied to them, and the death squads." See United States Institute of Peace, *From Madness to Hope: the 12-year war in El Salvador: Report of the Commission on the Truth for El Salvador*, page 36.

Guatemala: See page 228 of this volume.

Honduras: Comisionado Nacional de los Derechos Humanos, "'Los hechos hablan por si mismos': Informe preliminar sobre los desaparecidos en Honduras 1980–1993"

Iran: The Islamic Republic executed supporters of the leftist People's Mujahedin of Iran, as well as the Tudeh and Fedaian Organization. Amnesty International gives a range of 4,672–4,969. See "Blood-Soaked Secrets: Why Iran's 1988 Prison Massacres are Ongoing Crimes Against Humanity."

Indonesia: See page 155 of this volume.

Iraq: For 1963 numbers, see Patrick Cockburn, "Revealed: how the West set Saddam on the bloody road to power," *The Independent*, June 29, 1997; The renewed crackdown in 1978 helped increase Saddam's popularity in Washington before he invaded Iraq (1980) and re-formed an alliance with the US. Prashad, *Darker Nations*, 160.

Mexico: During Mexico's "Dirty War," security forces and the military eliminated individuals accused of being part of one of the dozens of groups of armed leftists operating in the country, and massacred protesters at Tlatelolco in 1968. Security forces collaborated with US officials, as well as with the Brazilian dictatorship. See Adela Cedillo and Fernando Herrera Calderón, "Introduction: The Unknown Mexican Dirty War" in Cedillo and Herrera Calderón, eds., *Challenging Authoritarianism in Mexico: Revolutionary Struggles and the Dirty War, 1964–1982* (London: Routledge, 2012), 8; Gladys McCormick, "The Last Door: Political Prisoners and the Use of Torture in Mexico's Dirty War," *The Americas* 74:1 (January 2017), 57–81; and Alexander Aviña, *Specters of Revolution*, (New York: Oxford University Press, 2014), 151–55, 176–80.

Nicaragua: Loose estimates are 10,000 for 1979–1981, and 40,000 more for 1981–1989. Bethany Lacina. "The PRIO Battle Deaths Dataset, 1946–2008, Version 3.0: Documentation of Coding Decisions," *Peace Research Institute Oslo*.

The Philippines: Amnesty International, "Statement on Ferdinand Marcos' Burial at LNMB," November 18, 2016. www.amnesty.org.ph/news/statement-on-ferdinand-marcos-burial-at-lnmb/.

South Korea: This estimate includes the Jeju massacre (1948) as well as the communists and members of the Bodo League executed in 1950. Đỗ Khiem and Kim Sung-soo, "Crimes, Concealment and South Korea's Truth and Reconciliation Commission," *Japan Focus: The Asia-Pacific Journal*, August 1, 2008.

Sudan: The SCP itself recorded 37 state executions of Party members, but allows for more deaths from causes other than hanging, including among the 5,000 people detained, and those harmed outside the official legal structure.

Taiwan: Burke, *Revolutionaries for the Right*, 14.

Thailand: Jularat Damrongviteetham, "Narratives of the 'Red Barrel' Incident: Collective and Individual Memories in Lamsin, Southern Thailand" in Seng Loh, Dobbs and Koh eds., *Oral History in Southeast Asia*, p. 101.

Venezuela: Records of extrajudicial killings start in 1959, for example with Manuel Cabieses Donoso, *Venezuela, okey!* (Caracas: Ediciones del Litoral, 1963), 269, and *La desaparición forzada en Venezuela, 1960–1969* by Agustín J. Arzola Castellanos should have fuller treatment. At the launch of that book, José Vicente Rangel said that "disappearances" started in Venezuela during the presidency of Raul Leoni (1964–1969). Notably, John P. Longan, the US official discussed on page 164 of this volume, was active in both Guatemala and Venezuela. For Rangel's remarks, see "Rangel asegura que desapariciones forzosas de América Latina comenzaron en Venezuela" in *Chamosaurio.*

Vietnam: Ian G. R. Shaw, "Scorched Atmospheres: The Violent Geography of the Vietnam War and the Rise of Drone Warfare," *Annals of the American Association of Geographers*, 106 no. 3 (2016), 698.

All numbers are estimates.

Vincent Bevins is an award-winning journalist and correspondent. He covered Southeast Asia for the *Washington Post*, reporting from across the entire region and paying special attention to the legacy of the 1965 massacre in Indonesia. He previously served as the Brazil correspondent for the *Los Angeles Times*, also covering nearby parts of South America, and before that he worked for the *Financial Times* in London.

Among the other publications he has written for are the *New York Times*, *The Atlantic*, *The Economist*, the *Guardian*, *Foreign Policy*, the *New York Review of Books*, *Folha de S.Paulo*, *The New Republic*, *The New Inquiry*, *The Awl*, *The Baffler*, and *New York* magazine. Vincent was born and raised in California and spent the last few years living in Jakarta.

PublicAffairs is a publishing house founded in 1997. It is a tribute to the standards, values, and flair of three persons who have served as mentors to countless reporters, writers, editors, and book people of all kinds, including me.

I. F. STONE, proprietor of *I. F. Stone's Weekly*, combined a commitment to the First Amendment with entrepreneurial zeal and reporting skill and became one of the great independent journalists in American history. At the age of eighty, Izzy published *The Trial of Socrates*, which was a national bestseller. He wrote the book after he taught himself ancient Greek.

BENJAMIN C. BRADLEE was for nearly thirty years the charismatic editorial leader of *The Washington Post*. It was Ben who gave the *Post* the range and courage to pursue such historic issues as Watergate. He supported his reporters with a tenacity that made them fearless and it is no accident that so many became authors of influential, best-selling books.

ROBERT L. BERNSTEIN, the chief executive of Random House for more than a quarter century, guided one of the nation's premier publishing houses. Bob was personally responsible for many books of political dissent and argument that challenged tyranny around the globe. He is also the founder and longtime chair of Human Rights Watch, one of the most respected human rights organizations in the world.

·　　·　　·

For fifty years, the banner of Public Affairs Press was carried by its owner Morris B. Schnapper, who published Gandhi, Nasser, Toynbee, Truman, and about 1,500 other authors. In 1983, Schnapper was described by *The Washington Post* as "a redoubtable gadfly." His legacy will endure in the books to come.

Peter Osnos, *Founder*